Francis X. Clooney and John Berthrong (Eds.)

European Perspectives on the New Comparative Theology

This book is, with exception of the concluding chapter by Perry Schmidt-Leukel, a reprint of the special issue that appeared in the online open access journal *Religions* (ISSN 2077-1444) from 2012–2013 (available at: http://www.mdpi.com/journal/religions/special_issues/new_comparative).

Guest Editors
Francis X. Clooney
Harvard Divinity School
Cambridge, MA, USA

John Berthrong
School of Theology, Boston University
Boston, MA, USA

Editorial Offices
MDPI AG
Klybeckstrasse 64
Basel, Switzerland

Publisher
Shu-Kun Lin

Production Editor
Martyn Rittman

1. Edition 2014

MDPI • Basel • Beijing • Wuhan

ISBN 978-3-906980-45-4 (PDF)
ISBN 978-3-906980-44-7 (Hbk)

© 2014 by the authors; licensee MDPI AG, Basel, Switzerland. All articles in this volume are Open Access distributed under the Creative Commons Attribution 3.0 license (http://creativecommons.org/licenses/by/3.0/), which allows users to download, copy and build upon published articles, even for commercial purposes, as long as the author and publisher are properly credited. This ensures maximum dissemination and a wider impact for our publications. The dissemination and distribution of copies of this book as a whole, however, is restricted to MDPI AG, Basel, Switzerland.

Table of Contents

Preface ix

John Berthrong and Francis X. Clooney
Editors' Introduction to "European Perspectives on the New Comparative Theology" 1
Reprinted from *Religions* **2012**, *3*, 1195–1197; doi:10.3390/rel3041195
http://www.mdpi.com/2077-1444/3/4/1195

Ulrich Winkler
Reasons for and Contexts of Deep Theological Engagement with Other Religious Traditions in Europe: Toward a Comparative Theology 5
Reprinted from *Religions* **2012**, *3*, 1180–1194; doi:10.3390/rel3041180
http://www.mdpi.com/2077-1444/3/4/1180

Reinhold Bernhardt
Comparative Theology: Between Theology and Religious Studies 21
Reprinted from *Religions* **2012**, *3*, 964–972; doi:10.3390/rel3040964
http://www.mdpi.com/2077-1444/3/4/964

Klaus von Stosch
Comparative Theology as Liberal and Confessional Theology 31
Reprinted from *Religions* **2012**, *3*, 983–992; doi:10.3390/rel3040983
http://www.mdpi.com/2077-1444/3/4/983

Ulrich Dehn
A European (German) View on Comparative Theology: Dialogue with My Own Past 42
Reprinted from *Religions* **2012**, *3*, 1085–1093; doi:10.3390/rel3041085
http://www.mdpi.com/2077-1444/3/4/1085

Paul Hedges
The Old and New Comparative Theologies: Discourses on Religion, the Theology of Religions, Orientalism and the Boundaries of Traditions 52
Reprinted from *Religions* **2012**, *3*, 1120–1137; doi:10.3390/rel3041120
http://www.mdpi.com/2077-1444/3/4/1120

Rose Drew
Challenging Truths: Reflections on the Theological Dimension of Comparative Theology 71
Reprinted from *Religions* **2012**, *3*, 1041–1053; doi:10.3390/rel3041041
http://www.mdpi.com/2077-1444/3/4/1041

Claudia Bickmann
The Idea of a Highest Divine Principle—Founding Reason and Spirituality. A Necessary Concept of a Comparative Philosophy? 85
Reprinted from *Religions* **2012**, *3*, 1025–1040; doi:10.3390/rel3041025
http://www.mdpi.com/2077-1444/3/4/1025

Marianne Moyaert
On Vulnerability: Probing the Ethical Dimensions of Comparative Theology 102
Reprinted from *Religions* **2012**, *3*, 1144–1161; doi:10.3390/rel3041144
http://www.mdpi.com/2077-1444/3/4/1144

Jacques Scheuer
Comparative Theology and Religious Studies in a Non-religious Environment 121
Reprinted from *Religions* **2012**, *3*, 973–982; doi:10.3390/rel3040973
http://www.mdpi.com/2077-1444/3/4/973

Martin Ganeri
Tradition with a New Identity: Thomist Engagement with Non-Christian Thought as a Model for the New Comparative Theology in Europe 131
Reprinted from *Religions* **2012**, *3*, 1054–1074; doi:10.3390/rel3041054
http://www.mdpi.com/2077-1444/3/4/1054

Mouhanad Khorchide and Ufuk Topkara
A Contribution to Comparative Theology: Probing the Depth of Islamic Thought 153
Reprinted from *Religions* **2013**, *4*, 67–76; doi:10.3390/rel4010067
http://www.mdpi.com/2077-1444/4/1/67

Perry Schmidt-Leukel
Scholars in Europe on the New Comparative Theology. A Pluralist's Rejoinder 163

List of Contributors

Reinhold Bernhardt is Professor for Systematic Theology/Dogmatics at the University of Basel, Switzerland. His publications include *Der Absolutheitsanspruch des Christentums. Von der Aufklärung bis zur Pluralistischen Religionstheologie* (Gütersloher Verlagshaus 1990) and *Was heisst „Handeln Gottes"? Eine Rekonstruktion der Lehre von der Vorsehung* (Gütersloher Verlagshaus/Chr. Kaiser 1999 / LIT 2008). He is the editor of the series *Beiträge zu einer Theologie der Religionen* and of the periodical *Theologische Zeitschrift*. He is also the co-editor of the series *Scientia & Religio* and *Studien zur systematischen Theologie und Ethik*. His research interests are the theology of religions, divine action, and the relation of theology and science.

John Berthrong, educated in Sinology at the University of Chicago, has taught comparative philosophy and theology at Boston University since 1989. He is also an adjunct faculty member at the Beijing Language and Culture University in Beijing, China. His teaching and research interests include interreligious dialogue, Chinese religions and philosophy, and comparative philosophy and theology. His publications comprise *All under Heaven: Transforming Paradigms in Confucian-Christian Dialogue* (SUNY Press 1994) and *Expanding Process: Exploring Philosophical and Theological Transformations in China and the West* (SUNY Press 2008).

Claudia Bickmann is Professor of Philosophy at Cologne University, Germany. Her areas of research and publications are aimed at Transcendental Philosophy, Classical Philosophy from Kant to Heidegger with regard to Plato, Aristotle and Plotinus, Metaphysics, Philosophy of Religion, and Comparative Philosophy. She is the founding editor and editor-in-chief (with Markus Wirtz) of the cross-cultural book-series *World-Philosophies in a dialogue* (*Weltphilosophien im Gespräch*, Verlag Traugott Bautz). She is also president of the international *Society of Intercultural Philosophy* (GIP).

Francis X. Clooney, S.J., is Parkman Professor of Divinity and Professor of Comparative Theology and Director of the Center for the Study of World Religions. After earning his doctorate in South Asian languages and civilizations (University of Chicago, 1984), he taught at Boston College for 21 years, until coming to Harvard. His primary areas of scholarship are theological commentarial writings in the Sanskrit and Tamil traditions of Hindu India, and the developing field of comparative theology. He has also written on the Jesuit missionary tradition, particularly in India, and the dynamics of dialogue in the contemporary world. Clooney is the author of numerous articles and books, including *Comparative Theology: Deep Learning across Religious Borders* (Wiley-Blackwell 2010). In 2010 he was elected a Fellow of the British Academy.

Ulrich Dehn was born in 1954 in Duesseldorf (at that time, West-Germany). He studied Protestant Theology at several German universities and at the UTC Bangalore (South India) and worked eight years (1986–1994) at the Tomisaka Christian Center in Tokyo. He wrote his doctoral dissertation on (Christian) theology of liberation in India (1985). His post-doc research (habilitation) focused on Nichiren Buddhism in Japan (1992). Since 2006 he holds the Chair of World Christianity and Religious Studies at the University of Hamburg. He published several monographs and articles and is editor of the periodical *Interkulturelle Theologie*.

Martin Ganeri, O.P., is Vice Regent of Blackfriars Hall, University of Oxford and Director of the Centre for Christianity and Interreligious Dialogue at Heythrop College, University of London. His special area of interest is the Christian theological engagement with classical Hindu thought. His research has focused especially on the theology of Rāmānuja and Thomas Aquinas. His recent publications include "Two Pedagogies for Happiness: healing goals and healing methods in the *Summa Theologiae* of Thomas Aquinas and the *Śrī Bhāṣya* of Rāmānuja", in: *Philosophy as Therapeia* (Cambridge University Press 2010), "Theology and Non-Western Philosophy" in: *Theology and Philosophie: Faith and Reason* (Bloomsbury 2012). He is currently working on a monograph, *Indian Philosophy and Western Theism: Rāmānuja and Aquinas,* for Routledge.

Rose Drew completed her doctorate in 2008. She has since lectured in interfaith studies and Buddhism at the University of Glasgow, UK, and in 2011 held a research scholarship at Uppsala University, Sweden. Her research interests are predominantly in interreligious dialogue (especially Buddhist-Christian dialogue) and the theology of religions. Her monograph, *Buddhist and Christian? An Exploration of Dual Belonging* (Routledge 2011), focuses on the question of whether, and to what extent, it is possible for an individual to be both an authentic Buddhist and an authentic Christian. In addition to her academic work, she has been involved in practical interfaith work for a number of years and currently works full-time for the charity Interfaith Scotland, managing a new project to support and develop positive engagement between faith communities in the city of Glasgow.

Paul Hedges is Programme Leader in Theology, Religion and Ethics at the University of Winchester, UK, and has taught for other British, Canadian and Chinese universities. Books include *Preparation and Fulfilment: A History and Study of Fulfilment Theology in Modern British Thought in the Indian Context* (Peter Lang 2001) and *Controversies in Interreligious Dialogue and the Theology of Religions* (SCM Press 2010). He is also general editor of a forthcoming three volume reference set entitled *Controversies in Contemporary Religion* (Praeger 2014). He researches and teaches in areas such as Interreligious Studies, theologies of religions, modern and contemporary Christian theology, Asian religions, and meta-theory in the study of religion and theology. He has been editor of the *Australian Religion Studies Review / Journal for the Academic Study of Religion* (Equinox), and is on the editorial board of *The Journal of Religious History* (Wiley-Blackwell).

Mouhanad Khorchide is Associate Director of the Center of Religious Studies, Director of the Centre for Islamic Theology (CIT) and Professor of Islamic Religious Education at Münster University (Westfälische Wilhelms-Universität Münster). He studied both at the Al-Imam Al-Ouzai University for Islamic Studies in Lebanon and at the University of Vienna, Austria, where he handed in his doctoral dissertation in 2008. He is the author of *Islam ist Barmherzigkeit: Grundzüge einer modernen Religion* (Verlag Herder 2012) and *Scharia - der missverstandene Gott: Der Weg zu einer modernen islamischen Ethik* (Verlag Herder 2013).

Marianne Moyaert holds the Fenna Diemer Lindeboom Chair of Comparative theology and hermeneutics of interreligious dialogue at the Free University of Amsterdam, The Netherlands. She also teaches courses at the KU Leuven, Belgium. She has authored two books, including *Fragile Identities: Towards a Theology of Interreligious Hospitality* (Rodopi 2011), and has edited three others, including, with Didier Pollefeyt, *Never Revoked: Nostra Aetate as Ongoing Challenge for Jewish Christian Dialogue* (Peeters 2010). In addition, she has published over fifty articles, approximately half of which appeared in peer-reviewed journals, in both English and Dutch. These have treated a wide range of topics relating to interreligious dialogue, hermeneutics, and comparative theology.

Jacques Scheuer, S.J., is Professor Emeritus of Asian philosophies and religions at the Université catholique de Louvain, Louvain-la-Neuve, Belgium. His main areas of interest are Hinduism and Buddhism as well as Comparative Culture and Religion. His doctoral dissertation at the Ecole pratique des hautes études, under the direction of Madeleine Biardeau, was published as *Siva dans le Mahâbhârata* (Presses Universitaires de France 1982). He recently authored *Un chrétien dans les pas du Bouddha* (Lessius 2010) and *L'Inde, entre hindouisme et bouddhisme: quinze siècles d'échanges* (Académie royale de Belgique 2013).

Perry Schmidt-Leukel taught at the Universities of Munich, Innsbruck, Salzburg and Glasgow. Since 2009 he is Professor of Religious Studies and Intercultural Theology at the University of Münster/Germany. His main interest is in the fields of inter-faith relations, Buddhist-Christian dialogue, pluralist theologies of religions and – most recently – inter-faith theology. He published more than 20 books in different languages. Among his more recent publications are: *Understanding Buddhism* (Dunedin Academic Press 2006), *Transformation by Integration. How Inter-faith Encounter Changes Christianity* (SCM Press 2009), (ed.) *Buddhism and Religious Diversity*, 4 vols. (Routledge 2012), and (ed.) *Religious Diversity in Chinese Thought* (Palgrave 2013).

Klaus von Stosch is Professor for Systematic Theology and chairman of the Centre for Comparative Theology and Cultural Studies at the University of Paderborn. He is the author of the monograph *Komparative Theologie als Wegweiser in der Welt der Religionen* (Ferdinand Schöningh 2012) and co-author (with Reinhold Bernhardt) of *Komparative Theologie. Interreligiöse Vergleiche als Weg der Religionstheologie* (Theologischer Verlag Zürich 2009).

Ufuk Topkara is currently enrolled as a PhD Student with the Post Graduate Program in Islamic Theology (Stiftung Mercator), and is affiliated with the Center for Comparative Theology at the University of Paderborn. He received a Magister Artium (M.A.) degree in History and Philosophy from Humboldt University Berlin. His doctoral dissertation focuses on the convergence of reason and faith in Islam.

Ulrich Winkler is Professor of Systematic Theology, Initiator and Co-Director of the Center for Intercultural Theology and the Study of Religions at the Paris Lodron University of Salzburg, Austria. He is director of the University Study Course 'Spiritual Theology in the Process of Interreligious Dialogue and Encounter.' His research focuses on the Theology of Religions and Comparative Theology. He is editor of the book series *Salzburger Theologische Studien – interkulturell* and founding editor of the journal *Salzburger Theologische Zeitschrift* (SaThZ). He recently published his monograph *Wege der Religionstheologie. Von der Erwählung zur komparativen Theologie* (Salzburger Theologische Studien 46, Tyrolia 2013).

Preface

We were delighted to be approached by the editors of *Religions* to serve as guest editors for a thematic issue of the journal related to comparative theology. We soon settled on "European Perspectives on the New Comparative Theology" as an important and interesting focus that would expand what has, in many ways, been primarily a North American conversation. The thematic issue serves also to highlight the work of some of the European scholars who have already been thinking creatively and critically about this discipline. The complete set of essays had appeared on line by the end of 2012, and as such served to constitute an impressive conversation on comparative theology, raising many issues deserving scholarly attention. By no means speaking with one voice or in agreement with one another, our authors did the great service of thinking through and rethinking the discipline according to the history, priorities, and needs of European theologians and scholars of religion today.

Given the value and importance of the collection, we were similarly pleased when the opportunity arose to publish them as a volume with MDPI, thus furthering the audience for this important discussion. We decided that it would be fair and valuable to preserve the same features that went into the original publication, and so the essays appear in this volume largely as they appeared online. We have thus hoped to preserve the freshness and diversity of the conversation. Readers will notice, as is to be expected, traces of the online origins of the project, wherein the essays were published serially, as they were ready, and without an overall consideration of their continuity in theme and style, taken as a whole.

However, it is also fair enough to expect that a book has some greater focus, by virtue of the work of consolidation such that helps the reader to make overall sense of the conversation. We decided therefore that it would be appropriate for the book to balance our introduction with a response essay that would step back and look at what our authors have proposed and argued across the eleven essays. In this regard, we are very grateful to Perry Schmidt-Leukel (Münster) for writing, on relatively short notice, a response to these essays. Unable to accept our original invitation to write for the thematic issue itself, this distinguished theologian and scholar of religions promptly and generously accepted our invitation. His response essay reflects upon the set of essays as a whole and sorts out its various strands of reflection on comparative theology in the European context. He addresses some of the key questions our authors raised but also, appropriately enough, adds still others to the discussion. He assesses this volume's mapping and assessment of comparative theology, its possibilities and problems, noting carefully what is reflected in the essays and re-reading them in light of his own personal views on the matter. Thus, he chose to cast his reflections as a "pluralist's rejoinder" and thereby to enhance our original vision of the project by crystalizing and predicting where comparative theology is going as a discipline in Europe and beyond.

Francis X. Clooney and John Berthrong
Guest Editors

Reprinted from *Religions*. Cite as: Berthrong, John, Clooney, Francis X. "Editor's Introduction to 'European Perspectives on the New Comparative Theology.'" *Religions* 3 (2012): 1195-1197.

Editorial

Editors' Introduction to "European Perspectives on the New Comparative Theology"

John Berthrong [1,]* and Francis X. Clooney [2,]*

[1] School of Theology, Boston University, One Silber Way, Boston, MA 02215, USA
[2] Harvard Divinity School, 45 Francis Avenue, Cambridge, MA 02138, USA

* Authors to whom correspondence should be addressed; E-Mails: jhb@bu.edu (J.B.); fclooney@hds.harvard.edu (F.X.C.).

Received: 19 November 2012 / Accepted: 14 December 2012 / Published: 18 December 2012

This thematic issue of *Religions*, "European Perspectives on the New Comparative Theology," asks how comparative theology—an old discipline that has been infused with new energy in recent decades and merited new attention—has been received, understood, and critiqued among theologians and scholars of religions in Europe today. How does comparative theology look in light of current understandings of theology, the study of religions, and comparative studies, and the politics of learning in the churches today? In taking on the project, we were eager to open up a new conversation on comparative theology with a wide range of European scholars. These essays vindicate our hope, as they make the case that comparative theology needs to be situated in relation to the study of religions and comparative religion on the one side, and the mainstream of theological discourse on the other. For the sake of cohesion in the conversation, at the start we suggested to the invited authors that they take Francis Clooney's 2010 *Comparative Theology* as a reference point, with reference not just to his ideas but also to the authors he reviews in his third chapter. The point was not to agree or disagree with Clooney, but to take his view of comparative theology as a starting point for the project. Aware that our own work as editors was likely to be under scrutiny in the essays, we agreed from that start that our job was not to sway the authors one way or another, but simply to give them a fair space in which to express important ideas deserving the attention of us all. We therefore very much appreciate all that is said in the essays, even when we ourselves might put the matter rather differently. Moreover, even after the work of these essays, we readily admit that no single understanding of comparative theology in Europe emerges here; our authors do not speak with a single "European voice." Nevertheless, certain questions about presuppositions, method, and the theology of religions repeatedly arise and a careful study of these contributions will help us to shape the field more coherently.

Pluralism raises questions not only about the content of theology, but also about the institutional support of theological education and research. In question too is how deeply theology, comparative or not, should or will remain a denominational discipline rooted in a specific (Christian) community or, particularly if comparative, will move away from such roots. If disciplines like comparative theology blur the boundaries among Christian communities and between the Christian and non-Christian, such as theology is no longer a uniquely Christian discipline that can be divided into its Protestant and Catholic portions, then the institutional effects too will be large. In the German context in particular, there is clearly a sharp sense of what is at stake as theology's institutional supports are shifting, and state and even ecclesial sponsorship of Christian theology is diminishing. (Winkler, Salzburg)

In the German-speaking academy, for instance, there is still rivalry between theology and religious studies; comparative theology may from one perspective seem less than theological, but from another, too theological. Whether a judicious compromise can be worked out is at issue in these essays, such that the actual work of comparison belong to the world of religious studies, and evaluation to the realm of theology, is an interesting challenge but still an open question. (Bernhardt, Basel)

As for substance, one might argue that comparative theology is in fact one of the best fruits of liberal theology and of a Wittgensteinian interpretation of transcendental philosophy; as such and even apart from what is learned in actual comparisons, it is already opening new perspectives for confessional theology (von Stosch, Paderborn). Or one might see comparative theology as an alternative to pluralist theology, and one that enables a more responsible engagement with other religions (Dehn, Hamburg). Yet caution is wise, since claiming that today's comparative theology is "new" may be unfair to earlier instantiations of the comparative project, and may also conceal continuities that make today's comparative theology possibly, for better or worse, simply a continuation of older evident and implicit Christian theological reflection on other religions (Hedges, Winchester).

Several contributors accentuate what comparative theology seems to leave undone with respect to disclosing its own underpinnings, particularly the suspected theology of religions that it is supposed to presuppose if it is to justify the work of comparison. One might even assert that comparative theology implies some version of a pluralist theology of religions. So why don't the comparativists spell out their theology of religions? This may be due to a certain stubborn practicality—you will know my theology by observing how I do it—but there may also, here too, be ecclesial dynamics at work. Thus it may be that the currently understated—under-theorized—nature of comparative theology has much to do with the position of practitioners of it, such as Clooney and Fredericks, within a Catholic Church where authorities seem ever suspicious of ways of engaging pluralism that actually make a theological difference (Drew, Glasgow).

In any case, it is worthwhile to consider more closely the distinction, directly or indirectly addressed in many of the essays, between the theology of religion and comparative theology. To put it simply: the older study of theology of religion based its methods and modes of evaluation on the doctrines and the teaching of the various churches. In this sense its subsequent attention to other religions tended at times to be an *a priori* enterprise even when its practitioners were determined to treat partners in dialogue with complete respect. Today's comparative theology is more tentative, for it works with the view that before any normative theological statements can be made, there is need for an extended engagement with the texts and/or praxis of those other religions. Hence, comparative theology is an *a posteriori* approach to the intercultural study of religion and declines to make any normative judgments prior to an extended and deep reflection on the texts and practices of the religions under comparison. Ironically—or by a kind of symmetry—it may at times seem that just as the theology of religions postpones actual engagement with other religions, comparative theology postpones the explication of some expected, allied theology of religions. More to the point, one may also observe that only if comparative theology maintains, and appears to maintain, theological rigor, will it hold its own in the larger theological conversation. For that rigor, those interested in comparative theology must pay attention to the philosophical underpinnings of comparative work; without a strong enough sense of comparison as a discipline with philosophical implications, what is at stake in comparative theology may remain less than fully understood even by its practitioners (Bickmann, Köln).

Marianne Moyaert addresses a different dimension of comparative theology by asking about the kind of learning exemplified in Clooney's comparative theology. Vulnerable learning seems to be an inner requirement of this kind of theological comparison, its true inner measure. However, if one stresses too strongly the attitudes and acts of empathy and vulnerability and sees as comparison's primary goal a fostering of mutual understanding, then responsibility to Christian communities and Christian theology may be attenuated and neglected, and the Christian intellectual challenge to other traditions blunted. Comparative theology may then seem to erode distinguishing features of theology itself, attenuating bonds to authorities and communities. It would indeed be disappointing were comparative theology to become the last refuge for religious nostalgia, a way of evading the challenges of indifference, agnosticism, or atheism (Scheuer, Louvain-la-Neuve). Comparative theology therefore needs robust theological explanation, explicit in its debt to and continuity with tradition, if it is to hold its place in theological conversations (Ganeri, London).

Mouhanad Khorchide and Ufuk Topkara (Münster) write from a Muslim perspective. They do some of the necessary foundational work for thinking through comparative theology in Islam tradition. Moreover, getting particular, they offer a constructive example of an Islamic contribution to comparative theological study, by reflections on divine compassion. In this way they engage a topic central and familiar in the Jewish and Christian contexts, and invite further comparative study on the part of Muslims and by Jewish and Christian theologians likewise wishing to understand God's compassion more deeply across religious boundaries. More broadly, their contribution signals the necessary work of hearing from scholars in other religious traditions, about whether and how they see comparative theology as relevant to their own distinctive religious communities too.

In closing, we again express our gratitude to our authors. Their essays are invaluable in raising substantive questions and opening new possibilities while at the same time urging those of us interested in comparative theology to explain and defend more fully the practices we already employ.

The essays—in the end just a sample of what is potentially a much larger body of authors and reflections—aid us in moving forward in a wider theological conversation that reaches beyond local contexts such as North America or Western Europe. In the end, we are all the more convinced that theology in the 21st century needs to be comparative theology, and that comparative theology itself needs to be intercontinental, global, and interreligious, if these are to remain vital disciplines.

Reprinted from *Religions*. Cite as: Winkler, Ulrich. "Reasons for and Contexts of Deep Theological Engagement with Other Religious Traditions in Europe: Toward a Comparative Theology." *Religions* 3 (2012): 1180-1194.

Article

Reasons for and Contexts of Deep Theological Engagement with Other Religious Traditions in Europe: Toward a Comparative Theology

Ulrich Winkler

Center for Intercultural Theology and the Study of Religions, Paris Lodron University Salzburg, Universitaetsplatz 1, 5020 Salzburg, Austria; E-Mail: Ulrich.Winkler@sbg.ac.at

Received: 6 November 2012; in revised form: 13 December 2012 / Accepted: 17 December 2012 / Published: 18 December 2012

Abstract: The different contexts of America and Europe have a significant impact on the development of comparative theology, especially in the German-speaking countries. The latter have found other solutions to the problem of religious pluralism that are not really conducive to comparative theology. Hence, the double responsibility of Catholic theology in particular toward the university and toward the Church is a part of the discourse policy of theology, which affects the theology of religions and comparative theology. On the one hand, theology is under the protection of the state, and on the other hand theology is threatened by the risk of unreliability due to ecclesiastical paternalism. But the theology of religions and comparative theology do not evade into science of religion or neo-orthodoxy, rather, they take a risk in a theological engagement with other religions, bringing one's own faith into a deep encounter with other religions and their faiths while delving into points of detail. After giving short descriptions of these tasks, this article shows some examples of practice in comparative theology and gives a prospect into potential further developments of comparative theology in theories of difference and spaces.

Keywords: theology of religions; comparative theology; Second Vatican Council—Nostra Aetate; postcolonial studies; German catholic theology; church-state relations; spirituality; apologetics; third space; theory of difference

1. Reciprocations, Attributions, and Constructions

Comparative theology in Europe can only be described as a host of individual and personal perspectives. This lies in the nature of both comparative theology and "Europe". It makes a big difference whether one is addressing a German-speaking community, scholars in the USA, or a primarily Muslim audience as I did two years ago at Gadja Mada University in Yogyakarta, Indonesia. When addressing such groups, we try to correlate the different contexts and to respond to our dialogue partners.

This sounds like a truism not worth mentioning. However, the matter becomes more complex if we ask: What is the source of our knowledge about the context of our dialogue partners or our listeners and readers? The simplest problem is the inevitable and abiding narrowness of our knowledge. The lessons we learned from postcolonial studies, after Edward Said's deconstruction of the invention of the Orient, are much more serious. Our view of the other issues, attributions of identity, and constructions of the *other*'s identity, marked by our blindly presupposed and only more or less consciously assumed power constellations and rankings. Our cultural maps guide our epistemic pre-decisions, and the choice of the parameters we regard as essential for our understanding of the *other* is informed by these attributions.

Therefore, it is to be expected that my experiences in the American context and my choices about what I want to explain to my American audience and international readers about the European context deliver more insights about my epistemic pre-decisions and about my cultural matrix. We cannot shake off this matrix, but we can analyze and understand its blind dynamics, and by deconstructing it we can diminish its impact on the process of our cultural construction. We may begin to see through our implicit apologetics. We cannot escape our mapping procedures or attributions, but we can be attentive to them and cast some light on their hidden dynamics.

This introduction would still be trivial, and no more than a briefing on the commonplaces of cultural and postcolonial studies, if this epistemological problem were not essential to comparative theology. This is because, however praxis-oriented and interested in details comparative theology may want to be, it is always caught in this methodological and epistemic maelstrom, struggling not to get drawn into the depths and drown. What are the attributions and identity constructions of the *other* with which comparative theology views the other traditions? Does it acknowledge its hidden dynamics and can it elucidate them? I find the best way to avoid this danger is to honestly and humbly disclose one's own horizon and the narrow field one cultivates. This is what I want to try here: to give a very brief look at my work, theory, and view of comparative theology from a European, especially German-speaking, and Catholic perspective. I will conclude this introduction with the following thesis: *The exchange between the continents as well as that between religious traditions must be sensitive to the issues of postcolonial studies and attentive to the mutual attributions of identity, which are marked by constellations of power and implicit—perhaps apologetic—conceptions of their relationships.*

2. The European and the American Contexts of Comparative Theology

The driving force behind Europe was, and is, its great diversity of cultures, which also brought about very diverse forms of religion to the public sphere: modernity, secularization, a radical decrease in the importance of established religions, laicism and atheism of the state on the one hand, and postmodernity, postsecularism, a new interest in religion and spirituality on the other. What role can comparative theology play here? After the great religious unity of the past, it can keep up with the growing religious diversity today. But there are also critical questions to be posed: Why should we study traditional religions at this time and expend a lot of energy in comparative theology on languages and detailed studies? Do we want to slow the rapid pace of postmodernity toward more and more plurality, individuality and an ever greater complexity ("Unübersichtlichkeit," Jürgen Habermas), by at least concentrating on the great world religions, if Christianity and our churches can no longer take refuge in their claim to uniqueness? Is it about mitigating the loss of religion's importance in the secular world of the almighty economy? Are we looking for new resources of salvation in the kaleidoscopic colorfulness of the religions, far away in the more distant land of authenticity? Are we not, indeed, merely taken in by the dynamics of exoticism (Tzvetan Todorov) and Orientalism with comparative theology? Are we then not in danger of repeating the power strategies of dominating and instrumentalizing the *others*? These are very serious questions that call for a *theological* answer.

(Christian) religious diversity is formative for the United States. The modern history of Europe, and therefore of the USA, cannot be understood without understanding religious violence—the *Mayflower* sailed to the new continent at the beginning of the Thirty Years' War when nearly half of the population in Central Europe was about to be wiped out by a religious war. The pathos of liberty and religious freedom in the USA cannot be understood without attention to the confessional and religious constraints in Europe. So, I am already doing what I just described—applying a cartography of the *other*, the USA, in order to construct my own Europe. I am mapping the field by attributing what I believe to be important information on Europe to American and international readers. I can observe myself in the process of constructing the *other*. This process is irreducible and inevitable, which is why I think it is essential to bring it into the light and reflect on it, and thus disclose one's own constructing principles. I will now continue.

The comparison is tricky: (a) On the one hand, one meets a fascinating diversity of religious voices in the USA, as I encountered them, for example, at AAR conferences, where groups marginalized in Europe like gays and lesbians are represented in religious discourses as a matter of course. (b) On the other hand, a strict official separation between church and state is anchored in the American Constitution, although this does not prevent religions from exerting influence in politics. The personal belief of a presidential candidate has great importance in the public eye. In most European countries it would be rather awkward for a journalist to report and write about a topic of that kind. Religion in Europe is more of a private affair, whereas religion in the United States is something public but officially separate from the state. (c) In Europe and in the German speaking countries, *i.e.*, Germany,

Switzerland, and Austria, in particular, the separation is combined with state privileges by so-called concordats, treaties between a state and the Vatican or other forms of church leadership.

These different contexts have an enormous impact on the specific development of comparative theology in Europe and especially in the German-speaking countries. The latter have found other solutions for the problem of religious pluralism that are not really conducive to comparative theology.

3. Theology in German-Speaking Countries

At the beginning of the 20th century, these German-speaking states realized—unlike laicist states, like France—that the program of the Enlightenment and the displacement of religion to the private sphere underestimated the religions. Therefore, the states became interested in bringing religious discourse into the public sphere while, through concordats, contractually committing to fund the education of clergy in public university faculties. Religions cannot eke out an existence as arcane disciplines in back alleys but must enter the light of the public sphere and prove themselves to the academic community of universities. Inherent in religions is an immense potential for good and for violence, and therefore religion continues to be a public affair. We theologians profit immensely by this outcome, and in the three countries mentioned above—to which I will limit myself here—we have excellent and excellently equipped state-run theological faculties.

At the same time, the states conceded to the churches the right of sharing in the decision about the appointment of professors. The Catholic Church must give its *nihil obstat* ("no objection") and the refusal to do so bars a candidate. In case of conflict, the Church can withdraw the candidate's ecclesiastical license to teach as a Roman Catholic theologian (*missio canonica*) while exercising his or her profession.

Thus, Catholic theology in particular has a double responsibility: toward the university and toward the Church. On the one hand, theology is under the protection of the state—up to now the majority of professors have either been public officials with tenure or had quite solid contracts—with the commitment and freedom to truth even if it is uncomfortable. On the other hand, because of the responsibility toward its own faith community and the possibilities of interference by the Church, theology is threatened by the risk of unreliability due to ecclesiastical paternalism. At the universities, theology wants to appear to be committed solely to rationality, science, and truth, but in practice each theologian is dependent on not losing his or her ecclesiastical teaching license. In order not to betray itself theology has to be able to parry this suspicion in a decisive way.

This is a part of the discourse policy of theology, which affects in particular the theology of religions and comparative theology. It is a discreet part of theology that is gladly kept shrouded in mist in the public sphere. Fierce conversations about it take place only in private; public debates are rare [1].

Up until now, there have been at least two strategies for resolving the tension of this double responsibility: (a) On the one hand, there is the strategy of liberating theology from the Church while still having it be protected by the state. This led in the 18th and 19th centuries, for example, to an independent, very anti-theological and anti-ecclesiastical science of religion. Also, after the Second Vatican Council, there was a group of theologians critical of the church that lost their ecclesiastical license to teach and who would go on teaching independently from the Church at state universities. The most famous is Hans Küng. (b) On the other hand, one can find growing opposite strategies—an unbidden neo-orthodoxy and an overzealous ecclesiastical obedience. One could call them strategies of ecclesiastical ingratiation. Only those discourses believed to be ecclesiastically beyond suspicion are honored. The best known example is the exclusion of some sensitive questions in sexual ethics by many Catholic moral theologians.

Both strategies can be observed in the field of theological engagement with other religions. First, attempts to force theologians who are close to the pluralistic theology of religions out of ecclesiastical teaching positions are causing a stir [2]. Yet, there are also theologians who distance themselves from the Church. Second, and more discreet, however, are the procedures of marginalization and ghettoization.

4. Consequences for Comparative Theology

Comparative theology is caught in these constellations, with the following consequences.

(a) *Governmental* sponsorship is providing liberty and security for comparative theology as well. The *institutional* confessionalization of theology emphasizes the ecclesiastical perspective of theology. The above-mentioned escapist strategies in favor of only one side are not viable paths for comparative theology because comparative theology profits from both sides. It can be creative and outline entirely new issues while also, as practiced from a faith perspective, respects the authority of the church. It does not just remain an irrelevant academic hobby. Only when this tension is not suspended—by having its freedom taken away through ecclesiastical paternalism or by comparative theologians fleeing the church—only then can comparative theology be a good answer to both an insular neo-orthodoxy as well as a science of religion that is both critical of theology and anti-ecclesiastical. Then it will also be an advocate for religious diversity and respect for other religious traditions.

(b) The *institutional* confessionalization of theology in the form of theological faculties is mainly limited to Protestant and Catholic theologies, and thus does not represent the multiplicity of religious traditions. The few Jewish theologians are intensively engaged with dialog projects. Great efforts are being made at select universities to establish Islamic theology. It remains to be seen if the monolithic and hermetic situation of theology can be dissolved. The situation in Germany now has gone so far that Catholics cannot study Protestant theology and Protestants cannot study Catholic theology. Comparative theology, however, requires internal knowledge of other religions. The German-speaking countries still have a long way to go before students of Catholic theology, for example, are able to study Buddhist theology at the same time and thereby acquire interreligious theological competence.

Comparative theology, in contrast to comparative religion, is a *theological engagement with other religions*, bringing one's own faith into a deep encounter with other religions and their faiths while delving into points of detail. The results cannot be anticipated *a priori*. Theology has to take a risk in these encounters; otherwise they are not real encounters. Does this venture go directly against one's own faith, or are there good reasons for that faith to take this risk? I think this is the decisive question that lies ahead for comparative theology. The stakes are high for comparative theology as well as for the Catholic Church.

Many are looking anxiously to the pope, expecting a dramatic decision concerning the Society of St. Pius X and thus the validity of the Second Vatican Council and especially the Declaration on Religious Freedom (*Dignitatis Humanae*) and relations with the other religions (*Nostra Aetate*). We have to keep the consequences of such decisions for the Society of St. Pius X in mind and consider which positions would regain validity with a partial revision of the Second Vatican Council: there cannot be any truth, sanctity, and spiritual gifts in other religions, but everything that seems to be such could at the most be signs and preparation, at worst lies, deception and the deceit of the devil in order to divert souls from the true faith of the Catholic Church; it would be forbidden to recommend the salvation of the other to God [3] because they are excluded *a priori* from salvation; in short, all pagans, Jews, heretics and schismatics—as defined by the Magisterium—are condemned to hell (Council of Florence). These are not just arbitrary decisions and issues of personal taste, but a decision concerning other religions that is centrally linked to the content of the Christian faith.

5. Deconstructing the Apologetic Tradition of the Church

It is not surprising that many Catholics, from laypeople to the Church leadership, are suspicious about positive relations with other religions and see their own faith as threatened. Those who only see a failure of Second Vatican Council's pedagogy here fall short. One must look rather for the subtext of Catholic identity construction. Although the pre-conciliar theological handbooks vanished from the lists of study literature, post-Tridentine theology and especially the concise didactics of neo-scholasticism still form the basis of Catholic self-conception. That is why it is worthwhile to look critically at the dynamics of these identity attributions.

The theological discipline called apologetics used to perform the task of describing and defending the identity of Catholic doctrine and the Church against outside relations in a systematic way. A *societas perfecta* should be completely safeguarded from the outside. This is not an unusual procedure for constructing identity. But here attitude is crucial. In this system one's own truth and superiority were certain from the outset—before any *a priori* experience—and could be substantiated by cogent proofs.

Apologetics is composed of three parts: (a) The *demonstratio religiosa* argues for the possibility of religion and the possibility of a natural knowledge of God and supernatural revelation. This part secures the identity of faith *against* the Enlightenment and atheists. (b) The *demonstratio christiana* argues *against* other religions via the revelation in Jesus Christ. Christianity is proven to be the true religion. The fulfilled promises are quoted against the Jews, the miracles and the empty grave against the heathens. (c) Finally in the *demonstratio catholica* or *ecclesiae* the legitimacy of the *Catholic* faith *against* other churches and denominations is proven through the arguments of the foundation of the church and the miracle of the global presence and holiness of the Catholic Church.

Both comparative theology and apologetics have chosen a theological view of the outside. The big difference lies in the signature of both disciplines, describing the *attitude* in which they engage in the argument: (a) one's own truth and superiority applied *a priori*; (b) the outside was not a source of truth; (c) the interest in and study of the others was aimed at knowing their weaknesses. (d) This form of apologetics was condescending and entertained mutual suspicion; (e) the arguments seemed aimed at compelling assent (f) an epistemology of a faith informed by mercy was missing, and (g) there was no reconnection to dogmatic theology and spirituality [4]. Apologetics of this kind is an iron suit of armor. In times of change, there is a desire for fixed identities, and comparative theology has to reckon with this. It is therefore important for comparative theology to argue convincingly for a reversal of the suspicion of other religions toward an attitude of truth assumption. This is the task of theology of religions.

6. Theology of Religions

The assumption of the presence of truth cannot be based on the research findings of comparative theology itself because these findings are subject to interpretation. To this day, many examples can be cited from the field of missiology in which the painstaking study of other religious traditions only served to demonstrate the superiority of the gospel and Christianity.

Allow me to cite an example of my visit to the predominantly Catholic St. Mary's County (Maryland, USA). Susan, a pious Christian owner of a bed & breakfast there, recently tried to convince me with great consternation to return to the right path because all my Muslim and Hindu friends will surely show their true natures by luring me to destruction. She was not impressed when I told her about my enriching encounters and my theological work in the field of Judaism. For her, all this only confirmed that Satan exercises a highly sophisticated art of infatuation.

Underlying such positions are the dynamics of apologetics, of suspicion, and downgrading that inscribe themselves, like original sin, into all our relations with other religions to this day. The crude stories of guilt hopefully belong to the past, but the subtle stories of guilt are still operative. Theology of religions has to perform this postcolonial task of deconstructing traditional or at least neo-scholastic attributions of Catholic identity and show how theological pre-decisions mold one's view of other religions fundamentally.

In my view, the genitive in "theology of religions" or "theology of religious pluralism" is—this is *the first part of my definition*—is to be understood in the sense of a *genitivus objectivus*, *i.e.*, theological reflection *on* other religions. But this reflection is done on the basis of the self-understanding of the religions and their "theologies," *i.e.*, in the sense of a *genitivus subjectivus*, the theology that other religions have. Since theology is the reflection of one's own faith, theology of religions inquiries into one's own faith for the attitude and the relation to other religious traditions. In this case, there is the essential question as to the reasons in one's own faith that argue for a positive relationship and an attitude of the assumption of truth toward other religions. The Second Vatican Council, for example, speaks explicitly about issues of attitudes toward other religions in *Nostra Aetate* under the term "de habitudine."

But some exponents of comparative theology, however, maintain strong reservations regarding theology of religions for quite different reasons. Theology of religions can have quite different levels of discourse, e.g., systematic, philosophical, practical, and discourse political dimensions. To me, it seems important to identify which discourse level the different arguments against theology of religions are to be allocated to. It may then show that some reasons can be respected on one level without affecting all dimensions or theology of religions as a whole. (a) In most criticisms, theology of religions is confined to a model competition between exclusivism, inclusivism, and pluralism. This, however, is only one area of theology of religions that has in the meantime found sufficient treatment. (b) Or, theology of religions is regarded as futile theory, whereas comparative theology is fertile praxis that should not be impeded by the theoretical work of theologians of religion. But history gives ample lessons on how a good praxis can result in unwanted or dangerous consequences because of a bad theory; therefore, there is always the need for resilient theories. Theory and praxis must not be separated. Comparative theology itself produces many theoretical premises [5]. (c) Another objection against most theologies of religions is that it is abstract, giving the impression that nothing much needs to be known about other religions before judging them. (d) Again, other causes might be connected to the tenuous ecclesiastical discourse-political situation mentioned above in theology of religions. It could be a respectable strategy not to lead comparative theology up the garden path and save it from the limelight or shadows of this dispute. (e) This is so because, assuming that it is just a competition of models, only very little theological research is done in the field of theology of religions, and because the *aporia* between one's own positionality of faith and the appreciation of others cannot be solved satisfactorily. (f) Finally, it should not be concealed that there are naturally grave problems in the prominent approaches of pluralistic theology of religions that comparative theologian are not very eager to adopt.

Therefore, I want to list a few of these objections to the pluralistic theology of religions that are relevant for comparative theology. (a) Does it really make sense to want to compare religions and their truth content? (b) Can truth claims be compared, or do creeds work like grammatical sentences or rules that can be adopted and adhered to but cannot be argued, whereas truth can be tested only within these rules [6]? (c) Are not religions far too complex entities with the multiplicity of their expressions and their believers, if we consider too their vast historical changes from their millennial past to an open future? These judgments must be very vague and in any case open. (d) A related topic is the discussion as to whether judgments made here are empirical or hypothetical. The misunderstanding or allegation of an empirical judgment is rampant. It is clear on methodical grounds that such a judgment cannot be made. (e) The pluralistic theology of religions is searching for models of unity in order to understand multiplicity, thus demanding serious alterations in the self-understanding of the religions. (f) In conjunction with this is a tendency to grade confessional positions. (g) Many objections against the pluralistic theology of religions identify pluralism with John Hick's variant, and especially his epistemic premises of *noumenon* and *phenomenon*. (h) An objection that is rarely raised and on which I elaborated is the lack of a theology of Israel. From a Christian perspective, a theology of religions must take Christianity's uniquely close relationship to Judaism into account. It is unacceptable that both mega discourses of theology of religions and the theology of Israel are isolated from each other. (i) The next objection is popular, but reflects a certain ignorance and unacceptable: the pluralistic theology of religions holds that all religions—indiscriminately—are equally valid, often resorting to the German pun that, due to the pluralistic theology of religions, all truth claims are *gleichgültig* (a reference to both their equal value and meaning and thus ho-hum insignificance). I do not know any pluralistic theologian who sees all religions as equally valid, true, and salvific. (j) I see a serious problem in the fact that theories that cover all religions tend to draw attention away from differences between religions. I could word my critique like this: the pluralistic theology of religions is not pluralistic enough; it has too narrow a concept of the incredible plurality of religions, their mutual differences and contradictions. In contrast, for comparative theology, the differences must be viewed as the assets of the religions to be worked with copiously.

In spite of the many objections to theology of religions and especially its pluralistic version, I hold the theology of religions to be indispensable. Therefore, I will supplement the first part of my *definition of the theology of religions* as follows: theology of religions thus deals with assessing the relationship toward other religions and it conceives of one's own faith and constructs one's own self-understanding in terms and conditions of religious pluralism. Furthermore, a choice has to be made. I hold that the option of a partial and potential pluralistic theology of religions is an indispensable pre-condition for comparative theology. (a) Theological inference from my own belief in the Trinitarian God make me think it is possible to invest in an assumption of truth in other religious traditions because God's history of salvation is universal and at the same time multiple. From the beginning, from creation until consummation, God is the source, the way, and the goal of our salvation. (b) Therefore, I think it is possible to find truth, holiness, and spiritual gifts in other religious traditions [7] from which we can learn. (c) It is impossible, unnecessary, and senseless to define the relations among religions in a general way. Rather, we should, in the sense of comparative theology, focus on particular issues. That is why I call the definition of relations *partial*. (d) And it is *potential* because the results of the comparisons and encounters are not clear *a priori*, despite the assumption of truth. So I am not reversing the apologetic *a priori* assumption of the inferiority of other religions into an *a priori* assumption of their superiority. I remain open for surprises. (e) Comparative theology must take the *pluralistic* option, if its goal is not to learn from the mistakes of others but instead yearns to learn from the surprising treasures that "a generous God has distributed among the nations of the earth" (Vat. II, AG 11). Comparative theology believes there may be things to discover in other religious traditions in which salvation, revelation and truth can be found in a form *equally valid, successful*, or *superior* to that in one's own religion because the equal validity or superiority of one or more faith traditions constitutes the definition of a pluralistic theology of religions. At the same time, it reckons with a history of guilt in one's own and likewise in other religious traditions. It is possible to learn from one another. (f) Comparative theology cannot be neutral toward theology of religions. Even if it is intended to include much more than a discussion of models, it cannot avoid taking a—*pluralistic*—option. There must be a discussion regarding which worldview, which theological epistemic premise, one presupposes before one deals with detail issues. It makes a difference whether I engage with other religions on the basis of an exclusivistic, an inclusivistic, or a pluralistic view, whether I feel there is no truth in them at all, only to be exposed, or that the other faith can automatically only be deficient and inferior, or if I think it possible that it can have equally valid or superior truths on certain points that challenge me, that there can be faith I can encounter at eye level and appreciate. We are not serious about learning from others if we do not take that into account. (g) The strongest attempts at persuasion in favor of comparative theology need to be made in advance by the theology of religions. In times when clear orientation and definite identities are called for, opening hearts for the experiences of other faith traditions is one of the larger challenges facing churches, religions, and theology. That is why the issues of theology of religions must not be concealed but pushed courageously. (h) Comparative theology will be limited to a small circle of experts. It will have its impact on society, churches, and faith communities through theology of religions through which it can exert its influence on changing attitudes and general convictions about other religions. Its research findings may encourage people in widely different fields to meet other believers with openness and a willingness to learn.

7. Features and Projects

(1) Beyond the relationship between comparative theology and theology of religions I want to list some features of my understanding of comparative theology. (a) Theology is the reflection of faith bound to the perspective of one's own religion. Since a living faith can only exist in conjunction with faith content and a personal life of faith (*fides quae* and *fides qua*), one's own faith praxis plays an important role—or, in other words, one's own spirituality. That is why I place the role of spirituality as first for comparative theology. Spirituality flows into the work of a theologian. Although the theology of religions option can be supported by good arguments, it is ultimately a stance of faith or a spiritual stance. It is a spiritual stance of mindfulness and appreciation. (b) Comparative theology does not carry out objective outside analyses of other religions but tries to enter into dialogue with the inside perspectives and self-understandings of other religions. Comparative theology is the dialogue of participant perspectives. Therefore, one has to look for ways how faith attitudes can meet one another and how comparative theologians can enter into the inner spaces of religions, how theologians can participate in the faith of others. For example, purely philological studies will not suffice. Creative ways are needed, which also include spiritual encounters. (c) In addition to the most diverse legitimate methods of comparative theology, I find biographies of people who were or are living on the threshold of two religions especially enlightening. (d) Theologians, and therefore also comparative theologians, usually write texts. There are, however, other forms of theology, oral theologies like personal encounters and discussions, for example, or common academic courses. (e) For a Christian, no matter what tradition one focuses on, dialogue with Jews should—in my opinion—never be completely absent.

(2) This leads me to my second point in which I give a brief selection of projects in which comparative theology is relevant.

(a) Every year for the past 20 years, the Center for Intercultural Theology and the Study of Religion at the University of Salzburg [8], of which I am one of the founding members, has invited guest professors from other cultures or religions to teach and do research at the theological faculty within the theological curriculum. Theological dialogue with colleagues of other religious traditions and friendships that have developed belong essentially and centrally to the pillars of the Center and the study of theology. Here we practice mutual exchange at eye level.

(b) As director of the University Study Program "Spiritual Theology in the Process of Interreligious Dialogue and Encounter," I am in charge of a 3-year Master's program offered by the University of Salzburg, both in Salzburg and in Switzerland. Participants study in closed groups, and most of them have full-time positions in their professions. In these programs, academic study is combined more intensively with personal encounters and spiritual maturing processes. It is quite extraordinary that professors from different religions are not only willing to present their expertise but also bring their own personality into this study program. Teaching their religion and representing their course in a different environment and setting of communication from regular classes at university can be sometimes surprising and challenging at times. Relating religious knowledge in religion to spiritual participant's questions can encourage a new attitude toward teaching and thinking about their own approaches toward their own tradition through these encounters. The success of this study program shows that spirituality is not limited to wellness but can also be connected with a high intellectual standard. Comparative theology emerges within the creativity of these settings.

(c) The following example is quite another format. I am a board member of ESITIS, the European Society for Intercultural Theology and Interreligious Studies [9] that was formed in northwestern Europe. There is a wide variety of approaches among the board members reflecting the different European traditions. Our biannual meetings bring together about 100 or more scholars. In addition to a major focus on the sociology of religion and the present shape of religions in Europe, we emphasize the study of concrete detail issues of religious traditions and the actual practicing of their religious life today. Though comparative theology does not fall under the main tasks of ESITIS, it is nonetheless a framework in which such a theology arises. More and more young scholars are responding to the call for papers and bringing perspectives of this research into this kind of community.

(d) Finally, here is an example of a practical regional interchange between academic theology and the concrete life of faith communities: Occurso—Institute for Interreligious and Intercultural Encounter. [10] An initiative of Martin Rötting, [11] the institute is intended to facilitate and academically chaperone dialogue between people of different religions and cultures in a way that is close to actual life by creating spaces for encounter. Its work includes dialogue praxis, the training of dialogue facilitators, and education in academic research. Practical experiences are reflected upon theologically, and, in return, theological research and studies in the science of religion flows back into educational and dialogical practice [12]. Comparative theology arises in these small contexts.

8. Perspectives: Theories of Difference and Spaces

It would be presumptuous to want to propose future perspectives for comparative theology in Europe. I would like to touch on only two questions here that I intend to pursue further.

(1) The fundamental methodical works of the Cross-Cultural Comparative Religious Ideas Project [13] in Boston 1995–1999 and especially the works of Robert C. Neville show that the creative methodology of comparative theology aims at common ground. On its journeys of discovery comparative theology wants to be surprised by similarities and analogies. What about the differences? Are they a challenge for comparative theology? Will they be a cause of embarrassment for

comparative theology? Will it be upset by them? Is comparative theology successful only when it bridges differences? This would be a misapprehension of comparative theology, since it would establish the epistemic presupposition that all differences can be negotiated and resolved in the end. Thus, comparative theology would once more be a strategy of uniformity. But it is not. Comparative theology attempts to note differences that show up especially in the study of details. Here comparative theology reaches the limits of understanding and interpretation because the differences may be unbridgeable or because there is no longer any language for naming the differences. Differences can make us clueless and speechless. Is the collapse of theology, of God-talk, hence inevitable or is there also a theology that can be done in the midst of this speechlessness? This is where theories of difference come into view.

There are real differences between religions and they are not explained away. These spaces between religions are not only a problem; they can be viewed as *loci* of theology. This is not a postmodern invention but a grammar of differences that is in fact inscribed deeply into the doctrine of ecclesiastical tradition.

(a) By way of example, I refer to Christian religious differences from and special relation with Judaism. The differences cannot be resolved, yet Judaism is constitutive for Christianity as an abiding *other*. Jesus was a Jew, he was born as a Jew, and he believed, lived, and died as a Jew. He never had the intention of leaving Judaism.

(b) In its Trinitarian and Christological theology, the Church opted for a relational grammar of difference. Trinitarian thought states: unity in essence, difference in persons; and Christology holds: unity in person, difference in the two essences. Both grammars have in common the fact that a difference is made between relation and blending in unity, differentiation, and division. A grammar of difference is inscribed into the identity logic of an unrelated single divine essence and the identity logic of a Christological single essence.

(c) The above displays the nature of theological language. Its symbolizations no longer aim at the establishment of an identity and at fixation. Rather, the history of theology and dogma must be read and critically analyzed with regard to *openness to the ungraspability of the ungraspable* and with respect to *new but ever revisable understandings*. Moreover, signs never just declare themselves but do so always in relation to other signs and only in a process of a continual updating and engrafting of the signs.

(d) Comparative theology assumes difference hermeneutically in that one's own faith is never given in a fixed logic of identity but is set up with respect to the most diverse figures of difference. Therefore, it need not remain stuck in identity logic when it engages other religions.

(e) Differences are not just challenges to be overcome by learning; differences also name the spaces of the unspeakable. The unspeakable differences between religions can be a signature of God-talk in religiously pluralistic times. Perhaps they have to be kept open as empty spaces, free, still, silent, and speechless so one can hear the indeterminable totally *other*. The differences from other faiths and other believers are no longer under the pressure of the identity logic of unification or the alternative between truth and lie, but become the place of a theology hermeneutically conscious of difference listening to the infinite silence. Comparative theology is the art of subtle nuances.

(2) Hence, comparative theology opens up new spaces, spaces of understanding and mediation, spaces of surprise as well as diffuse spaces and empty spaces. A standard polemic against so-called postmodernity from the church governing body is that individual religious freedom of choice leads to arbitrariness and non-commitment. Following a consumerist model, people choose the most popular products to compose a colorful and comfortable shopping basket. These misgivings also affect comparative theology, if it is seen as a self-inventing haven of arbitrariness. These self-made spaces of faith are said to lack religious commitment and people avoid the demands of religions. People supposedly construct a *third space as a place of escape beyond the traditions* for themselves. Are private esoteric churches and conventicles really emerging? Then what about the space opened up by comparative theology?

(a) There are many answers to these questions. I already mentioned the confessional commitment of comparative theology and the differences inscribed in one's own identity. Other answers could also be added. Here I will only suggest a perspective.

(b) The question about the new spaces [14] can be misunderstood if one tries to comprehend it via inappropriate theoretical instruments. If we conceive of space as a three-dimensional container, as was done in antiquity, we imagine that we can set up many subspaces. But modern physics already teaches us that there is no space as such—rather, spaces are relational entities determined by their mutual relationships and the variables of time and movement. In the cultural studies approach we understand spaces as constituted by human action [15].

The geographical notion of space has also been changed from definition by topographical borders to that of cultural spaces: Spaces are affected by social practice, by lingual and visual representations [16]. We experience spaces as discursive constructions [17] of our cultural memory, which is inscribed in texts and images, and which governs the awareness of self and others in different cultures. These spaces are not the inventions of individual persons or indications of individual arbitrariness, but instead endowments of our cultural, economic, social, *etc.* treasure of memories.

(c) Postcolonial cultural geography and theories of mapping have abandoned the dichotomies of center and periphery, deconstructed the orientations of space toward the overriding north of the colonial powers, and revealed the sphere of interest of Orientalism (Edward Said). The partitioning of public space in citadel and cathedral, and the division into national spheres of governance of the confessions (*cuius regio, eius religio*) and religions (e.g., Pakistan, India) have become obsolete. The briefly hinted at *spatial turn* in cultural studies and the turning toward a "Thirdspace" (Edward Soja) and "Third space" (Homi K. Bhabha), especially Bhabha's version, reveal the turning of the category of space toward discursivity and epistemology.

(d) Symbols can be understood only by means of a "third" (Charles Sanders Peirce). A sign finds its meaning only in the triangle of signifier, signified, and interpreter. Furthermore, semiotic communication can never be closed down because signs receive their meaning through the designation with the help of other signs. This process modifies their meaning. A sign thus functions only in difference and in relation to other signs ("semiosis," Umberto Eco; "difference," Jacques Derrida). Making a critical connection with that, Homi K. Bhabha understands the *third space* as an epistemological term. Spaces cease to have unalterable meanings and do not accommodate fixed representations. The thought of pure cultures is rendered impossible. The notion of hybridity becomes central: "[T]he theoretical recognition of the split-space of enunciation may open the way to conceptualizing an international culture, based not on the exoticism or multiculturalism of the diversity of cultures but on the inscription and articulation of culture's hybridity. …. by exploring this hybridity, this 'Third Space', we may elude the politics of polarity and emerge as the others of ourselves." [18] In multiculturalism there is a competition between identities, thus the word becomes either a threatening phantom or a *fascinosum* of exoticism. The hybridity of the "third space" inscribes discourses of difference into identity, not just of plurality.

Against this background, comparative theology could take on a significant meaning through responsibly and competently leading these discourses. Ever existing discourses are implemented and deepened. No new imperiums of third spaces will be established as places of refuge beyond the traditions according to antiquated theories of space established. With the help of comparative theology, the Church could step out of the nightmare of retreat and defense and bring its faith to light again under the conditions of hybridity and religious pluralism.

Conflicts of Interest

The author declares no conflict of interest.

References and Notes

1. For example, I have no knowledge of any bibliography of all the publications—they are numerous—that were demanded from many prospective theologians by the Vatican Congregation for the Doctrine of the Faith and for Catholic Education to establish their orthodoxy. The epistemic status of this genre of theological literature is not discussed anywhere. These contributions are silently indexed under regular theological research without posing the questions of power constellations, *etc.* of postcolonial studies. I do not challenge the right of the Church to request information from theologians about the ecclesial status of their theology, but I do ask that these discourses be held openly and transparently on both sides. Power constellations cannot be eliminated, but it is possible to contribute toward deconstructing them and making them somewhat more transparent.

2. The majority of doctrinal complaints in the recent past were linked to the topic of other religions and the plurality of other faiths: Anthony de Mello SJ (1931–1987) from India, 1995 posthumously posted; Tissa Balasuriya O.M.I. (b.1924) from Sri Lanka, condemnation and excommunication 1997, rehabilitation 1998; Jacques Dupuis SJ (1923–2004), Belgian Jesuit and professor of dogmatics at *Vidyajyoti College of Theology*, Delhi, and at the Pontifical Gregorian University in Rome: investigation 1998, rehabilitation with notification 2001; Roger Haight SJ, b. 1937, Weston Jesuit School of Theology in Cambridge, MA; now at Union Theological Seminary/New York, 2000 investigation, condemnation 2004 with a ban on writing and speaking; Peter C. Phan, b. 1946, Georgetown University in Washington, 2004 investigation, 2007 doctrinal complaint by the US Commission of Doctrine; Perry Schmidt-Leukel, b. 1954, now at the University of Münster, Germany, was refused the *nihil obstat* in 1997. His most important opponent at the University of Munich was Professor Gerhard Ludwig Müller, who has just become the Prefect of the Congregation for the Doctrine of the Faith. The problem of religious pluralism and the theological examination of other religions lies in the focus of attention within the Catholic Church.
3. In the *Syllabus errorum* of 1864 Pope Pius IX condemned the following sentence (no. 1) 7. "Good hope at least is to be entertained of the eternal salvation of all those who are not at all in the true Church of Christ." (DS 2917). To entertain good hope for Christians means to pray to God for one's eternal salvation. The church states: this is forbidden in view of the conviction *extra ecclesiam nulla salus* ("outside the Church there is no salvation").
4. See Ulrich Winkler. Kniende Theologie—Eine religionstheologische Besinnung auf eine Spiritualität komparativer Theologie. In *Wagnis der Freiheit. Perspektiven geistlicher Theologie. FS Paul Imhof*, edited by Friedrich Erich Dobberahn and Johanna Imhof. Strukturen der Wirklichkeit 4. Scheidegg: Via Verbis Verlag, 2009, 162–198.
5. The whole of F.X. Clooney's last book talks quite rightly and most clearly about these theological, theoretical, *etc.* premises: Francis X. Clooney. *Comparative Theology. Deep Learning Across Religious Borders*. Chichester: Wiley-Blackwell, 2010.
6. Cf. Klaus von Stosch. *Komparative Theologie als Wegweiser in der Welt der Religionen.* Beiträge zur Komparativen Theologie 6. Paderborn et alii: Ferdinand Schönigh, 2012.
7. Second Vatican Council, *Nostra Aetate* 2: "that is true and holy in these religions,", "the good things, spiritual," in Latin: "bona spiritualia." goods things given by the Holy Spirit.
8. Center for Intercultural Theology and Study of Religions. "Statement." http://www.uni-salzburg.at/ztkr.
9. The European Society for Intercultural Theology and Interreligious Studies. http://www.esitis.org.
10. http://www.occurso.de. The Latin *occursare* means "to encounter." I myself recently joined as a board member.

11. Martin Rötting. *Interreligiöses Lernen im buddhistisch-christlichen Dialog* [Interreligious Learning in Buddhist-Christian Dialoge, PhD-thesis]. St. Ottilien: Eos Verlag, 2007; Martin Rötting. *Interreligiöse Spiritualität. Verantwortungsvoller Umgang der Religionen* [Interreligious Spirituality. A Responsible Encounter of Religions], St. Ottilien. Eos Verlag, 2008.
12. For example, one recent study conducted by Martin Rötting examined by interviews various experiences of people involved in interreligious dialogues by interviewing them. The results of this research flow back into the very sort of dialogue that we are encouraging people to engage in and that we are organizing by making them sensitive and aware of what's going on in dialogue processes in particular in the case of different kinds of partners, circumstances, social and life period contexts *etc*. Therefore new dialogues will profit from former experiences. Martin Rötting. *Religion in Bewegung. Dialog-Typen und Prozess im interreligiösen Lernen*. Interreligiöse Begegnungen, Studien und Projekte 9. Berlin et alii: Lit-Verlag, 2011.
13. Cf. Robert Cummings Neville, ed. *The Human Condition*. Foreword by Peter L. Berger. The Comparative Religious Ideas Project 1. New York: Suny Press, 2001; id., *Ultimate Realities*. Foreword by Tu Weiming. The Comparative Religious Ideas Project 2. New York: Suny Press, 2001; id., *Religious Truth*. Foreword by Jonathan Z. Smith. The Comparative Religious Ideas Project 3. New York: Suny Press, 2001.
14. In the following I am referring to lectures of Birgit Wagner: *Einführung in die Kulturwissenschaften*, Vienna 2010 [Introduction to Cultural Sciences].
15. Cf. Michel de Certeau. "Walking in the City." In *The Cultural Studies Reader*, edited by Simon During. London/New York: Routledge 1993, 151–160.
16. Cf. Henri Lefebvre. *La production de l'espace*. Paris: Anthropos, 1974. Engl. *The Production of Space*. Malden: Blackwell, 1974.
17. Cf. Harvey David. *Justice, Nature and the Geography of Difference*. Cambridge, MA/Oxford: Blackwell 1996.
18. Homi K. Bhabha. "Cultural Diversity and Cultural Differences." In *The Post-Colonial Studies Reader*, edited by B. Ashcroft, G. Griffiths and H. Tiffin. London: Routledge 1995, 206–09, here 209; see: Homi K. Bhabha. *The Location of Culture*. London/New York: Routledge, 1994.

> Reprinted from *Religions*. Cite as: Bernhardt, Reinhold. "Comparative Theology: Between Theology and Religious Studies." *Religions* 3 (2012): 964-972.

Article

Comparative Theology:
Between Theology and Religious Studies

Reinhold Bernhardt

Chair of Systematic Theology/Dogmatics, Theological Faculty, University of Basel (CH), Heuberg 33, CH-4051 Basel, Switzerland; E-Mail: Reinhold.Bernhardt@unibas.ch; Tel.: +41-061-267-04-93

Received: 26 July 2012; in revised form: 10 October 2012 / Accepted: 12 October 2012 / Published: 15 October 2012

Abstract: In the German-speaking academy there is a widespread rivalry between theology and religious studies. "Comparative Theology" provokes suspicions from both sides. This contribution first takes a look at the history of the rivalry, refers then to the criticism from both sides against "Comparative Theology" and suggests a way of positioning it between the two stools. It pleads for distinguishing between the levels of (analytical) method and (constructive) interpretation as far as possible. The comparative approach should be understood and used as a method of comparative analysis in accordance with the standards of religious studies, while theological reflection should constitute the hermeneutical frame of motivation and interpretation.

Keywords: Comparative Theology; religious studies; religious truth-claims

---

1. Introduction

In the German-speaking academy there is not only a split but sometimes a harsh sibling rivalry between the disciplines of theology and religious studies. "Comparative Theology" (CTh) falls between the two stools and comes under scrutiny and even suspicion from both sides. In order to understand that tension we need to take a brief look back in the history of the relationship between the siblings.

2. Sibling Rivalry between Theology and Religious-Studies

Before religious studies developed as an academic discipline of its own the related questions were dealt with in other departments: in theology (often associated with Old Testament studies or Mission-studies) on the one hand and in ethnology and philology (especially Orientalism) which were rooted in the humanities on the other. In Tübingen, for example, the Indologist and Orientalist Rudolf von Roth (1821–1895) regularly lectured on "Allgemeinen und Vergleichenden Religionswissenschaft" ("General and Comparative Studies of Religion"). Friedrich Max Müller can be considered as the very originator of "Comparative Studies of Religions" ("Vergleichende Religionswissenschaft") in the 19th century [1].

A first attempt to integrate the studies of the history of religions into theology (especially in the exegesis of biblical text) was undertaken by the "Religionsgeschichtliche Schule" at the turn from the 19th to the 20th century—which had its center at the theological faculty of Göttingen. The scholars who adhered to that movement analyzed the Bible in the context of studies on the ancient Jewish, Babylonian, Persian and Hellenistic culture and religion. Their motivation for research was a theological one. They strived for a deeper understanding of the emergence and development of the sacred texts of Christianity. Ernst Troeltsch, who was called the "theologist of the Religionsgeschichtlichen Schule" went even further in trying to show on the basis of historical studies that in Christianity the highest values of the history of religions are realized. It was not the least such an apologetic application of religious studies which provoked the emancipation of that discipline from theology.

The company between the uneven siblings parted after World War I. Both turned away from each other. The model of integration was replaced by a model of independence or even dissociation.

On the one hand Karl Barth and the other proponents of the Dialectic-theology movement regarded religious studies as irrelevant for theology. They focussed on the revelation of God in Jesus Christ as it is witnessed in the Bible. Religion was regarded as an epitome of the sinful human and set in strong opposition to faith which is the gift of God alone. As a consequence studies of the history of religion were regarded as research on the historical manifestations of human striving for transcendence and thus to be located in the humanities.

On the other hand scholars of religious studies like Joachim Wach claimed independence for their discipline. In his 1924 published reflections on the epistemological foundations of religious studies [2] he drew a clear and sharp line of demarcation between theology (including the philosophy of religion) and the new discipline which he called with emphasis *science* of religion ("Religions*wissenschaft*"). Following Max Weber's ideal of an "empirical science" he stressed the empirical method in studying religious phenomena. "The task of *Religionswissenschaft* is the exploration and depiction of the empirical religions" [3]. He criticized the "Religionsgeschichtliche Schule" for being centered in Christianity and for pocketing the studies of religious history into theology. In contrast to theology religious studies has to follow a non-confessional agenda, to be ideologically neutral, non-positional and non-normative. It has to keep methodological distance as well to the religious attitudes of the researcher as to the religious phenomena which are the objects of its research. It is obliged to dispense with any value-judgments ("epochè").

In his 1988 published introduction "Was ist Religionswissenschaft?" Hans-Jürgen Greschat—who taught history of religions at the University of Marburg—established a similar borderline between theology and religious studies: While the latter apprehends her objects of study according to their own categories and standards theology applies categories which are coined by the Christian tradition. He stated that if religious studies are conducted by theologians non-Christian phenomena will probably become assimilated to a Christian hermeneutical frame of reference and thus be usurped. The cultural turn of religious studies, its methodological paradigm-shift from a phenomenological to a culture-analytic approach has deepened the gap between the siblings.

The more religious studies emancipated from the inclusion into theology and developed as a distinct academic discipline, the more the chairs for religious studies tended to leave the theological faculties and institutionalize itself in the humanities as an own branch of historical and cultural studies. In this process of emancipation it formed its academic self-understanding frequently in a sharp and sometimes even polemical distinction from theology. Theology became regarded as an ideological enterprise which lacks scientific integrity. That argument quite often is used to demand for institutional (including financial) support of religious studies by the universities at the cost of theology.

CTh now seems to be located right in the middle of religious studies and theology and thus gets entangled in their rivalry. It claims to be a theological enterprise which is rooted *in* religion as opposed to stand beyond and teach *about* religion. It sticks to the truth-claims of Christian faith and asks—like Ernst Troeltsch did—for the validity of religious ideas and practices, as well as for criteria of judging religious phenomena. Thus it does not strive for religious neutrality [4] but presents itself as a normative approach. It differs from the 'old' CTh (which originated from Schleiermacher and found its fully developed form in Troeltsch) by turning to specific phenomena and does not try to create "ideal-types". Its method is micrologic, not macrologic. It shares that methodological turn with present comparative religious studies ("Vergleichende Religionswissenschaft") which also works on the microlevel, asking from there for functions and structures of religious appearances.

The critical questions from both sides—from the side of religious studies and from the side of theology—are similar to those which were addressed by Ernst Troeltsch and his companions.

3. Criticism from the Side of Religious Studies

Scholars of religious studies ask critically: Does CTh 'theologize' the comparative method of religious studies and—as a consequence—lead to a backlash of the emancipation of religious studies from theology in the 20th century? CTh seems to restore the model of integration and to revitalize the agenda of the "Religionsgeschichtliche Schule". The difference to that movement lies in its reference not so much to the history of religions but to its present manifestations. But that makes things even worse in the eyes of the critics.

Jürgen Mohn, who teaches religious studies at the University of Basel, states a clear cut difference between comparative religious studies and CTh. It relates to the truth-question and concerns the method of CTh as he noticed it in the work of James Fredericks [5]. In his comparisons between the notions of "person" in the Buddhist philosophy of Dōgen and in Trinitarian theology [6] Fredericks—according to Mohn—relates the Buddhist tradition immediately to 'his' Christian tradition and thus enters into a *dialogue*. As distinct from a dialogue, a comparison (and all the more a methodological testable comparison) needs a third level (*tertium comparationis*). It needs a perspective which is different from the self-understanding of the traditions and it needs categories which are not interwoven by them. Otherwise one falls back into what Mohn calls a "self-comparison" of the 'own' with the 'other' ("Selbstvergleich mit dem Fremden" [7]), which on the basis of the own religious tradition tries to determine similarities and differences in the other tradition, in order to deepen the understanding of the own tradition. The problem of such a method of relating the 'other' to the 'own' lies in transferring tradition-specific concepts like "ontology" or "salvation" to the other tradition to which they do not comply. The result may be a better understanding of the one's tradition but at the cost of possibly misunderstanding the other.

Robert C. Neville and Klaus von Stosch are aware of that jeopardy. Thus von Stosch pleads for introducing the role of a "third" participant in interreligious comparisons ("Instanz des Dritten") [8] and refers to Robert C. Nevilles postulation of a "cloud of witnesses" [9]. It is interesting to compare the suggestions of Mohn, von Stosch, and Neville. While for Mohn the "third" is the acting subject who conducts the comparison, for von Stosch and Neville he/she plays only the role of a critical observant who has to guarantee that the actors who conduct the comparison do not diminish the differences, respect the otherness of phenomena from the other tradition and prevent assimilations. The acting subjects for them are adherents of the respective religious traditions (mostly theologians) while for Mohn it is the 'neutral' scholar of religious studies. According to Neville the "cloud of witnesses" consists of the scientific community in the theologies of the religious traditions and in religious studies in the present and the past. Von Stosch assigns the role of the "third" to anyone who is not member of the religious traditions which are to be related to each other. He/she can be an atheist or an agnostic or an adherent of another religion or a scholar of cultural studies. It is crucial that he/she represents another basis idea ("hinreichend verschiedene Grundidee" [10]). For Mohn the "third" is the "first". The "third" is not primarily a personalized but stands for a method. Mohn's reflections on that issue are not located on the level of interreligious communication but are part of a theory of science ("Wissenschaftstheorie") of the religious studies. They refer to the epistemological basis of that discipline and describe the setting of the comparison, the structure of the 'room' in which it takes place. For the comparison it does not need the persons who belong to specific religious traditions but only the scholar of religious studies. The adherents who represent the traditions in their specific way (including the truth-claims of those traditions) are *objects* of comparison.

The epistemological and methodological difference between comparative religious studies and CTh correlates a different attitude towards the truth-question. While religious studies—according to Mohn—are basically abstinent to religious truth-claims CTh shares the truth-claims of the Christian tradition. The "third" level is truth-laden. Klaus von Stosch does not take truth as something given which is exclusively represented in that tradition. Although it is grounded in God's revelation in Christ

Christian faith and theology cannot claim to possess the truth in its plentitude. That is due to the universal und eschatological nature of that truth. It exceeds beyond the Christian tradition and its consummation is yet to come. Thus Christians have to be open for its ongoing self-manifestation which includes other religious traditions as well. Only on this epistemological premise the project of CTh is possible—in contrast to the absolute truth-claims on one side and to abandoning the question of truth on the other. Interreligious encounters are means of discovering that truth.

This avowal to truth not the least is supposed to protect CTh against the charge of relativism as it is raised frequently against the pluralist model of the theology of religions. But what does it mean in the concrete work of CTh? All the case studies I know of do not try to evaluate religious phenomena—neither those of the Christian religion nor those of other religions. They practice a "passing over and coming back" (John S. Dunne) but they do not ask for truth. Does that dissonance between programmatic sketches and the real performance indicate a methodological problem? Some proponents of the CTh offer sets of criteria evaluating religious phenomena [11] but those reflections remain on a rather abstract philosophical level. They are not applied to specific interreligious comparisons and probably not easy applicable. If such an application is supposed to be the way of seeking for truth then this does not happen here.

If it would happen the question occurs how to relate CTh to theology of religions. If truth-seeking presupposes that the seekers have a pre-conception ("Vorverständnis") of what they seek so that they can identify truth in what they have found and if that pre-conception is coined by Christian beliefs then an inclusivism in terms of theology of religion is unavoidable.

Concerning the question of truth the positions of the Comparative theologians are not in accord. Keith Ward distinguishes between confessional and comparative theology. Confessional theology is restricted to the Christian tradition, tries to unfold its content in order to foster its reception. It is based on the assumption that this tradition roots in an authentic revelation of God und thus leads into the salvific truth of God. Comparative theology, however, relates the Christian belief to the beliefs and religious practices of other religions. According to Ward CTh is "an intellectual discipline which enquires into ideas of the ultimate reality and goal of human life, as they have been perceived and expressed in a variety of religious traditions" [12]. Its task is to discover similarities and differences between different religious beliefs and practices. The question of truth is not crucial for that endeavor. CTh "does not, as such, and like confessional theology, presuppose the truth of one tradition, and see the others from its own point of view" [13]. It is a method of relating religious phenomena which does not presuppose the claim that the own religions tradition manifests the truth. It abstains from value-judgments and thus does not need to develop and apply criteria for assessing truth-claims. It is theology inasmuch as it refers to a transcendent reality and not only to empirical religious phenomena, and as much as it refers to the religious traditions as assumed manifestation of that reality.

To describe the task of CTh in that way obviously differs from Clooneys, Fredericks and von Stosch's understanding. The difference may be—at least partly—explainable by taking into account that those three are roman-catholic theologians look for an alternative to the pluralist theology of religions as it was condemned by the "Congregation for the Doctrine of the Faith" (CDF), especially in the declaration "Dominus Iesus" (2000). As many of their colleagues they strive for creating a theological foundation of interreligious dialogue while not arousing suspicion of being a pluralist or—even worse—a relativist. Thus they stress the importance of being loyal to the truth as it is manifest in the Christian tradition but goes beyond. As an Anglican, Ward, however, is free from such considerations. He does not need to attune his theological position with the normative standards of the ecclesiastical magisterium. That is not to say that for the Catholic proponents of CTh there are no other motivations for creating and developing that approach. Clooney, like Ward, points to his biographical experience of religious diversity [14]. Ward felt challenged by that plurality and compelled to answer the question why humans who seek the one truth differ so deeply in their perceptions of it. So he asked: Is there a way of mediating between those differences? [15] For Ward, as for the other Comparative Theologians, to mediate between religious traditions is not primarily a question of theological programs, located in the debate on theology of religions (on that level Ward tends to be a pluralist), but a matter of the credibility and of intellectual integrity of his Christian faith. But it is obvious that especially the Roman-Catholic proponents of CTh try to proof the theological legitimacy of that approach by stressing that it is to be practiced *within* confessional theology [16], while Ward regards CTh as a method which widens the horizon of confessional theology and stands in tension over against it.

4. Criticism from the Side of Theology

While the critical questions from the side of the religious studies focus on the "Standortgebundenheit" of CTh, on being tied to the normative position and perspective of Christian belief, the objections from the side of theology appeal to its alleged tendency to dissolve confessional into an interreligious theology. The crucial question here concerns the epistemological basis of Christian belief and theology: Is no longer the Scripture alone (*sola scriptura*) or the Scripture (as the *norma normans*) plus the confessions of faith (as the *norma normata*) and/or (for Roman-Catholic believers) the magisterium the source of belief and theology? Is it also the encounter of religions?

The critics may point to Klaus von Stosch's statement that interreligious dialogue is the *basis* for CTh [17]—and thus for theology in general, because theology altogether should be done in a comparative way. It is a theology *of* dialogue. Von Stosch does not intend to create a new theology but to do confessional theology as comparative theology. On the other hand, he stresses that the traditional confessional theologies will undergo transformations. How is that to be understood? Are the non-Christian traditions *sources* of authentic theological knowledge or are they regarded merely as hermeneutical *frames* for interpreting the Christian tradition?

More radical is the suggestion of Keith Ward to strive for a "global" theology [18]. For him the whole history of religions constitutes the epistemic source of theology. In that respect his program overlaps with the demand for an interreligious theology as it is raised by some proponents of a 'pluralist theology of religion' like Perry Schmidt-Leukel [19] or Rose Drew who worked with him at Glasgow University [20]. The critics may blame Ward and all those who try to extend the epistemological basis of theology for betraying the revelation in Christ by looking for 'revelations' elsewhere.

Clooney is more cautious inasmuch as his normative point of reference is the revelation in Christ. He does not strive for a global theology but for an "inter-theology", as Norbert Hintersteiner puts it [21]. But even here the question arises: How are the non-Christian traditions—in his case: the Hindu traditions—to be qualified in terms of a theological epistemology? For the "deep learning across religious borders" advocated by Clooney needs a double or multiple religious loyalty on the side of the Comparative Theologian. Is that an asymmetrical loyalty?

This is not the least a dispute on 'apologetics'. Ward regards global theology as an alternative to an 'apologetic' way of doing theology. Other proponents of CTh share that aversion to apologetics. Friedemann Eissler by contrast claims that an apologetic attitude necessarily is tied to holding on to the truth of Christian faith as Francis Clooney, James Fredericks and Klaus von Stosch intend to do. Apologetics should not become discredited as a polemical distortion of other religious beliefs and practices in order to demonstrate the superiority of the Christian religion [22]. Paul Tillich qualified theology as a whole as an apologetic endeavor in the sense of giving answers to the existential questions of the contemporaries.

Eissler insist that there is a qualitative difference between showing *respect* towards adherents of other religions traditions (and towards the traditions itself) and *acknowledging* those traditions (including their truth-claims) theologically. He claims to distinguish between successful communication and normative relevance. Is it possible—Eissler asks—to turn to another religion on the level of normative relevance without departing from ones one?

A closely related question concerns in regard to witnessing the Christian faith towards people of other (or no) religious faith and thereby touches the issue of 'mission', which was and is a vital manifestation of Christian faith since its very origins. If CTh is not only a subdiscipline of theology but is supposed to become the new paradigm for theology as a whole—as Klaus von Stosch insists—doesn't that marginalize or even exclude missionary efforts in the sense of inviting communication of Christian faith? What about the claims of *universality* which are inherent in the gospel of Jesus Christ and which go beyond the Christian language-games? What about the *provocation* of that message which according to Paul is a stumblingblock unto the Jews, and foolishness unto the Greeks (1Co 1:23)? How in general does the "proprium" (the characteristic, crucial features) of this message, in which it is fundamentally distinguished from other forms of faith, come into play? The more we turn to the core of it the more a comparison becomes difficult because it lacks a *tertitum comparationis*. It is possible to give witness of such core-beliefs in a dialogical communication—but is it possible (or at least fruitful) to compare them?

5. CTh as a Bridge between Religious Studies and Theology

In his "Introduction to the science of religion" Max Müller states that there is "a doctrine more unchristian than any that could be found in the pages of the religious books of antiquity, viz. that all the nations of the earth before the rise of Christianity, were mere outcasts, forsaken and forgotten of their Father in heaven, without a knowledge of God, without a hope of salvation. If a comparative study of the religions of the world produced but this one result, that it drove this godless heresy out of every Christian heart, and made us see again in the whole history of the world the eternal wisdom and love of God towards all His creatures, it would have done a good work" [23].

Müller's statement is as relevant today as it was in 1870, when he gave his lectures on the "Science of Religion" and pleaded for a comparative approach in the study of religion. He hoped that such an approach would overcome the "heresy" of exclusivism. To call exclusivism a heresy means to see it in contradiction to fundamental convictions of Christian faith.

If CTh wants to assert its claim to be a *theological* enterprise it needs to enroot the comparative approach in a theology of religions which shows that from the very heart of the Christian faith we can expect God's salvific presence to be present not only in the Christian tradition. That creates an attitude of 'theological curiosity' which expects to meet those representations in other forms of faiths. From a Christian perspective they can be identified as such—as formations of grace—in the light of the Christ-revelation. Such a hermeneutical inclusivism cannot be avoided. And it need not be avoided because it has nothing to do with a claim of superiority. The adherents of other religious tradition will use *their* normative worldviews to decipher manifestations of the transcendent reality in the immanent reality of nature and history. That leads to a *mutual* hermeneutical inclusivism. The different faith-perspectives can be set in a dialogical relation.

On that hermeneutical basis and in the frame of a theology of religion (which should not become reduced to the debate on the 'models' of exclusivism, inclusivism und pluralism) interreligious comparisons on the micro-level seem possible and useful. The individual and communal faith-perspectives on the medium-level cannot be the object of a methodological comparison and the faith traditions as a whole on the macro-level still less.

6. Conclusions

I suggest that interreligious comparisons are to be conducted by the standards of religious studies. That is not a theological endeavor in itself. Like historical exegesis of biblical texts it is a method of philological and cultural studies which can and should be applied by theology. Theological reasoning comes into play first, on the level of motivation which precedes the comparison, and second, on the level of interpretation which follows it. Thus theology creates the frame of the comparison but does not interfere with it methodologically. Such a distinction of levels should invalidate criticisms from the side of religious studies and help to defend CTh against becoming charged of reducing theology to cultural studies by abandoning the truth claim of Christian faith. According to that gradation CTh is to be regarded as a method which can be applied to every religion. The method stays the same while the frame can change.

Conflicts of Interest

The author declares no conflict of interest.

References and Notes

1. Friedrich M. Müller. *Einleitung in die vergleichende Religionswissenschaft*, 1st German ed. 1874. Reprint: Saarbrücken: Verlag Classic Edition, 2010.
2. Joachim Wach. *Religionswissenschaft. Prolegomena zu ihrer wissenschaftstheoretischen Grundlegung*. Leipzig: J. C. Hinrichs'sche Buchhandlung, 1924. See also: Rainer Flasche. *Die Religionswissenschaft Joachim Wachs*, Berlin: De Gruyter, 1978.
3. Wach, 68 (translation R.B.).
4. Klaus von Stosch. *Komparative Theologie als Wegweiser in der Welt der Religionen*. Beiträge zur Komparativen Theologie 6. Paderborn et alii: Ferdinand Schönigh, 2012, 231; Cf. Keith Ward. *Religion and Revelation. A Theology of Revelation in the World's Religions*. Oxford: Clarendon Press, 1994, 40.
5. Jürgen Mohn. "Komparatistik als Position und Gegenstand der Religionswissenschaft." In *Komparative Theologie. Interreligiöse Vergleiche als Weg der Religionstheologie*, edited by Reinhold Bernhardt and Klaus von Stosch. Beiträge zu einer Theologie der Religionen 7. Zürich: Theologischer Verlag Zürich, 2009, 225–276.
6. James Fredericks. Das Selbst vergessen: Buddhistische Reflexionen zur Trinität. In *Komparative Theologie*, edited by Reinhold Bernhardt and Klaus von Stosch. 203–223.
7. Mohn, 269.
8. Von Stosch, 208–211.
9. Robert Cummings Neville. Philosophische Grundlagen und Methoden der Komparativen Theologie. In *Komparative Theologie*, edited by Reinhold Bernhardt and Klaus von Stosch. 42.
10. Von Stosch, 209.
11. Von Stosch, 293–316.
12. Ward. Religion and Revelation, 40.
13. Quoted from the English version of the paper which was published as: Keith Ward. Programm, Perspektiven und Ziele Komparativer Theologie. In *Komparative Theologie*, edited by Reinhold Bernhardt and Klaus von Stosch. 55–68. The German translation reads: „Sie setzt als solche weder die Wahrheit einer Tradition voraus, wie es in der konfessionellen Theologie geschieht, noch betrachtet sie die anderen nur aus der eigenen Perspektive." 63.
14. Francis X. Clooney. *Comparative Theology. Deep Learning across Religious Borders*. Malden, MA: Wiley-Blackwell, 2010, 1–23.
15. Ward. Programm, 59.
16. Von Stosch, 211f. Clooney, 111ff.
17. Von Stosch, 212.
18. Keith Ward. The Idea of 'God' in Global Theology. In *Naming and Thinking God in Europe Today*, edited by Norbert Hintersteiner. Amsterdam/New York: Rodopi, 2007, 377–388.
19. Perry Schmidt-Leukel. "Interkulturelle Theologie als interreligiöse Theologie." *Evangelische Theologie* 1 (2011): 4–15.

20. See her contribution to this issue. See also: José. María Vigil, ed. *Toward a Planetary Theology* (Along the Many Paths of God V). Montreal: Dunamis Publishers, 2010.
21. See: Norbert Hintersteiner. Interkulturelle Übersetzung in religiöser Mehrsprachigkeit. Reflexionen zu Ort und Ansatz der Komparativen Theologie. In *Komparative Theologie*, edited by Reinhold Bernhardt and Klaus von Stosch. 114.
22. Friedemann Eißler: "Komparative Theologie. Eine Alternative zu bisherigen religionstheologischen Konzepten?" *Zeitschrift für Religions- und Weltanschauungsfragen* 12 (2011): 449–455.
23. Friedrich Max Müller. *Introduction to the Science of Religion* (1870). London: Longmans, Green, and Co., 1882. Reprint: Elibron Classic Replica Edition, Boston: Adamant Media Corporation 2005, 149.

Reprinted from *Religions*. Cite as: Stosch, Klaus von. "Comparative Theology as Liberal and Confessional Theology." *Religions* 3 (2012): 983-992.

Article

Comparative Theology as Liberal and Confessional Theology

Klaus von Stosch

Universität Paderborn, Warburgerstraße 100, 33098 Paderborn, Germany;
E-Mail: klaus.von.stosch@uni-paderborn.de; Tel.: +49-5251-602362

Received: 14 September 2012; in revised form: 10 October 2012 / Accepted: 15 October 2012 / Published: 22 October 2012

Abstract: For most European scholars, the scope of Comparative Theology is not very clear. They see big differences between the notion of Comparative Theology among its protagonists, e.g., between Keith Ward or Robert Neville and Francis Clooney or James Fredericks. That is why I will try to define a certain understanding of Comparative Theology which can be defended in accordance with strong European theological traditions. I want to show that Comparative Theology can be understood as one of the best fruits of liberal theology and of a Wittgensteinian interpretation of transcendental philosophy—and that it opens new perspectives for confessional theology. The current development of Islamic theology in Germany is especially challenging for Comparative Theology and the best opportunity to develop it into a project undertaken by scholars of different religions and different intellectual traditions. I will argue that Comparative Theology is not a new discipline within the old disciplines of theology, but that it can give new perspectives to all theological disciplines and thoroughly change their character.

Keywords: liberal theology; postliberal theology; comparative theology; global theology; confessional theology; German theology; Kant; Wittgenstein

1. Comparative Theology and the Dispute between Liberal and Postliberal Theologies

Christian Theology in Germany is highly influenced by philosophers from the enlightenment era, such as Immanuel Kant, as well as certain aspects of German idealism, in particular the philosophy of free will. The basic idea underlying this philosophy is to provide insight into the senselessness of the traditional metaphysical debates on both the nature and perceptibility of reality. Kant explains that there is no scientific possibility of solving the debate between empiricism and rationalism within a metaphysical framework. Thus, a continuation of traditional metaphysics in line with Plato or Aristotle would lead to the end of metaphysics as science; it is therefore necessary to reshape metaphysical inquiry in a way that allows for the achievement of results which can be falsified. In this vein, theology has to change its outlook from metaphysical doctrine to considerations *sub specie humanitatis* [1] and critical engagement [2].

I call this a critical theology, which understands human free will and human rights as the basic principles underlying all theological considerations. In essence, such critical theology posits a positive relationship to modernity as liberal theology. Characteristic of liberal theology as such is the universal struggle for the liberation of humans.

This liberal, critical and public theology seems, however, to have two different branches. One branch understands its own approach and theories as universal, at times driven to establish a sort of world or global theology [3]. It is revisionist towards many traditional parts of Christian belief and thus highly disputed. The overwhelming majority of contemporary Catholic theologians in Germany do not agree with this tradition because they insist on the denominational or creedal character of theology. This liberal theology is based on philosophers and theologians like Friedrich Daniel Ernst Schleiermacher and Ernst Troeltsch.

The other branch of liberal theology has at once a universalist character combined with an acceptance that people in different cultures, times and denominations have varying approaches to theology. Unlike postliberals, these theologians believe that these differences do not consequently lead to incommensurability among religious language games. They avoid any kind of relativistic or pluralistic movements without establishing one global theory or super language game in theology. They understand their theology as public theology, not because they think that everybody has to share it, but rather because they want to provide evidence pertaining to all contexts. The public character of liberal theology as such consists of the claim to translate theological ideas in all kinds of language games without using only one method or one language in realizing this task. Paul Tillich and Karl Rahner are two of the most important theologians engaged in such a form of liberal theology, or "contextual theology." In contemporary intellectual thought, Wolfgang Huber (who has developed concepts of communicative freedom and public theology [4]) and Jürgen Werbick (who has outlined an idea of non-foundationalist foundation of Christian belief [5]) seem to continue this tradition. One could argue that this is the most influential type of theology in Germany today.

There are also postliberal and postmodern thinkers who criticize the universalist tendencies of both kinds of liberal theology, armed with the belief that theology must first and foremost express the belief of the church, shaping our world by the message of the Bible. Postliberals perceive a gap between the world and the church, and find that it is decisive for theology to adopt the perspective of the Church and the Bible. In the Catholic tradition, postliberals have established a sort of coalition with anti-liberal, neo-conservative, sometimes neo-scholastical thinkers. In the Protestant tradition, they share much with the Evangelicals. Postliberals are an increasing minority in the German academic context.

If we are looking at the attitude towards the emerging field of comparative theology espoused by these various groups, according to a postliberal perspective, it does not make sense for theologians to contribute to comparative studies. This arises from their position that any form of theological reasoning must arise from the Bible, which they perceive as the first (and most important) Christian theology [6]. Although the Bible also deals with people of other religious paths and although postliberals draw on a wide range of Western philosophical, literary and theological resources, they always want to use the Bible as the starting point to debate religion. Of course it is also possible to establish a comparative theology of sorts from a postliberal standpoint, which allows Christians both to explain Christianity and to speak with adherents of other religions who explain their theologies. In the end, however, any attempt to establish a postliberal comparative theology will end up in apologetic movements or in relativism, since a postliberal framework cannot provide the criteria that allow theologians to modify their own theological insights in the light of other religions or philosophical theories. At least in this perspective such a modification cannot be grounded in reason. A postliberal movement tends to think that other religions are inferior to the religion of the scholar or that they simply cannot be understood.

Both ideas—the claim to incommensurability and the lack of possible appreciation of other religions—contradict the basic principles of comparative theology and the attitudes that Catherine Cornille recommends for interreligious dialogue. Cornille invites theologians to search for a way to welcome the differences of the other and to find a common ground for understanding [7]. As comparative theology seems to be in a sort of tension with postliberal thinking, it can be explained in the tradition of liberal theology. This is why it is so important to decide which branch of liberal theology should be distinctive for comparative theology. The key question underlying this task is whether comparative theology is another term for world, global or interreligious theology, or instead a movement within confessional theology/theologies?

2. Comparative Theology and the Dispute between Global and Confessional Theology

In the U.S., Robert Cummings Neville is one of the most important proponents of comparative theology as a global theology and as a public theology without the necessity of denominational attachment. Neville believes that basic theological ideas can be defended from a purely philosophical perspective. If you consider Neville's *Cross-Cultural Comparative Religious Ideas Project*, which was organized in the late 1990s at Boston University [8], it is striking that religious insider perspectives are usually avoided, in order to prevent any kind of apologetics, although some of the participants of the project like Clooney argued within the volumes for the necessity of insider views. Neville himself seems to think that truth is found in avoiding insider views and searching for neutral and objective perspectives. This directly connects to the first branch of liberal theology.

The problem with religious convictions from the perspective of contextual liberal theology, however, is that they cannot be adequately understood from the outside, and they experience shifts in meaning if they are translated into secular contexts or outsider views. They have not only a cognitive, but also regulative and expressive dimensions, *i.e.*, they express values and attitudes of religious believers and they highly influence their form of life and have to be understood within this context [9]. It is thus imperative to include religious believers as theologians who explain their own theologies in any project of comparative theology.

Of course, Neville knows how diverse and differing religious worldviews are and how difficult it is to translate them across cultures and strands of thought. Yet he thinks that we all have 'to operate within a public that integrates reflections from as many of the world's philosophic traditions as possible' [10]. The problem with this idea of a globalized theology or philosophy, which integrates all kinds of theological and philosophical systems, is that it ignores the impossibility of translating all language games in one system of reference. Although each religion has a possibility of finding ways to understand others' worldviews, the ways of understanding can be very different; they have to be found in different ways within different cultural and philosophical contexts. Each world religion can identify numerous commonalities and differences with other world religions, and thus there is no way of integrating all of them into one theory or perspective. This is the truth of postmodernism. However—and this is why modernity cannot simply be replaced by postmodernism—different ways of establishing comparative theologies that integrate diverse theories and worldviews can always be found—albeit one can never engage all of them at the same time.

Wittgenstein employs the metaphor of 'family resemblances' to explain this point (PI 65-71). This metaphor explains that while you can compare every member of a family with any other member because of certain resemblances, there is no single characteristic shared by all members of a family. Some will have the same nose, others have some similar movements, others share an accent. Thus, there is always a way to know that somebody belongs to a certain family. Returning to the theological applications of such relational understanding, the bridges to this knowledge are very different across cultures and perspectives—and, even more problematically, are not necessarily even comprehensible from other perspectives. This underlies why we need so many different approaches to theology, which cannot be harmonized in one super language game. The quality of a comparative theology is not dependent on the number of internalized theories, but rather on its capacity to create networks and to enter into dialogue with other perspectives, *i.e.*, to search for truth in different contexts.

If we avoid understanding comparative theology as global theology, we can begin to appreciate the attention to particulars characteristic of the comparative work of Francis X. Clooney or James L. Fredericks. In this branch of comparative theology, theologians try to 'do theology' in dialogue with one other religious tradition while maintaining a particular framework aimed at answering key questions. The goal is not *one* coherent theology that integrates all strands of comparative work. Nor is the aim a global theology that integrates as many worldviews as possible. The aim is simply to deal with case studies in order to produce a preliminary survey of a certain kind of problem. This type of comparative theology seeks to create a dialogue between different theologies in diverse contexts. This concept is, however, inevitably in danger of postmodern relativism or theological irrelevance if it does not explain convincingly the choice of its subjects. It is important to connect it with the central research tasks of theological inquiry of today. The challenge of the next years will be to develop this 'micrological' kind of inquiry in a more systematic way, without turning to postmodernism or liberal theology characteristic of classical 19th century German liberal theology. European comparative theology provides the opportunity to reflect through the second branch of liberal theology, which I explored above.

3. Challenges for Comparative Theology

A European perspective, in particular the German tradition of confessional theology, could help comparative theology strike a balance between the temptation of (supra-denominational) global theology and a postliberal language game approach. Three challenges remain at the core of comparative theology:

3.1. The Challenge of Non-christian Theologies

One challenge is quite obvious. It consists of the emerging field of non-Christian theologies, in particular that of Muslim theology in countries like Germany. After many years of ignorance towards the sizable Muslim community in Germany, the federal government has recently established (and funded) the discipline of Islamic Theology at German universities. This has led to a burgeoning attempt to connect this new, developing theology with comparative theology, most strikingly evident in the Center for Comparative Theology and Cultural Studies at Paderborn University. It will be decisive for the future of denominational theology in general whether Muslim and Christian theologies will succeed in finding ways to cooperate fruitfully, thereby transcending religious borders without losing their respective religious identities. The methods of comparative theology can undoubtedly contribute significantly to this endeavor.

3.2. The Challenge of the Orientation towards Problems and Needs

My second point is related to the question of the selection of examples within the concentration on particular case studies in comparative theology. It seems important in this respect that comparative theology succeeds in giving orientation to actual, posed questions and that it remains—in the words of the Second Vatican Council—concerned with the 'the joys and the hopes, the grief and the anxieties of the men of this age, especially those who are poor or in any way afflicted' [11].

Although comparative theology unites and contrasts, the selection of cases is not arbitrary. It must instead be geared to anthropological and theological problems. And it must engage questions about sense, salvation and truth, as well as critical challenges. Without the careful selection of cases, comparative theology could become a playground for detail-loving eccentrics who meticulously compare irrelevant subjects. Just as comparing random linguistic details is not analytic philosophy, comparing religious traditions is not automatically comparative theology. As time is finite and as not all problems can be solved, it is also important to reflect on which questions should be first on the agenda of comparative theology. Thus, theologians of different religions have to decide together on the problems on which their work should focus.

In comparative theology as in other branches of theology, it is important that intellectual questions are addressed from different viewpoints of religious and non-religious traditions. The critique of religion is meaningful in this discipline. Of course, there does not exist as a uniform canon of questions to be universally addressed by all comparative theologies in the world. And yet through concrete research, one should identify shared problems as both belonging to—and perhaps existing beyond—a certain cultural context.

Thus, I am not sure whether, in comparative theology, it is really sufficient just to 'go forward by intuitive leaps, according to instinct' [12]. Perhaps this appearance of arbitrariness is one of the reasons why comparative theology is still regarded suspiciously by mainstream theology in Europe [13]. Instead of following one's own intuition it may be useful to build on current theoretical strands and to try to get fresh insights through comparative work. This is already occurring in the field of comparative theology—for example, in an article by Jim Fredericks, which deals with the doctrine of trinity in the context of Buddhism [14]. However, even in Fredericks's expansive work, his insights could be connected more closely to recent discussions in the different areas of theology. On the one hand, the aim should be to struggle with the main challenges of theology as a whole through comparative theology. On the other hand, work should be carried out on current social problems, as well as religious conflicts—including the potential of violence between religions [15].

As some younger scholars in comparative theology have pointed out, comparative theology has much to learn from theological movements like liberation theology or feminist theology. Such theological movements can help comparative work demonstrate and address the distress of the marginalized and become aware of hidden consequences of their own reasoning [16]. When focusing on classical texts arising out of different theological traditions, for example, it is important to keep in mind what these texts mean not just for insiders, but also for outsiders—and the marginalized, in particular. Feminist theology could provide guidance in this area [17]. Clooney is right in emphasizing our need for a mutual process of critique at this point; in other words, feminist theology also has to seriously engage interreligious and intercultural strands of intellectual thought, which could be accomplished through dialogue with comparative theology [18]. Nonetheless, the key point here is that comparative theology needs an ideologically critical process in determining both its research areas and methods. The systematic development of a large variety of methods and theological approaches in the different sub-disciplines within theology can help to better pinpoint necessary areas of study, and thereby help to initiate emancipatory processes [19].

The orientation of theology towards the problems and needs, the grief and anxieties of humans, does not mean that the micrological method or the attention to detail in comparative work must be relinquished. Comparative theology must consist of a large variety of case studies, rather than be engaged as a meta-theory. These case studies are not independent from human needs, but instead have to care for them. They are not value-free, but rather engaged for the sake of humankind. Comparative theology—from my perspective—wants to empower people to orientate their lives and to set them free. In order to participate in such liberating processes, it has to begin from a certain creedal perspective or a certain worldview; and it has to become increasingly sensitive to the needs and the possibilities of world development. The aim of theology should not be a competition among different theological approaches, in order to determine which account or which religion is best at solving a problem. The aim should rather be to solve problems together and to encourage people to solve them. Ecology is the best example of a pan-human problem beyond the range of any one or even two religions to solve. It needs everyone, religious and non-religious as well. If religions can understand that they have certain tasks to fulfill in and for the world, they can find a way out of an orientation, which seeks for the weaknesses of the other. Instead of showing the strength of one's own religion against others, it is important to empower the strengths of the other religion to solve our common problems [20].

The Muslim scholar Farid Esack, for example, explains in a moving way how the shared commitment of Christians, Muslims and atheists against the apartheid regime led to a new appreciation of others [21]. In a similar vein, Dietrich Bonhoeffer realized that non-Christians, e.g., communists, were some of his most important combatants against the terror of the Nazis [22]. Obviously, there are commonalities between different worldviews, which at times reflect religious commonalities and which can be both understood and enacted through united actions. Sometimes on a deeper level of understanding, that Wittgenstein calls the level of depth grammar (PI 664), reconciliation and existential understanding across religious borders becomes possible. This too can be reflected in comparative theology. In order to achieve such a constructive, common attitude beyond the borders of different worldviews, a lot of work has to be done in comparative theology; many theoretical problems seem to impede such an engagement. Perhaps the most important step in this context is the insight in the above-mentioned regulative and expressive dimension of worldviews and of religious beliefs [8] and the willingness to give up any essentialist understanding of religion. This general attitude can only be a first step. The decisive points are detailed case studies showing new possibilities of relating religious worldviews and revealing their common challenges.

If comparative theology really concerns the recent problems of people, however, and intends to deal with current theological questions, there is always the danger of projection. Some of the greatest problems of humankind have been caused by people who wanted to solve the problems of the world. There is always the danger of imposing an individual perspective on the other. Furthermore, even if comparative theology is developed in dialogue with other positions and worldviews, there is always a third position that is not taken into account.

3.3. The Challenge of the Third Position

In Europe, theology is very much accustomed to developing its theories in dialogue with secular, agnostic and atheistic people [23]. Every argument is examined from ideologically critical perspectives, but for many years Christian theologians did not adequately take the contributions of non-Christian theologians into account. Thus, the perspective of non-Christian or non-Western-theologies did not contribute to the initial development of theology on the continent. However, European theology informed by atheism can help remind comparative theology not to forget the importance of secular questions and ideas. As it is not possible to integrate all perspectives, we always have to reflect which perspective is ignored in the setting of a research project. The instance of a third position can help us to avoid blind spots in theology. The integration of such third positions therefore presents the third great challenge for comparative theology.

Mutual-including processes of understanding fundamental to comparative theology bear the threat of making reciprocal arrangements and agreements in order to disguise certain problems. If two confessional inner-perspectives focus on a particular problem, there exists an increased risk of trivializing the problem on the basis of shared convictions. As Franz Kafka puts it, those that engage in this process run the risk of becoming a „community of scoundrels". For instance, conservative Muslims and conservative Christians can easily agree on condemning sexual relationships of gays, and it is very important that they take into consideration the perspective of aggrieved parties in their judgements.

Modern theology tends to underestimate this threat with reference to autonomous philosophical reason and the attempt to develop religion-external criteriology. However, since the linguistic turn, this endeavour has been challenged. Metaphysical and transcendental-philosophical oriented attempts to develop such a criteriology are often considered rather unhelpful, with the whole idea of religion-external criteriology highly disputed. Nonetheless, I recommend that such a criteriology can and needs to be developed on a formal level. At least to some extent, the instance of a third position could be established by the position of a philosophically autonomous, critical, external perspective.

Unfortunately, two opposing problems appear in attempting to engage the third perspective or third way. On the one hand, this criteriology is necessarily too pluralistic, since it cannot answer orientation problems and must comprehend contradicting truth claims as equally rational. On the other, this criteriology is not pluralistic enough, since it is based on a reasonable understanding within a certain philosophical tradition and therefore rejects religious positions from a philosophical point of view.

The third position cannot therefore simply be an abstract philosophy or criteriology, but must instead be concrete and be able to observe and control, the dialogue of the other two positions in play. To avoid an 'expanded community of scoundrels', it seems essential that the third position holds a continuing moment of critique on the processed problems. This third position could thus be atheistic or agnostic. Depending on the dialogue context, a follower of a third religious tradition can also (or instead) be consulted if: (1) the religion espouses a sufficiently different basic idea of the question at hand, and (2) the follower is able to confront the issue with respectively critical, skilled arguments. For example, it can be a decisive progress for Christian-Muslim dialogue if the Jewish perspective is taken into account on certain issues [24].

If theologians of two religious traditions manage to find a common grammar or a common set of assumptions, they always have to remain open to the perspectives of theologians from other religious traditions, because otherwise the new commonality can produce injustice towards others. In all comparative work—not only in theology—it is important to look for a third point of reference to avoid any kind of one-sidedness or bias [25]. This third point of reference does not hint at a privileged point of view from a sort of supervisor of comparative processes, which could be adopted by a highly critical philosopher. Rather, the aim of the third position to consult scientific processes external to the movement of dialogue and mutual exchange. This position can help to illuminate the blind spots of reasoning and critically review all results.

At this point, Robert C. Neville is speaking of a 'great cloud of witnesses' that can consist of very different approaches [26]. Only all witnesses together can fulfill the task of creating a critical comparative theology. Neville admits that it is not possible to satisfy or even to hear all witnesses at the same time, but he insists, quite convincingly, on the necessity of always being prepared to answer to a witness. As I explained above I am not convinced that comparative theology can be formulated in a way to integrate all questions of such third positions. Nonetheless I think that it is decisive to take into account at least a concrete third position in the comparative movements.

Finally, the third position also has to integrate the diversity not only between, but also within religions. Comparative theology has to be an ecumenical endeavor with different insiders from each denomination, if it wants to achieve representative results [27]. Only the participation of different actors of various denominations can show at the same time the possibility of reconciliation among religions and the vulnerability of all achieved results. As the possibility of direct participation cannot be given to everybody, it is very important that in different countries and different universities the idea of the third position is fulfilled in varying ways, which will effectively stimulate and strengthen this field.

Conflicts of Interest

The author declares no conflict of interest.

References and Notes

1. Peter M.S. Hacker. *Insight and Illusion. Themes in the Philosophy of Wittgenstein.* Reprint of the revised and corrected 1989 edition. Bristol: St. Augustine's Press, 1997, 146.
2. Cf. Klaus von Stosch. "Transzendental Kritizismus und Wahrheitsfrage." In *Kant und die moderne Theologie*, edited by Georg Essen and Magnus Striet. WBG: Darmstadt, 2005, 46–94.
3. Cf. Rose Drew's paper in this volume; Keith Ward. "The *idea* of "God" in global theology." In *Naming and Thinking God in Europe Today. Theology in Global Dialogue*, edited by Norbert Hintersteiner. Amsterdam-New York: Rodopi, 2007 (Currents of Encounter—Studies on the contact between Christianity and other religions, beliefs and cultures; 32), 377–388.
4. Cf. Wolfgang Huber. *Von der Freiheit. Perspektiven für eine solidarische Welt*, edited by Helga Kuhlmann and Tobias Reitmeier. Beck: München, 2012.
5. Cf. Jürgen Werbick. *Den Glauben verantworten. Eine Fundamentaltheologie*, 3rd ed; Freiburg-Basel-Wien: Herder, 2005.
6. Cf. Peter Hofmann. *Die Bibel ist die Erste Theologie. Ein fundamentaltheologischer Ansatz.* Paderborn: Schöningh, 2006.
7. Cf. Catherine Cornille. *The Im-possibility of Interreligious Dialogue*; Crossroad Publ.: New York, NY, USA, 2008.

8. Cf. Robert Cummings Neville, ed. *The Human Condition*. Albany: State University of New York Press, 2001; *Ultimate Realities*. Albany: State University of New York Press, 2001; *Religious Truth*. Albany: State University of New York Press, 2001.
9. Cf. Klaus von Stosch. "Was sind religiöse Überzeugungen?" In *Was sind religiöse Überzeugungen?* edited by Hans Joas. Göttingen: Wallstein, 2003 (Preisschriften des Forschungsinstituts für Philosophie Hannover; 1), 103–146.
10. Robert Cummings Neville. *Ritual and Deference. Extending Chinese Philosophy in a Comparative Context*. Albany: State University of New York Press, 2008, 142.
11. Gaudium et Spes 1.
12. Cf. Francis X. Clooney. *Comparative Theology. Deep Learning Across Religious Borders*. Malden/MA-Oxford: Wiley-Blackwell, 2010, 96.
13. Cf. Felix Körner. "Der Gott Israels, Jesu und Mammads? Trinitätstheologie als Regula im interreligiösen Gespräch." *Gr.* 92 (2011): 139–158, 151.
14. Cf. James L. Fredericks. "Das Selbst vergessen. Buddhistische Reflexionen zur Trinität." In *Komparative Theologie. Interreligiöse Vergleiche als Weg der Religionstheologie*, edited by Reinhold Bernhardt and Klaus von Stosch. Zürich: TVZ, 2009 (Beiträge zu einer Theologie der Religionen; 7), 203–223.
15. Cf. the projects of the comparative theology-group in the cluster of excellence on religion and violence at Münster. Jürgen Werbick, Muhammad Sven Kalisch, and Klaus von Stosch, eds. *Glaubensgewissheit und Gewalt. Eschatologische Erkundungen in Islam und Christentum*. Paderborn: Schöningh, 2011 (Beiträge zur Komparativen Theologie; 3); *Verwundete Gewissheit. Strategien zum Umgang mit Verunsicherung in Islam und Christentum*. Paderborn: Schöningh, 2010 (Beiträge zur Komparativen Theologie; 1).
16. Cf. Klaus von Stosch, and Muna Tatari, ed. *Gott und Befreiung. Befreiungstheologische Konzepte in Islam und Christentum*. Paderborn: Schöningh, 2012 (Beiträge zur Komparativen Theologie; 5).
17. Cf. Michelle Voss Roberts. "Gendering comparative theology." In *The New Comparative Theology. Interreligious Insights from the Next Generation*, edited by Francis X. Clooney. London-New York: T&T Clark, 2010, 109–128, 127.
18. Cf. F. Clooney. "Response." In *ibid.*, 197.
19. Cf. Tracy Sayuki Tiemeier. "Comparative theology as a theology of liberation." In *ibid.*, 129–149, 141f.
20. Cf. Jürgen Werbick. *Vergewisserungen im interreligiösen Feld*, Münster: Lit, 2011 (Religion—Geschichte—Gesellschaft; 49), 189.
21. Cf. Farid Esack. *Qur'an, Liberation and Pluralism. An Islamic Perspective of Interreligious Solidarity against Oppression*. Oxford: Oneworld, 1997 (Repr. 2002).
22. Cf. Dietrich Bonhoeffer. *Widerstand und Ergebung. Briefe und Aufzeichnungen aus der Haft*, 15th ed. Gütersloh: Chr. Kaiser, 1994.
23. Cf. the contribution of Jacques Scheuer in this volume.

24. Cf. Klaus von Stosch. *Offenbarung*. Paderborn: UTB, 2010, 96–122, where I explain for the context of revelation why Jewish theology is so helpful for Christian-Muslim dialogue. Certainly this obligation to the third position applies to all theologians—including comparativists. But there is not any special burden for comparative theology in this respect, although other third positions than those in non-comparativist contexts might make more sense in this field because both sides have to agree which third position should be chosen.
25. Cf. Elizabeth McKeown. "Inside out and in between. Comparing the comparativists." *Method and Theory of in the Study of Religion* 20 (2008): 259–269, 260, referring to Jonathan Z. Smith. *Relating Religion. Essays in the Study of Religion.* Chicago: University of Chicago Press, 2004, 239.
26. Robert C. Neville. "Philosophische Grundlagen und Methoden der Komparativen Theologie." In *Komparative Theologie. Interreligiöse Vergleiche als Weg der Religionstheologie*, edited by Reinhold Bernhardt and Klaus von Stosch. Zürich: TVZ, 2009, 35–54, 42.
27. Christiane Tietz. "Dialogkonzepte in der Komparativen Theologie." In *ibid.*, 315–338, 331.

Reprinted from *Religions*. Cite as: Dehn, Ulrich. "A European (German) View on Comparative Theology: Dialogue with My Own Past." *Religions* 3 (2012): 1085-1093.

Article

A European (German) View on Comparative Theology: Dialogue with My Own Past

Ulrich Dehn

Chair of Missiology, Ecumenics, and Religious Studies, Department of Protestant Theology, Faculty of the Humanities, Hamburg University, Sedanstr. 19, D-20146 Hamburg, Germany; E-Mail: ulrich.dehn@uni-hamburg.de; Tel.: +49-40-42838-3776

Received: 1 September 2012; in revised form: 5 November 2012 / Accepted: 12 November 2012 / Published: 14 November 2012

Abstract: For the last couple of years, particularly after the publication of the (German) book "Comparative Theology" by Bernhold Reinhardt and Klaus von Stosch, there was a significant attentiveness of this subject amongst German scholars. For many, it was the long anticipated antithesis/alternative to the pluralist theology of religions, even if it had not been devised explicitly to serve as such an alternative. For others, it has been an appropriate way to express their desire for a substantial interreligious dialogue in a theologically responsible way. This paper tries to review some of the major German contributions (being read alongside international ones) and reactions to Comparative Theology and to search for the motive behind its sudden popularity in some circles. It will also try to reconstruct the possibilities for Comparative Theology within the wider setting of the process and development of religious traditions as they grow and change in never-ending interaction and communication within the history of religions, ideas and society.

Keywords: comparative theology; theology of religions; history of religions; truth claim; heterogeneity; inter-religious dialogue

Introduction

The title of my paper[1] suggests that there is a particular perception of comparative theology in Germany, but this may not be the case. It remains to be seen whether the German discussion adds aspects to the general debate that has been intensifying for around the last 10 years but has had forerunners for some decades. I use 'forerunners' in the sense that comparative theology offers and formulates a model of doing inter-religious research and dialogue which may be found in many activities as early as in medieval times—even Nicolaus of Cues' *Cribratio alkorani* (1460/61) may be counted here as he is doing comparative research about the Quran from a Christian perspective, even though he did not do this from a dialogical, but rather a polemical perspective. The polemical outlook was true for most medieval theologians due to a lack of knowledge of the other religions, their holy scriptures, their rites and their background, in general. 'Comparison' and 'dialogue' were the modes and methods to convince the public of the irrationality of the other religion and to prove the truth of the Christian dogma. This was the case with Petrus Abaelard (12th century), Ramon Lull (13th century), and for Martin Luther knowledge of the Quran was helpful in order to know more about the enemy. A turn of religious thinking started only at the end of the 18th and the beginning of 19th century when Enlightenment thinking and European language translations of scriptures were in reach and the general climate started to change towards a discovery of peaceful potentials of religions and mutual tolerance [1]. The term itself came in to use in the 19th century, at that time in contrast to 'theoretical' theology, or indicating the study of religious doctrines ([2], p. 521). Already in 1699, James Garden used the term 'theologia comparativa' in distinction from an absolute theology.[2]

In my paper I will try to think about a couple of questions and problems regarding comparative theology, including the concepts and answers that have been offered in my research so far. This will include some simplifications as the conceptual offers are so widespread and different from each other that one may hardly believe that they fit under the one umbrella of 'comparative theology'. Giving the title 'European' or 'German' I do not mean to work only with references from this part of the world. Rather I will present my views which—whether I like it or not—probably are very German, but I will refer to all contributions known to me and relevant to my judgment.

Let me first of all try to summarize some of the claims of C.T. being raised, although they are not necessarily all shared by all C.T. representatives and some major issues which shall be treated in this paper.

– Some advocates of C.T. (e.g., Klaus von Stosch) claim to bypass the 'dilemma' of a theology of religions by asserting that it does not need one but to construct the hermeneutics and framework of inter-religious interaction in the process of doing dialogical work. It remains to be analyzed whether C.T. is really a 'theoretical virgin' and is able to start dialogue and comparisons in a theoretical vacuum.

---

[1] At this point I would like to heartfully thank John H. Berthrong and Francis X. Clooney for their extremely helpful comments to my essay. I learnt a lot from their ideas, and from this culture of scholarly sharing (quite different from the German way).
[2] I thank Francis Clooney for this hint.

– Within the German discussion about a confessional and theological way of doing dialogue of religions, on one side, and doing research about religions using empirical and sociological methods without adhering to a particular faith on the other, C.T. is considered a theological method with a confessional position, a claim which would put it in a contradictory position with the theologies of religion. It remains to be seen whether in scholarly hermeneutics there is such a thing as the distinction of theological and empirical methods with regard to religions and, if so, on which side we would find the C.T.

– Within the many variations of C.T., what are the marking points which are common to them? What is the core of C.T.?

– The major antagonist to C.T., besides a secular study of religion and the quest for a 'pure' and non-comparative Christian theology, seems to be the pluralist theology of religions, particularly its most prominent exponent John Hick and his most outspoken follower Perry Schmidt-Leukel. What are the main points in favor of agreement, where can they be reconciled, where are the everlasting differences, if any?

– What purpose does C.T. serve beyond that which dialogical research has previously served for a long time? What is the surplus of saying 'comparative' instead of 'dialogical'?

This last section will offer some conceptional ideas about C.T. and its function within the history of religions.

C.T. and the Theology of Religions

In order to clarify the relation of C.T. to the field of a theology of religions and whether it is a substitute for it or renders it obsolete, there needs to be clarity about what the purpose of the theology of religions is. According to various authors (e.g., Perry Schmidt-Leukel, Reinhold Bernhardt, Klaus v. Stosch), a theology of religions tries to give an idea about how one religious system, in our case Christian faith, can define its relation to other religions and at the same time has its self-reflection and continuous self-reconstruction encouraged by the encounter with other religions. The details of a theology of religions give criteria about whether another religion is to be considered inferior to my own faith, of equal spiritual rights or including elements which may be identified as being similar to my own tradition. Some religious traditions have the privilege, due to their age, to look back on older religions and define their basis in relation to their holy scriptures, such as Islam (looking back on, e.g., Judaism and Christianity) and Baha'i, considering themselves as the crown of the history of religion. Others, like Christianity, need a posteriori theological constructions to put themselves into an innovative and dialogical theological relationship if ever they think it necessary. This type of theological activity has two components, as is pinpointed by v. Stosch and others: On one hand, it tries to support the reality of a coexistence and plurality of religions which cannot but interact with each other respectfully, on the other, it needs to take account of the unbroken affirmation of my faith's truth and the central position of Jesus Christ which poses a challenge to the way I look at other religions equally claiming to hold the truth. Whether these two components can coexist in a theologically responsible way or will exclude each other and become an impasse (as v. Stosch thinks) needs to be discussed. I suggest making use of the idea that my personal affirmation of my faith as the truth which is the one relevant aspect for me (and my faith community) (as the inter-subjective 'absoluteness' of Christian truth) does not exclude the intellectual and mental recognition that there exist other religious traditions and truth claims in their own right and dignity and harboring their own inter-subjective truth and possibly being in contrast to particular contents of my tradition (such as the crucifixion of Jesus Christ being denied by Quran sura 4,157–159 and again being interpreted differently by the Ahmadiyya community—both versions have their reasonable position in the history of interreligious interaction[3]). Following this argumentation there should not be a substantial incompatibility of 'my truth' and the acceptance of the truth of the other as they do represent a truth which is true in an inter-subjective sense and is the authentic truth for each single person and community. Here I like to borrow from the pragmatic truth concept of Charles S. Peirce being further elaborated by William James and John Dewey [4,5], as I suppose that a Ptolemaic idea of truth would not carry me far in inter-religious interaction and comparative studies. Nevertheless, this is a modification on a purely pragmatic idea of truth which would only stress its viability and its competence to be valuable for the life of truth-holders. It needs to be added that internal criteria like authenticity and faithfulness within one's own religion and the recognizability of one person adhering to a particular religious tradition should be part of accepting truth claims. Anyway, this clarification has only a limited function in considering whether a theology of religions should be there and where the place of C.T. might be. Nevertheless it makes me aware that truth is, on one hand, not an arbitrary issue of an every day new option, and on the other hand should not support exclusivistic standpoints.

To add one more thought: I make use of the terminology of truth-holders or believers and do this for one particular reason. Trying to find out something about the truth claims of 'religions' implies that one essentialises religions as monolithic entities without taking into account that they change, that a 'religion' can be identified, apart from the scriptures and other written traditions and architectural monuments, only in the life of the believers, in their rituals, in the communication of religious humans and communities. Any 'religion' is a mosaic piece of art changing its parts by every single step through history. A theology of religions, be it exclusivistic, inclusivistic, or pluralistic, necessarily finds itself trapped in the presupposition to handle fixed religious compounds and clarify their relation to each other, knowing that even within one such 'compound' there are elements being stressed in a different way by different denominations within one 'religion'. For example, the dogma of the trinity, a major element in Orthodox thinking, or, in contrast, Jesus' suffering and death on the cross as the center of most Protestant orientations, or, in Islam, Ali being a major factor in Shiite Islam which he is not in Sunnite Islam *etc*. I do not stress the logical incompatibility of doctrinal elements but try to think of a procedure to interact, comparing each other without sticking to whole religious systems but

---

[3] Klaus von Stosch in his writings frequently mentions the negation of Jesus' death on the cross in the Quran as one point not acceptable by the Christian partner in the process of a C.T. (e.g., [3], p. 32). This seems to me a big challenge to v. Stosch's concept of truth and to the dialogue competence of his idea of C.T. If a C.T. fails to constructively handle an issue like this—theological differences focusing on one common point—without hurting the dialogue partners, it is not worth the name.

looking for a case-by-case means of communicative hermeneutics. The above-described essentialisation of religion is what I consider the real impasse of a theology of religions, at least of most types I came across, and probably of most ways to think about religions. Being considered this way, a procedure according to C.T. should be able to celebrate religious diversity instead of being irritated by it and be hesitant to stick to a particular construction of religious relationship as a theology of religions would support.[4] In this regard even the suggestion to let the 'Abrahamic religions' (Judaism, Christianity, Islam) have a dialogue with each other sounds rather essentialising—and exclusive to those who might also like to be members of the club but do not have a focus on the Abraham tradition. In order to say it concisely: In a very broad sense, C.T., as I like to propose it, may be within the range of theology of religions, but as a type sui generis which will find its communicative place and structure case by case in the world of religious heterogeneity and not within the setting of exclusivism, inclusivism and pluralism.

This is the one dimension of C.T. that might as well be part of the general idea of interreligious dialogue. The other stage is to consider within my own dialoguing tradition what there is to be learnt from the partner in dialogue about our particular subject of comparative communication if ever the dialogue should go beyond what might be called comparative religion, respectively a purely phenomenological comparison, such as Schmidt-Leukel stresses ([6], p. 102). In what regards may transformations of my position be challenged? What does it mean to be a Christian theologian vis-à-vis other religious outlooks? In the process of reconsidering elements of the interaction and the impact they may have in form of a revision of my religious position, it is necessary for criteria to judge the gravity of challenges which poses the procedure close to the realm of a theology of religions. However, the criteria need to be generated out of the comparative process, not be transported by a preceding theological system of interreligious relations.[5]

---

[4] At this point, Perry Schmidt-Leukel needs to be contradicted as he writes: "... my bad news for Fredericks and his German followers is that 'comparative theology' will not lead out of the impasse of theology of religions but straight into it. The liberating good news, however, is that the theology of religions is not an impasse at all' ([6], p. 91). C.T., as I understand it, may very well be able to avoid any type of theology of religions and still be able to respond to the questions which a theology of religions is confronting—which Schmidt-Leukel doubts ([6], p. 91).

[5] Schmidt-Leukel claims: „And if the comparatist starts her work from a specific religious or confessional tradition, it is doubtless the case that she, as part of her own religious background, will already be influenced by those religious convictions that have their own implications on the truth claims entailed in the beliefs of others. To bracket or exclude the implications of one's own religious presuppositions would once again mean to fall back into the business of a purely phenomenological comparison—and apart from that, there are good reasons to doubt whether such a bracketing is possible at all." ([6], p. 102) Schmidt-Leukel is true in his supposition that there is no hermeneutical process without a 'package' of influences and impregnations which influence our perspective on texts and other objects of understanding. This is true and trivial at the same time, as all our perceptions bear the marks of our constructions.

Major Arguments towards Comparative Theology in German Speaking Theology

Christian Danz, a systematic theologian at Vienna University, in his introduction to the theology of religions [7] appreciatively summarizes major aspects of C.T. as an attempt to avoid the bird's eye view on religion(s). Instead he perceives their differences and renounces the concept of a 'common core' of religions. Danz notices C.T.'s attention to concrete issues between two religious traditions instead of performing global comparisons and using general concepts including side-stepping of ready-made theologies of religions. He also honors the conceptual intention of C.T. to evaluate a religion resp. elements of it only after having encountered it in the comparative process and to have it as a mirror for reflecting one's own tradition ([7], pp. 104–106). However, it is the latter point which Danz doubts: Will C.T. really be able to renounce the use of general concepts? Will it not at the end of the comparative process, when the moment of judgements has come, have to make use precisely of those concepts which it has at the beginning of the process denied to take into account? He claims that a C.T. will have to get back to general concepts if it does not want to resort to an 'intransparent empirism' ([7], pp. 106–107). Danz' criticism of C.T. is close to that of Schmidt-Leukel and has in common with him as well with v. Stosch that a hiatus between theological hermeneutics and 'empirism' resp. the 'purely' phenomenological comparison is asserted. This issue, a gap between theological hermeneutics and phenomenological comparison, we have to discuss later.

Friedmann Eissler[6] deals with the question whether C.T. may serve as an alternative to known theologies of religions. He introduces the thought of Clooney, Fredericks and v. Stosch and expresses appreciation of some of their major concerns, like the major impasse of all previous concepts of theology of religions, as v. Stosch has it, of the acceptance and appreciation of religious plurality on one hand, and the truth claim of one's own religion, on the other ([8], pp. 451–452). He doubts that if one is faithful to the truth claim of one's own religion (Christianity) whether there is a way to the acceptance of other truth claims—without converting to the other religion. Eissler demands a position which sticks to the Christian basics of faith (Bible, confessions) and upholds the claim to be true for all humankind. Citing Norbert Hintersteiner, who writes that C.T. 'implicates and asks for' an 'inter-religious community' no longer sticking to the faith of one particular community and its theological discourse[7], he feels that this bird's eye perspective may not be appropriate for religions coming into the horizon of comparison. Eissler's position, which includes a very narrow truth concept, leaves only a small space for constructive interreligious comparison, mutual appreciation and dialogue as it first of all stresses the apologetic and missionary part of interaction and does not even explicitly appreciate the chances of C.T. within a religiously plural world, as Danz does. For some authors, C.T.

---

[6] Eissler is working with the Protestant Institute for Religions and World Views (EZW, Berlin) of the Protestant Church in Germany (EKD).

[7] Quoted in [8], p. 454, from [9], p. 337. This idea of Hintersteiner seems unusual to me within the range of C.T. Christine Tietz who quotes Hintersteiner in her contribution 'Dialogkonzepte in der Komparativen Theologie' ([9], pp. 315–338) also does not feel comfortable with this position which overcharges the idea of C.T. and raises the threshold for participation.

seems to offer a way to escape the pluralist option even if they did not look closely at the intentions and concepts of C.T.

Juergen Werbick of Muenster University, a supporter of C.T., perceives that there should be a way to overcome the militant competitiveness of religions and instead find out what might make them partners and mutually discover not weaknesses but strong points as in certain concerns it will be the same challenges to be confronted, and thus a common interest to have the others as strong companions. The challenges, according to Werbick, are of human and social character, they concern human basic experiences and quests. In the comparative process we can discover how the others handle challenges, the specifics of one's own way of handling it, and learn from the ways others meet the challenges and judge and re-view our own way in relation to others. This does, as Werbick stresses, not automatically mean appreciating other ways uncritically but can result in critical evaluation. One possible outcome may be to discover our own religious tradition as the religious and cognitively superior one, but Werbick's major point is that militant competition is overruled and embraced by appreciating and honoring argumentation. This task has, according to Werbick, a dimension of common human and religious interest ([10], pp. 188–190).

Comparative Theology in the Context of the History of Religions

Beyond struggles with the truth problem and the issues of inclusiveness, acceptance and coherence, C.T. with its methods of comparison, dialogue, appreciation and evaluation opens a process of historical recapitulation. Religions, as indicated above, do not fall from heaven like monoliths and stay unchanged journeying through history. They start with people who feel an impasse with their religious environment and pick up a new reforming idea which comes into a forming process. The people transporting it encounter other ideas and start to walk a long way of formation, adaptation, stabilization, new encounters and challenges, establishing a community with rules and rituals, formulating a confessional code which defines who will or will not be one of them. Narratives are formed, myths which mark the ideas and stories to be important for the identity of the new group of believers. A religious movement is like a ball of clay which is thrown, collides, changes its form with every single collision and makes other loam balls change as well by meeting and 'communicating'. Such was the case when Buddhism met the world of the rural Hindu gods: reincarnation ideas of old Brahmanism, and, centuries, later the godhead families of East Asian pre-Buddhist religious worlds, influenced Hinduism and Buddhist ideas changed in themselves. In Japan it was the mutual penetration and re-figuration of Shinto and Buddhism which created new religious amalgams, the same being true for the Tibetan confluence of Indian Buddhism, Tantrism, Bon traditions and Chinese spiritual worlds [11,12].

This process is a never-ending one, only becoming slower and viscous because of institutionalization, competitive identity struggles and power games. The dialogical part of C.T. is a chance to reconstruct this movement and process and generate a new understanding of religious formation processes. It opens the horizon of various responses to the questions and challenges of humankind and life—in this regard I feel close to Werbick—and may develop to be a 'communicative theology' in the quest for new hermeneutics of religious processes. This quest first of all is a clarification process about how my religious tradition became what it is and who its mothers, fathers, sisters, brothers and other relatives are. It does not touch the truth issue in this stage as this is a cognitive search for the elements out of which truth shall be generated. Of course, beyond clarification, C.T. or communicative theology implicates the challenge whether it is a follow-up to historical clarifications or whether there is a need and an intuitive urge to be a different theology in the long run of the process of comparison and communication. Facing this question it comes to the point whether C.T. should be an intellectual game, a matter of historical reconstruction or a process of existential seriousness. I opt for the second one with elements of the third. Klaus von Stosch's claim of C.T. as 'main task of the theology of the future' being explicated in a complete reshuffle of theological faculties, e.g., establishing chairs for theologies other than Christian, having the challenge of the other religion(s) as a permanent background for theological reflection ([3], pp. 317–322, [9], pp. 29–31), sounds radical but to a large extent describes projects already on the move and being practiced in dialogically oriented inter-religious research and the way many theological suggestions for the last years have been considering the horizon of other religions [13,14].[8] Many of them did not seek the setting of a C.T. but might be judged as monological dialogues. Anyway they were aware that Christian theology can no longer be reflected in splendid isolation and is challenged for encounter by 'theologies' in other religions.

Making my last point, I doubt the validity of distinguishing an internal and an external view of religions in the scholarly process of C.T. Internal views may, beyond the 'facts', have a confessional and affectional aspect, but the 'facts' and the 'material' should be the same as with the external view—otherwise one of them is right and the other wrong. In any case it should be a good practice in teaching, learning and having dialogue to have adherents of a religion speak for their tradition instead of having Christians talk about Islam or Buddhism or the other way round. The results should be authentic communicative situations and an equal standing and representation of religious communities at universities (as has been the dream of f.e. Wilfred Cantwell Smith). However, there is no epistemological need to do this in order to have the 'correct views'.

C.T. will have the never-ending task of allowing humans of the different religious traditions search together for the answers to urgent questions of life and humankind. For this project which on different scales is underway in many places already, a fitting and congenial design at universities—particularly in Germany—is still a great need. One implication might be the establishment of multi-religious theological faculties which offer connections between the religions and for the flow of new ideas and mirror the religiously plural situation of the country.[9]

Conflicts of Interest

The author declares no conflict of interest.

---

[8] Also see the government support for establishment of chairs of Islamic theology and training of teachers for Islamic lessons.

[9] For ideas in this context see also [15].

References

1. Rainer Forst. *Toleranz im Konflikt*; Frankfurt am Main: Suhrkamp, 2003.
2. Francis X. Clooney. "Comparative Theology: A Review of Recent Books (1989-95)." *Theological Studies* 56, (1995): 521–550. http://www.bc.edu/schools/cas/theology/comparative/resources/articles/theolstudies.htm.
3. Klaus von Stosch. *Komparative Theologie als Wegweiser in der Welt der Religionen*; Paderborn: Schoeningh, 2012.
4. William James. The *Meaning of Truth—A Sequel to, Pragmatism'*. New York/London: Longmans, Green & Co, 1909.
5. Charles Hartshorne, Paul Weiss, and Arthur W. Burks, eds. "Pragmatism and Pragmaticism." 58th ed.; Collected Papers of Charles Sanders Peirce. Bristol: Thoemmes u. a., 1998, Vol. 5.
6. Perry Schmidt-Leukel. "Comparative Theology: Limits and Prospects." In *Transformation by Integration*. London: SCM Press, 2009, 90–104.
7. Christian Danz. *Einfuehrung in die Theologie der Religionen*. Wien: LIT, 2005.
8. Friedmann Eissler. "Komparative Theologie." *Materialdienst der EZW* 74 (2011): 449–455.
9. Reinhold Bernhardt, and Klaus von Stosch, eds. *Komparative Theologie*. Zuerich: Theologischer Verlag, 2009.
10. Juergen Werbick. *Vergewisserungen im interreligioesen Feld*. Muenster: LIT, 2011.
11. Kenji Matsuo. *A History of Japanese Buddhism*. Folkstone: Global Oriental, 2007.
12. Michael L. Walter. *Buddhism and Empire: The Political and Religious Culture of Early Tibet*. Leiden: Brill, 2009.
13. Hans-Martin Barth. *Dogmatik: Evangelischer Glaube im Kontext der Weltreligionen*. Guetersloh: Guetersloher Verlagshaus, 2001
14. Hans Waldenfels. *Kontextuelle Fundamentaltheologie*, 2nd ed. Paderborn: Schoeningh, 1988.
15. Ulrich Dehn. Religionswissenschaft als theologische Disziplin? In *Religionsdifferenzen und Religionsdialoge (= EZW-Texte No. 210)*, edited by Reinhard Hempelmann. Berlin: EZW, 2010, 90–100.

Selected Bibliographies Relevant to C.T.

Francis X. Clooney. *Theology after Vedanta: An Experiment in Comparative Theology*. Albany/New York: Orbis Books, 1996.

Francis X. Clooney. *The New Comparative Theology: Interreligious Insights from the Next Generation*. London: T&T Clark, 2010.

James L. Fredericks. "A Universal Religious Experience: Comparative Theology as an Alternative to a Theology of Religions." *Horizons* 22 (1995): 67–87.

Norbert Hintersteiner. *Traditionen überschreiten: Angloamerikanische Beiträge zur interkulturellen Traditionshermeneutik*. Wien: Universitätsverlag, 2001.

Norbert Hintersteiner. "Dialog der Religionen." In *Handbuch Religionswissenschaft*, edited by Johann Figl. Innsbruck/Goettingen: Tyrolia/Vandenhoeck & Ruprecht, 2003, 834–852.

Perry Schmidt-Leukel. *Gott ohne Grenzen*. Guetersloh: Guetersloher Verlagshaus, 2005.

Ulrich Dehn. "Einleitung: Brauchen wir fuer den interreligioesen Dialog eine Theologie der Religionen?" In *Handbuch Dialog der Religionen*, edited by U. Dehn. Frankfurt am Main: Lembeck, 2008, 13–27.

Wikipedia. "Komparative Theologie." http://de.wikipedia.org/wiki/Komparative_Theologie (accessed on 25 July 2012).

Wikipedia. "Comparative theology." http://en.wikipedia.org/wiki/Comparative_theology (accessed on 25 July 2012).

http://www.facebook.com/pages/Comparative-theology/112127335473352 (accessed on 25 July 2012).

ZeKK. http://kw.uni-paderborn.de/institute-einrichtungen/zekk (accessed on 1 August 2012).

Reprinted from *Religions*. Cite as: Hedges, Paul. "The old and New Comparative Theologies: Discourse on Religion, the Theology of Religions, Orientalism and the Boundaries of Traditions." *Religions* 3 (2012): 1120-1137.

Article

The Old and New Comparative Theologies: Discourses on Religion, the Theology of Religions, Orientalism and the Boundaries of Traditions

Paul Hedges

Programme Leader Theology and Religious Studies, Department of Theology and Religious Studies, University of Winchester, Sparkford Road, Winchester, SO22 4NR, UK;
E-Mail: Paul.Hedges@winchester.ac.uk

Received: 10 November 2012; in revised form: 1 December 2012 / Accepted: 3 December 2012 / Published: 4 December 2012

Abstract: This paper disputes that a strong contrast can be drawn between the Old Comparative Theology and the New Comparative Theology, looking particularly at the arguments of Hugh Nicholson as well as drawing on Francis Clooney. It disputes a simplistic and monolithic dismissal of the Old Comparative Theology as guilty of 'Orientalism', and seeks to show that in figures like Rowland Williams, as well as F. D. Maurice that the discipline was important in breaking down boundaries between traditions. Building on this, an argument is made that the New Comparative Theology should be seen as part of a lineage of progression and understanding that links it with the Old Comparative Theology and the Theology of Religions, and that any attempt to see these as different, or contrasting, discourses is based upon a distorted or partial historical understanding. In this the work of Tomoko Masuzawa is also assessed, and issues surrounding the terms 'religion' and 'world religion' are discussed. It is also suggested that the weight of history may be a factor as to why the New Comparative Theology came to prominence in the USA rather than in Europe, or at least the UK.

Keywords: comparative theology; Orientalism; Frederick Clooney; Hugh Nicholson; Frederick Denison Maurice; Rowland Williams; religion; Tomoko Masuzawa; theology of religion

Introduction

In her much commented on work *The Invention of World Religions*, Tomoko Masuzawa discusses the role of Comparative Theology in the creation of the category 'religion', and its concomitant term 'world religions' [1]. For her, Comparative Theology is a discipline complicit in the spread of a Christian theological worldview and ideology into the, apparently, neutral and pluralistic discourse of contemporary Religious Studies ([1], pp. 72–146, 259–328). Masuzawa's work is heavily utilized by Hugh Nicholson in drawing a contrast between the Old Comparative Theology (OCT) and the New Comparative Theology (NCT). We will examine the changing face of Comparative Theology, looking at the distinction drawn between the OCT and the NCT, where some advocates of the NCT have even suggested that we should see them as quite distinct enterprises. I will begin by outlining this argument, focusing upon the work of Nicholson and Francis Clooney, suggesting that a more nuanced history of the development of Christian encounter with the religious Other is needed. (At least in places, Nicholson and Clooney admit this heritage, as such my aim will not be simply to show these connections, rather I will take issue with the more theoretical contention that the OCT engaged in one type of discourse and the NCT another type of discourse that permits a radical distinction to be drawn). This will lead us to engage Masuzawa and, indirectly, other critics of 'religion'; her work has parallels with critiques made by such scholars as Timothy Fitzgerald, Talal Asad, and Russell McCutcheon amongst others [2–5], whose work is also employed by Nicholson ([6], pp. 26, 67–8, 87). Here, I will argue that the heritage shared by the OCT and the NCT is not inherently implicated within an Orientalist discourse as Nicholson and Masuzawa imply, rather, it may represent a process of increasing understanding in relation to religious diversity. (I employ the term 'Orientalism' herein in the post-Saidian sense (for a brief description see [1], pp. 20–1), however, in a way that is not uncritical). We will also consider the Theology of Religions (ToR), which is often drawn into the debate on what distinguishes the NCT from the OCT.

The NCT and Its Discourse on the OCT and the ToR

Nicholson has argued that the NCT exists today largely without reference to its nineteenth (and, indeed, we may also add early twentieth) century forbear ([7], p. 612). Yet, elsewhere he has admitted a continuity, suggesting it 'is not nearly as unprecedented as many of its exponents tend to assume' ([6], p. 22). Nevertheless, he still maintains that a sharp distinction remains between the OCT and the NCT, so while he uses Rudolf Otto's classic work as a model for his own, he nevertheless seeks to show that his own NCT has moved beyond the 'Orientalism' that characterizes Otto's work ([6], p. 105). As such when comparisons are made, it tends to be on the basis of distinguishing the new venture very sharply from the old, even referring to it as the 'antithesis' of the former ([7], p. 620). Indeed, in reviewing some older attempts at Comparative Theology in his general survey of the field, Clooney states that, 'I have included these examples to signal the history of comparative theology and to remind us of dangers to which it is liable' ([8], p. 34). A similar point is made by Nicholson who warns us that: 'By ignoring that history, contemporary theologians, particularly those who deal with interreligious issues, risk repeating some of the same mistakes' ([7], p. 610). Elsewhere, Clooney also highlights a distinction between the NCT and the OCT [9]. (We should note, though, that the term NCT is not one Clooney employs in this respect, and it is specifically Nicholson's term, nevertheless, the same sense of distance between the NCT and the OCT can, arguably, be detected in both).

In both Clooney and Nicholson we therefore see repeated the same message, that the OCT was a failed and flawed venture, and one which can clearly be distinguished from the NCT, although the latter, if unaware of these failings, may too become subject to such flaws. It should be noted, moreover, that while Clooney and Nicholson concede a lineage, both stress them as distinct, if not antithetical, approaches; Nicholson in particular arguing that a step-change or boundary breakage stops the OCT flowing naturally into the NCT [6]. This sense of the NCT as a different type of venture is also expressed in a contrast to the ToR. Both Clooney and James Fredericks explicitly draw a contrast between the work of the NCT and the ToR ([10], pp. 666–8; [11], p. 8). The latter is understood to be creating a stance on other religions based upon a typological paradigm, notably one based upon Race's classic Exclusivism-Inclusivism-Pluralism typology [12]; often seen today in the fourfold version of Exclusivisms-Inclusivisms-Pluralisms-Particularities ([13], pp. 17–30). Nicholson, moreover, draws a linkage from the OCT to the ToR, which he then contrasts with the NCT [7]. As such, it is suggested that the ToR shares in the same failings as the OCT and is, essentially, a failed and somewhat illegitimate venture (Fredericks, certainly, does not go this far and his suggestion for a moratorium on the ToR seems based upon its presumptuousness rather than its inherent failings ([14], p. 8).

However, the clear break hypothesis which suggests that parallels between the venture of the NCT and the OCT (and the ToR) are less significant than the discontinuities can be questioned. Therefore, I will outline the way that the OCT and the ToR is characterized by the writings of proponents of the NCT, and offer a discussion around this. In particular, I will focus upon the work of Nicholson who has, probably, most systematically discussed this distinction. It may be noted that, in his arguments here, Nicholson is not directly doing Comparative Theology, but working on the justification of the NCT in the light of critiques of the OCT, although this feeds into how he sets out his own Comparative Theology (*i.e.*, in its contrast with Otto).

Aspects of the OCT

Nicholson follows the lead of Masuzawa in selecting two particular figures as representative of the OCT ([1], pp. 75–9; [7], p. 612). These two selected paradigmatic examples of the OCT, one American and one British, are each exemplified by a particular text: James Freeman Clarke *Ten Great Religions: An Essay in Comparative Theology* (1871); and, F. D. Maurice's *Religions of the World and their Relations with Christianity* (1847) [14,15]. Both Freeman and Maurice were noted theologians, of a liberal inclination, in their own day, and their books enjoyed great popularity as accessible works discussing other religions from a Christian standpoint. Maurice's work had originally been delivered as a series of public lectures, while Clarke's work was an extension of articles originally delivered in the popular magazine *Atlantic Monthly* in 1868. In brief, both books argued that non-Christian religions mediated some form of worthy spiritual values to their devotees, but were, nevertheless, entirely eclipsed by Christianity. While these are just two examples, it is, perhaps, notable that here this is raised as a question in the UK before the US, which is perhaps indicative of the contemporary colonial interests of Britain, however, I make this here as a fairly speculative point.

Echoing Masuzawa's well-placed critique ([1], p. 79) Nicholson takes as a starting point the presupposition of Christian superiority found in both these writers, who work from a position that clearly seeks to show the advantages of their own tradition over those of others ([7], pp. 611–3). Indeed, in many ways it must be said that such a venture must be contrasted with the exponents of the NCT, figures like Clooney, Fredericks and Keith Ward, who do not set out in their work to show the advantages of the Christian tradition, but rather to lay each tradition side by side for the better to get an understanding of each, that the light shone in the venture may be that which illumines, rather than believing that there is any necessity to show that one's own position is, per se, better than the other [8,11,16]. In this sense, we do see a clear break between the OCT and the NCT. However, as I will argue this is part of an organic development from the OCT to the NCT, with the ToR playing a key part.

Nicholson sees the OCT as implicated in what he suggests is a typical liberal theological/theoretical approach: generalizing about religion ([7], p. 619). That is to say, religion was understood in fairly monochrome terms as something which approximated to the liberal theological expectations of the writers themselves and was assumed always to be fairly similar with linked characteristics ([17], p. 230). Commentating on such monolithic interpretations, John Thatamanil, utilizing the work of Paulo Gonçalves, suggests that generating homogeneity 'serves the interests of those who aspire to gain control over a tradition' ([18], p. 248).

Also, the OCT is underlain by a claim that the Christian religion alone is supreme, which Nicholson, following Masuzawa, argues is based on the belief that this judgment is the outcome of an objective comparison ([7], p. 612). As such, we may say, the theological prejudice of the writers becomes a factor in the comparative exercise itself. Indeed, Nicholson tells us, 'the older comparative theology, as we have seen, epitomizes the kind of theological hegemonism that one finds in the theology of religions' ([7], p. 620).

The NCT and the ToR

Another aspect of Nicholson's critique is that the ToR is simply a continuation of the liberal theological agenda found in the OCT, and from which the NCT can also be distinguished ([7], p. 621–2). His argument is that what Knitter calls an acceptance model differentiates it from a fulfilment model of inclusivism ([7], p. 623). However, this seems uncompelling for several reasons. Firstly, Knitter's acceptance model is very broad and encompasses a great variety of approaches [19], which includes what is often termed a particularist approach, which is far from the respectful recognition of religious difference which Nicholson uses to classify the NCT ([13], pp. 194–6; [20], pp. 127–30). Second, when Clooney defines himself as an inclusivist it is not clear he does so ([21], p. 66), in the way Nicholson suggests which separates itself from pluralist stances as a way that transcends it ([7], pp. 619–20), but rather presumably sees himself in line with older inclusivist lines of thought embedded in the thinking of Vatican II and figures like Karl Rahner (on such ideas, see [22]). Meanwhile, as has been argued, it is not clear that the NCT does not indeed play the same game as the ToR does, as it must make prejudgments about other religions ([13], pp. 52–5; [23], pp. 90–1, 96–104). That is to say, a judgment about the possibility of learning from the religious Other is made before one can even engage in Comparative Theology, as such the suggestion that it does not have the kind of pre-judgments and commitments of the ToR seems naïve or problematic. In part, what I am suggesting here is that it is by no means clear that the NCT occupies some privileged position which respects the religious Other, and which can be contrasted with other positions that do not; indeed, such an argument is made by Kristin Kiblinger [24]. Despite the compelling critiques, many proponents of the NCT understand their discipline as different and somehow 'beyond' what the ToR does.

The Political and the Religious Other

A key part of Nicholson's argument is that the liberal interpretation of religion, whether in the OCT or in the pluralist standpoint in the ToR effaces the political from view ([6], pp. 49ff). In each case, he argues, they see the religious as occupying a sublime position which in effect removes it from other discourses, where it might be seen as a sui generis concept. In contrast, he suggests, it is also thereby contrasted with a 'political' form of theology which it sees itself defined over and against. These are, respectively, an older and antagonistic apologetic or missionary theology, and an exclusivist or inclusivist approach in the ToR which is seen as harking back to a traditional sense of what he terms 'Christian Absolutism' ([25], p. 54). With regards to the NCT, Nicholson suggests that Fredericks, at least, tries to avoid this, however, he sees some aspects of the NCT as potentially involved in 'the liberal theological project of "depoliticizing" religion and theology' ([25], p. 55). Here, the NCT can be portrayed in terms of 'oppositional identity' whereby it operates against the ToR paradigms as a way of encountering the religious Other ([7], p. 621; [25], p. 55). However, the NCT, he argues, is capable of moving beyond this to a new position no longer be trapped in the denial of the political ([6], pp. 94ff). Despite the significance of this aspect for Nicholson's work our focus is not primarily upon his analysis and so having mentioned this as one part of his distinction we will not build further upon it here.

Improvements in the NCT

Having set out the key aspects of the way the OCT and the ToR are critiqued, we will turn to the positive suggestions for why the NCT goes beyond them. Nicholson gives different lists as to what he sees as the improvements between the NCT and the OCT which are synthesized here:

First, he suggests the NCT does not generalize about other religions, which he suggests is typical of both the OCT and the ToR. In particular he cites Clooney's work as part of its 'resistance to generalization' ([25], p. 58). That is, it deals with the particular and local, rather than making meta-statements about all aspects of specific religions.

Second, it also resists any claims to its own supremacy in a way that denies the truth of different religions. For Nicholson, this is part of its acceptance model of inclusivism, and he cites Kristin Kiblinger as a case in point ([25], p. 57). It should be noted, though, that contra Clooney, Fredericks and Nicholson who see the ToR and the NCT as different realms of activity, Kiblinger actually suggests, as noted above, that any form of Comparative Theology actually requires the ToR paradigms as a base mark [24]. Moreover, her notion of the 'new' inclusivism differs somewhat from Nicholson, while she suggests that both an improved form of inclusivism or pluralism could found a NCT approach ([24], p. 42). If Kiblinger is right, and her arguments certainly seem more cogent than the counter arguments, this destabilizes aspects, at the very least, of Nicholson's argument; this we will return to below.

Third, he also suggests that the NCT combines interreligious reflection and the practice of dialogue as parts of one principle ([25], p. 58). As such, instead of distinguishing the act of Christian thinking about the religious other from actually engaging with the religious Other, which he believes happens in the ToR, while the latter did not generally occur within the OCT, he believes the two are held as correlating poles in the NCT.

Finally, he suggests that whereas the OCT stood unaware of its own partisanship which informed its supposedly neutral and scientific judgments on other religions, the NCT openly acknowledges 'its own normative commitments and interests' ([25], p. 59). As such, instead of attempting to attain a phenomenological style of epoche and academic objectivity, the involvement of its practitioners as Christian theologians forms part of the engagement that takes place and so the bias is open. However, at the same time, instead of attempting to impose a Christian reading of the other religion, the NCT seeks to understand the religious Other as much as possible in its own terms, such that, to use Clooney's words, 'fresh theological insights' ([8], p. 10) are gained.

Assessing Discourse on the OCT and the NCT

Having seen the way that the NCT creates its discourse about its relationship to other disciplines, we will now turn to assessing whether this is a legitimate way to portray the arguments. Indeed, Nicholson at one place concedes that the distinction, here speaking about the ToR and the NCT, may be less, with the former 'a little less rigid and dogmatic', and the latter 'a little less flexible and open' than the rhetoric suggests ([25], p. 46–7). Indeed, I would suggest that in many cases the distinction is much more open than the claims we have seen made, and that the OCT can be seen as, in many ways, less prone to the kind of charges made against it.

I will extend my argument in three main parts: first, suggesting that the movement from the OCT and fulfilment theology to pluralism (in the ToR) to the NCT was not a series of jumps as Nicholson argues ([7], pp. 616–24), but represents a more continuous progression although one that is far more problematic and contoured than any kind of linear development; second, demonstrating that the portrayal of the OCT given by proponents of the NCT, and Masuzawa, is far too monolithic and generalizing and fails to take into account the particular writers and their contexts; and, third, developing out of our first point, I will suggest that the NCT exists in a history of engagement that encompasses the OCT and the ToR rather than being part of a story of different viewpoints. This will lead us on to some further points of analysis developing and extending the issues.

First, I would like to take issue with Nicholson's evolutionary model for the development of the NCT. This suggests that the development should not be seen as fairly linear, but marked instead by a series of step-changes or jumps ([7], pp. 616–24). In this way he suggests that the move from Fulfilment Theology to pluralism in the ToR to the NCT shows marked changes in each step. Tracing the whole of this history in the space within this article would be impossible, as such I will focus upon Fulfilment Theology and pluralism within the ToR to show some of the complications and nuances within it. Firstly, while sometimes referred to as a 'school of thought' Fulfilment Theology was a complex set of ideologies which were often quite contradictory or antagonistic. For instance, two representatives of mid to late nineteenth century Fulfilment Theology, Friedrich Max Müller and Monier Monier-Williams, both contemporaneous professors at Oxford, were poles apart theologically. The former's Fulfilment Theology being based upon what can be termed a 'liberal' Logos theology that saw religions developing in response to divine inspiration ([26], pp. 63–8). By contrast the latter's Fulfilment Theology was based in a 'conservative' strain ([26], pp. 58–63), he belonged to a notable evangelical family and tradition [27], that interpreted things from a pattern of decay from an original revelation ([26], p. 60). We see then that different strands underlie Fulfilment Theology itself (see [28], pp. 26–43). For a further example we can point to its best known proponent, John Nicol Farquhar, whose concept of fulfilment essentially meant the 'death' of Hindu ideas as they are replaced by Christian conceptions, as Hindu ideas 'died' to become improved Christian ones ([28], pp. 334–40; [29]). By way of contrast, his near contemporary Bernard Lucas advocated a form of Fulfilment Theology that moved into the development of a Christian Vedanta, where the Hindu scriptures are seen as a suitable replacement for the Old Testament in the Indian context ([28], pp. 383–7). As such, a far more positive appreciation of Hindu thought and what it could add spiritually could be seen. Therefore, while, on the one hand a 'jump' may be envisaged between the Fulfilment Theologies of figures like Monier-Williams and Farquhar to a pluralist position in the ToR, the often Logos inspired Fulfilment Theologies of figures like Müller and Rowland Williams (who we discuss more below) move by degrees into the theological position of figures like Lucas and the well known Charles Freer Andrews, whose Logos theology inspired him to give up any direct evangelization to live alongside the Hindu ([28], pp. 387–9). Yet, to see the two styles of Fulfilment Theology in opposition is problematic because we find many points of contact between those we have discussed ([26], p. 23). For instance, we discover the following of Farquhar and Andrews: 'in renouncing direct missionary work, Farquhar felt Andrews to be "grievously mistaken," but "Farquhar continued to be supportive of Andrews throughout the most troubled years, continuing to publish articles by him in *Young Men of India*"' ([28], p. 389; citing [30], p. 136), suggesting he did not see his position as antagonistic even if mistaken. As such, the theologian Ernst Troeltsch (who it has been argued moved towards a pluralistic position in his later writings ([31], p. 90), a figure discussed by Masuzawa ([1], pp. 309–27) and seen by Nicholson as part of a jump from the OCT to the ToR ([7], pp. 68–9), who it is said challenges Christianity's position as alone supreme and worthy to be presented as the single highest truth [32] stands not as a paradigm shift but in a line of development with figures like Lucas and Andrews, and therefore earlier proponents of the OCT. This brief account cannot, of necessity, do justice to the complexities of the situation, however, it is intended to suggest that Nicholson's portrayal of three stages of development in the liberal approach to the religious Other is too crude, and fails to notice the many differences, nuances, and altering patterns within each.

Second, the OCT is not so monolithic and generalizing as the portrayals of Nicholson and Masuzawa tend to imply. Certainly in regard to the examples given of Maurice and Clarke, there is a certain truth about the level of generality involved. Focusing upon Maurice, it cannot be denied that he tends to see all, at least non-Christian, religious traditions as being fairly static and unitary things each of which, he argues, posses a single overriding 'truth' or focus that they develop. So he speaks of, for instance, 'the great Mahometan truth' ([15], p. 165) which he tells us is that God is One. For the Hindu, he tells us: 'First, he has the deepest assurance that God must be an Absolute and Living Being, who can be satisfied with nothing less perfect than himself' ([15], pp. 60–1). Clearly here we see the sense that the OCT is generalizing, however, this claim itself generalizes about the OCT. While notwithstanding that both Maurice and Clarke were popular writers in the area they were not the only exponents, and in a figure like Rowland Williams we find a very different portrayal of the Hindu tradition [33]. In a work entitled *Paraméswara-jnyána-góshthí: A Dialogue of the Knowledge of the Supreme Lord in which are Compared the Claims of Christianity and Hinduism, and Various Questions of Indian Religion and Literature Fairly Discussed* (I will refer to it by the shorter title, which appears on its spine, *Christianity and Hinduism*) he sets out a detailed study of various schools of Hindu thought—including, as many at this time did, Buddhism—which later scholars of Hinduism have remarked upon as exhibiting a knowledge of these traditions quite remarkable for its time ([34], p. 52). Indeed, far from generalizing, Williams shows differences between each school and puts them in dialogue with each other as well as with Christianity. It will not serve our purpose here to provide a detailed account of Williams' text and the kind of comparisons he draws—work which can be found elsewhere ([28], pp. 64–85; [35]), while we will say more about Williams in due course. Nevertheless, Williams example demonstrates that the OCT is not limited simply to vague generalizations.

Third, and this is a theme developed further below, as well as being implicit in the first point here, the NCT I would argue is best seen as part of a process of engagement with the religious Other within modern and contemporary Western theologies. (It is, of course, the case that different or parallel engagements with the religious Other have been occurring in many Christian communities for centuries, see, for instance, [36] for evidence of this). While it may be strategically useful for exponents of the NCT to seek to distance themselves from the perceived Orientalism and colonialism of the OCT, and also from the pluralist stance within the ToR which has been attacked (not necessarily justly—but that is another debate, see [13], pp. 94–102, 129–33) as perpetuating a Western hegemony, the idea that this means insisting upon paradigm shifts rather than a process does not seem justified. To some degree I have argued for this sense of continuity above, and will engage it again below, which suggests it may be best to see an ongoing process (from the OCT, to the ToR, to the NCT—but recognizing that each overlaps and continues alongside the others, rather than being chronologically discontinuous) rather than a set of oppositional jumps, which stresses the inter-connectedness of changes.

Discussion on Religious Boundaries

We have, in this paper, approached a number of questions where to explore the scope of each would take us far beyond the space available. These include the question of the construction and reconstruction of the term 'religion' itself, as well as the way it is employed within the OCT, the NCT and the ToR. We have also raised questions about the way that the past is represented, or misrepresented, in contemporary scholarship, especially as we perceive the blind spots and prejudices of previous generations, yet can only do so from our own historical perspective (on this issue see [26], pp. 74–5). These are important questions, yet here we will restrict ourselves (although touching upon these other issues) to the way that the borders and boundaries of religious traditions are constructed and challenged by the changing discourse in the OCT and the NCT, mentioning the ToR as it becomes part of this discussion. In particular, the issue we confront is the construction of 'religion', and here it is useful to note that arguments of an extreme form that there is no such thing as 'religion' except as an academic construct tend to become dubious ([13], pp. 64–76, 81–7), and Nicholson seems to suspend judgment on such claims by Fitzgerald ([7], p. 616). We will return to this question in due course. Certainly, even critics of the colonial construction of the term 'religion' have suggested it may still be employed in new senses [37].

To some extent, at least, I would argue that the development we see from the OCT, to the ToR and the NCT does not primarily represent (contra Masuzawa, Fitzgerald *etc.*) the spread of a Christian theological hegemony into the discourse of religious plurality and the nature of religion, but the challenging of the boundaries and borders of the Christian tradition itself. Is it, we may ask, a theological victory or a victory over theology that this discourse bears witness to? (In this case understanding 'theology' within a narrow sectarian usage). Indeed, the development of the category 'religion' to mean not just Christianity, in its many denominations, but many traditions could be seen not as an extension of a Christian term to 'colonially' occupy the space of others, but, rather, a discovery that the limits of what may be termed 'religious' extend beyond those borders [13,23,38]. This accords with the arguments of the historian of thought J. J. Clarke who has cogently argued, even demonstrated, that the Western encounter with Eastern thought is not a one way street of interpretation, but has involved acts of what we may term 'subversion' of 'Western' categories by 'Eastern' thought [39]. That is to say, it has allowed counter narratives and alternative viewpoints to emerge. To take one example, while Theosophy absorbed and reinterpreted aspects of Hindu and Buddhist thought it found congenial, and so may be said to have partaken in a Western interpretation of the Orient, at the same time it helped to popularize concepts like reincarnation which were radically oppositional to what was, at that time, mainstream Christian discourse within most Western countries ([39], pp. 89–90; [40], pp. 44–5). The OCT and the ToR have also, at least in part, also been involved in such a process, which has come to challenge the borders and boundaries of religious understanding ([8]; [23], pp. 102–4).

While Masuzawa has rightly shown that certain political discourses may have been subtlety at work behind the various typologies of categorizing religion, such as the distinction between 'national' and 'universal' religion ([1], pp. 79–104, 207–56), this does not mean that they may not also have raised counter issues. We will return to Maurice and Williams for our examples.

Maurice, as we have seen, clearly wished to demonstrate that the genius, or overriding conception, in all of the non-Christian religions found its fulfilment within Christianity, indeed, Maurice's work is best understand as part of the development of what was later termed Fulfilment Theology (see [28], pp. 62–3). However, his work could also have been said to open a door between Christianity and other religions. As Maurice asserts, all religions were receptive to 'a Divine Spirit who awakens the thoughts, faculties, faith, hope, love in us, and directs them to an object above themselves, to a common object' ([41], p. 230). While he denies they have 'Revelation' (limited for him to pre-New Testament Jewish/ Israelite traditions and Christianity) they nevertheless are not entirely separated from the divine ([28], pp. 58ff.), while he suggests the core ideas of other religions, here speaking of Hinduism, provide 'a principle that is as characteristic of our faith as it is of the Hindoo' ([15], pp. 172–3). Despite a clear hierarchy of 'higher' and 'lower' between Christianity and the other religions of the world we see Maurice suggesting some form of kinship.

Williams, even more than Maurice, shows this relationship in his detailed study of various Hindu traditions. Particular focus is given by him to the concept of Vâch [*vac*], the divine word which he equates to both Logos and the Holy Spirit ([33], pp. 100–1; see also [28], pp. 79–81). Again, his work is underlain by the principles of Fulfilment Theology such that the 'truths' of Hinduism find their completion in the final form of Christianity ([28], pp. 70–5); although, unlike Maurice, he is prepared to see Revelation within Hinduism ([28], pp. 75–9). We see here a slippage of the boundaries between religions: if divine truth in some form is found outside of Christianity then we cannot simply bracket it as a category altogether differentiated from other religions. Karl Barth, of course, makes a similar point, that all 'religion'—Christianity as much as any other—is sinful and partial ([42], pp. 50–4). However, in contrast to Barth who sees this as related to sin and human failure, Williams, like Maurice, see all religions as partaking in truth and the Logos ([28], pp. 75–81); nevertheless, we may, to some extent, take Barth as an ally who calls into question the category of any religious system as alone supreme in truth and expression.[1] Williams, we may note, was also significant in another way. As an early British exponent of biblical criticism he made use of his knowledge of the methods of this 'higher criticism' to attack the Hindu scriptures showing their errors and inconsistencies; but, out of concern for fairness (and to show that Christianity need not fear it as others should) this led him to apply the principles not just to what he would term the Old Testament but to the New Testament as well [35]. It was, thus, the OCT that helped lead the way towards the comparison of religious texts on an equal basis.

Contrary, then, to the suggestion that the OCT perpetuated a discourse of Christian supremacy—although not denying that in both Maurice and Williams that this was the rationale—we see it as a means to start to level the playing field between religious traditions. Masuzawa is quite right

---

[1] I am grateful to Hendrik Vroom for alerting me to the way that Barth's theology can be used positively in this context.

to suggest that in a figure like Troeltsch we see a situation, just over half a century later, when Christian theologians could no longer assert their superiority by dictat and that a serious engagement with the religious Other was leading to a more pluralist form of expression ([1], p. 320). However, we can ask is she right therefore to assert that we see a Christian domination and takeover of the discourse on religious plurality? It is my contention that the assumptions of the Christian worldview had been, to some degree at least, shattered and reshaped by the encounter with the religious Other. Masuzawa's argument, at least partially, shares the problem that various critiques have found in Edward Said's Orientalism [43,44], that it portrays the Orient as a passive recipient of Western discourses [45], whereas it is a two-way street, as we have discussed in relation to Clarke above, a point made also by David Smith ([46], pp. 85–101). Likewise, we must ask, is it fair or reasonable to claim that it is Christian theology that is shaping the discourse on religious plurality or, in as far as it does, is it a Christian theology which has itself been shaped and changed in its response to religious diversity, and so we find a rather more subtle and complex set of webs to unravel. The challenge becomes then not simply to remove 'theology' from the discourse on religious plurality or Religious Studies—as Fitzgerald avers ([2], pp. 33–53)—for there is no pure or simple 'theology', in a thing as and of itself, underlying these debates.

Assessing the Relationship of the OCT and the NCT

This extended discussion on these themes should alert us, yet again, to the fact that the sharp distinction between the OCT and the NCT is overstated. In particular, I would like to pick up on two aspects of Nicholson's argument that they are different forms of discourse, first that the NCT, unlike the OCT, is aware of its own partisanship, and second that the OCT denies the truth of the other. Williams, at least, as we have suggested realized that the comparison must be even handed and fair and this lead him into questioning his own tradition in new ways in relation to critical scholarship. Likewise, both Maurice and Williams are at pains to stress the value of the other as a 'real' form of truth: Fulfilment Theology tends to stress an innate sentiment in humanity for certain religious truths so only in as far as the non-Christian religion can be said to hold something that answers to this can it ever be fulfilled by Christianity ([28], pp. 32–3).[2] Indeed, in as far as Clooney proposes an inclusivism as the basis for his NCT then we can see a clear link between this and the thought of Maurice and Williams—what is generally termed the inclusivist position in most versions of the ToR typology is generically called the 'fulfilment paradigm' in Knitter's version stressing how central such thinking is ([19], pp. 63ff.; see [13], p. 20). However, there is clearly a difference in the practice, with questions

---

[2] Certainly, a common critique made against 'Liberal Christianity' is that it assumes a common religious sentiment and this could be applied here, however, Fulfilment Theology in its various forms is far from a modern liberal tradition being found, as discussed above, in Evangelical and conservative traditions (which, arguably also develop a post-Enlightenment narrative), but also traces roots back through figures like Justin Martyr and others in the Christian tradition. The criticism we may not is also, arguably, fairly facile being prone to the genealogical fallacy—just because a tradition or concept arises at a certain point does not mean its ideas are limited to that context or subject to other failings of contemporary worldviews.

of truth being deferred in the practice of the NCT by Clooney and others, where religious ideas from different traditions are presented alongside one another [8] rather than in tension or competition. Nevertheless, it seems to make more sense to distinguish the OCT and the NCT by degree rather than by kind.

Religion, Orientalism and Comparative Theology

Our argument above raises the question therefore as to whether the NCT is guilty of perpetuating a theological and colonial representation of the Other if it exists as an extension of its forebear rather than a radical step change. This, possibly, lies behind the sometimes quite vehement denial of such a link by proponents of the NCT. Certainly, while Nicholson can see a certain heritage between himself and Rudolf Otto in his comparison of Shankara and Eckhart, a key argument that he invokes is that he is not captive to the Orientalist discourse of East-West dichotomies that he argues marked out Otto's work ([6], pp. 109ff.).

In his conclusion to *Comparative Theology and the Problem of Religious Rivalry*, Nicholson sets out clearly what he sees as distinct about the NCT. Speaking of 'scholars who reject comparison' he tells us that they do so because it is seen to 'exemplify the totalizing schemes and meta-narratives… identified as discourses of domination', where 'the cross-cultural similarities… are imagined, whereas the underlying cultural differences are real' ([6], p. 200). Whereas he suggests the NCT realizes 'that historical understanding is itself a creative process' ([6], p. 200). However, he argues that it is only when a tension is set up between 'a scientific, representational model' and a 'constructive' paradigm that we truly see comparison come to fruit, where we do not see it 'as a discourse of absolute truth, but rather pragmatically, as a political discourse of strategic intervention' ([6], p. 203).

I do not wish to develop one outcome of Nicholson's argument, as it seems to me, but feel it must be mentioned, which is that if we accept that it is only the historical interests of the scholar that guide the comparison, and so the act is undertaken 'strategically', then when he suggests that his reading highlights aspects of Shankara 'suppressed by the Orientalist characterizations' ([6], p. 198) of Otto, we have no reason to prefer his reading to that of Otto—each is merely the appeal of a scholar to the prejudices of his day. Leaving this aside, I think that Nicholson has nevertheless highlighted an important point about the constructive endeavour. Rather than being 'discourses of domination', the OCT by its very nature undermined the very domination that may, perhaps, have been the intention of it; both Maurice and Williams wrote their respective works on the OCT as commissions designed towards a missionary end ([28], p. 47). However, as argued above, particularly with regard to Williams, his deep study of the religious Other led to the application of critical theory more widely to Christian scriptures. While not to downplay the strong sense of Christian superiority found within his work it is notable that Williams' *Hinduism and Christianity* ends inconclusively, not with a conversion of the narrator from Hinduism to Christianity, but with him contemplating the various arguments—something which no doubt reflects Williams awareness that here lay a system with deep spiritual roots and strong intellectual validity [35]. As we have mentioned above, this is in accord with critics of a strong Orientalism, like J. J. Clarke and Smith, who have argued that the encounter was not simply a one-way process of Western domination, but one where the encountered Orient itself gave rise to counter narratives and new ways of thinking. It is my contention here that the OCT rather than being a simple discourse of Christian imperialism and hegemonic discourse was in fact part of a process that has led to a questioning of the borders and boundaries of the traditions. While we have shown that Williams' more nuanced attitude evidenced this, and challenged Christianity, we could even suggest parts of Clarke and Maurice do likewise. For instance, while Clarke sees Confucianism as inherently flawed by not speaking of God, he feels compelled to admit that the Chinese character has greatly benefitted under its tutelage ([14], pp. 58–61). Again, in relation to the Hindu tradition, which he terms Brahmanism, he argues that it has a 'special relation as a system of thought to Christianity' ([14], pp. 135), though flawed morally. While this fits within his own preoccupation to show the superiority of Christianity we find that he is led to admit points of contact, even congruence and great insights within other religious systems. As such, while, qua Said, power is asserted over the Other and the tradition placed in relation to Christianity, contra Said, it is as part of a process of giving of respect to the Other and recognizing, even if only by limited steps, that they hold great wisdom and insights.

I would like here to map some aspects of this. The categories 'religion' and 'world religion' are often questioned as simply being an imposition of a colonial or Christian template upon other traditions, worldviews and thought forms (to which the term 'religion' may not properly apply). Here critics like Masuzawa, Fitzgerald, McCutcehon and Asad share a focus on dismantling what they see as problematic construction of contemporary notions of 'religion' and the modern scholarship in the study of religions (Masuzawa, however, admits that she lacks knowledge of the contemporary scene both within the study of religion and theology and so focuses on the period that covers the origins of the OCT [1]), employing what may be seen as an archaeological, or genealogical, approach to uncovering the layers of meaning and discourse.[3] Space does not permit us to discuss the arguments fully here (however, I have engaged some of the arguments elsewhere ([13], pp. 64–87; [38]), but in relation to Masuzawa's specific point about the way that the OCT played a part in this process it is my suggestion that the narrative she presents needs to be, at the very least, problematized and presented with more nuance about how other discourses played into these representations. As I have argued above the OCT, as well as the ToR, are involved in complex ways with the representation of 'religion', and cannot be branded as guilty of a simple imposition of Christian hegemony. Again, debates around Orientalism post-Said are voluminous, and raise many questions about the representation of the Other, but in relation to what we have discussed above the invoking of the charge 'Orientalist' also needs to be presented with more nuance [39,44–46].

The above issues play into questions about borders, boundaries and changing discourses, and the way in which the OCT, the ToR and the NCT sit within a changing web of what is an acceptable position within Christian theology. This raises one question in particular, which is what does it mean to say that the creation of the term 'religion', or 'Religious studies' or contemporary thinking of

---

[3] The term 'archaeological' here suggesting a 'post-modern' suspicion of metanarratives and their construction that rests upon foundational work by Foucault and Lyotard. For a discussion of this ([47], pp. 12–16).

'religious plurality' owes some basis to a Christian theological position? Fitzgerald and Masuzawa both suggest that a liberal Christian theological position lay behind such terms and became assumed into what were often taken to be non-theological and neutral terms and ideologies. However, several points need to be raised, one of which is that there is not simply any single thing which encapsulates what 'liberal' theology is [48]. Even in relation to the religious Other we have seen that a variety of perspectives exist within figures like Maurice, Williams, Müller, Lucas, and Andrews. Meanwhile, Fulfilment Theology which is sometimes used as a touchstone of a liberal perspective for its time by Masuzawa and Nicholson [1,7] is endorsed as much by conservative evangelicals, like Monier-Williams and Farquhar, as it is by liberals [19,49]. Moreover, as argued above, the religious Other is not just represented by Christian theology but has a role in the very presentation and representation itself. We could speak of this as a subversion of 'theological' positionality, in that whatever 'Christian' position there was does not remain the same; however, and imperative in this, is the fact that there never was an 'original' pristine Christian theology; as Thatamanil warns us 'neither religion nor theology can be taken as universals' ([18], p. 251). Throughout its existence Christian theology has been in a process of cultural and interreligious engagement, and so to suggest that we have *a* Christian theology which imposes itself on others is itself problematic (see [13], pp. 31–44). At the same time, it cannot be denied that Western (in the Nineteenth century especially European and British) authority and worldviews were dominant and exerted an undeniable influence on the shaping of knowledge, which is part of Masuzawa's narrative [1]. Nevertheless, we must ask to what extent we can speak simply of Christian agency in the creation of these concepts. Here I would suggest that both the OCT and the NCT share common ground, for a claim made by a contemporary representative of the NCT, Thatamanil, that: '*Resources from other traditions must shape comparative theological method itself*' ([18], p. 253, italics in original). This, arguably, is found in relation to the category 'religion' itself, in that the notion of many 'religions' comes as a response to those other religions,[4] and as we have seen in relation to Williams this recognition led, even in the OCT, to a questioning of legitimate interpretations and critiques of the Christian tradition. As such, in creating 'religions', or 'world religions', as something to be seriously engaged, the OCT started to break the Western vision that only its own local truths are universal and something to be considered the norm. Therefore, we should join scholars who question the strong Orientalist thesis that we must reject developments like 'religion' as simply impositions ([18], p. 240; [37]), a stance that sometimes draws inspiration from Mandair [50,51].

Another issue that must be raised is the question of the disavowal of the past, which if we understand it as partaking in an 'Orientalist' discourse which we ourselves wish to disown may seem natural. However, as Nicholson suggests, we write from the perspective of our time just as others

---

[4] This, of course, begs the question of whether such things as 'religions' exist, but here I do not wish to insist upon any single or reified definition of what this means, but am simply referring to the various traditions which have come into dialogue, whatever specific term, or terms, we should apply to them. As has been argued elsewhere, even if we admit the term 'religion' is problematic and implicated in an Orientalist discourse we cannot avoid the historical fact that various traditions have apparently 'recognized' each other as occupying similar ground and have been in dialogue on related issues, which we might term 'an orientation to the transcendent' for many centuries ([38], pp. 297–8, 302ff.).

write from the perspective of theirs. In this context, as has been argued elsewhere about our own scholarly forebears:

> 'Our own interpretative strategies and, we may hope, greater self-reflexivity, is not divorced from their own attempts to look beyond themselves, but stands as part of an ongoing programme….No doubt future historians of religion will look back upon our attempts to interpret religion today and, with the benefit of hindsight, and their own agenda, pass judgement upon us. We can only ask what they will see, which we cannot see of ourselves?' ([26], p. 75).

We must therefore ask what can be left behind from the past, what can be learnt from the past, but always we must seek not to misrepresent the past, and terms such as 'Orientalist' lack the nuance and subtlety to understand the varied agendas and perspectives of figures like Williams, Maurice, Müller, Otto and others.

Europe, America and the OCT and the NCT

One final question arises, and which has given rise at least in part to this edition and its rationale—European responses to the NCT—which is why it is America in particular that has given rise to the discipline. Certainly it is not a uniquely American phenomenon, and scholars like Ward and others identify themselves with the label [16].[5] One line of enquiry may be to follow up Masuzawa's suggestion that the discourse on religious plurality became in the twentieth century a peculiarly American phenomenon ([1], pp. 268ff.). However, I am not convinced, the kind of discourse on World Religions—seen in textbooks and university courses—is just as much a British phenomenon (and I suspect more widespread in Europe and elsewhere) as it is American (something Masuzawa notes in her introduction ([1], p. 8)). Moreover, another claim Masuzawa makes is not entirely correct: she describes on the works of the OCT, and the surrounding literature and theology, as part of a strangely forgotten set of texts and ideas; certainly she makes little or no mention of surrounding secondary literature. However, while not a major scholarly industry there is a considerable set of writing, at least by British academics, on this period, and in monographs and period reviews it has been dealt with in a good number of sources (e.g., [28,52–56])—to mention but some of the works published prior to Masuzawa's monograph, and not including the considerable literature on Müller (see [28]). One hypothesis that comes to mind then is that perhaps the OCT remained a feature in the awareness of those within British academia such that a suspicion about embarking once again by something of this name (not that it would necessarily have been the tag used by, for instance, Maurice and Williams for their work). What may be described as the weight of history may perhaps have pressed more heavily in the 'old' world, such that the NCT could not come to fruition there. Speculating upon the reasons goes somewhat beyond the strictly historical analysis undertaken here, nevertheless, some points for contemplation may be made, however, they would require further research before being considered as secure arguments. We suggested above that, perhaps, theological articulation on the relationship

---

[5] The other articles in this edition testify to this, and reference many such scholars.

between religions may have been a factor in the UK before the US because of the former's colonial context. However, for the UK, and indeed many European countries, losing this in the twentieth century may also have impacted upon the further development of the discipline, while as a veritable melting-pot of cultures such reflection may have seemed more natural in the US. As has been suggested, the sense of the UK as a multi-religious nation has come only recently ([57], p. 11), so in some ways the weight of history as a Christian nation, which for the US is certainly later, and arguably therefore less embedded, especially in its becoming a more explicitly and clearly a multicultural society may have affected theological agendas.

Conclusions

In light of criticisms made of the OCT and the issues concerning 'Orientalism' raised against it, it is natural that proponents of the NCT should wish to disassociate their discipline from it, arguing that it represents a new arena of discourse. However, it is far from clear that such a clear distinction can be made, and as I have argued here there may not be grounds for seeking to make such a distinction. Rather than presenting a discontinuity between the OCT (and the ToR) and the NCT, it may be better to see them as part of a progressive challenge to a reigning hegemonic discourse in previous Christian theology (notwithstanding that, of course, legitimations for this approach are themselves founded in earlier, even foundational, Christian sources ([8], pp. 24ff.; [13], pp. 133–44; [23], pp. 146–70). Such an approach can be claimed to be not only more reflective of the actual circumstances of the development of ideas, but also presents further support to the critique of a strong 'Orientalist' thesis that portrays the 'Orient' as always subject to Occidental, especially Christian, dominionism, and fails to present the intercultural, and interreligious, history of ideas, which, I would argue, is essential to the project of Comparative Theology (and the ToR) in any form as a mature and self-reflective discourse.

Conflicts of Interest

The author declares no conflict of interest.

References

1. Masuzawa, Tomoko. *The Invention of World Religions*; Chicago University Press: Chicago, IL, USA, 2005.
2. Fitzgerald, Timothy. *The Ideology of Religious Studies*; Oxford University Press: Oxford, UK, 2000.
3. Fitzgerald, Timothy. *Discourse on Civility and Barbarity: A Critical History of Religion and Related Categories*; Oxford University Press: Oxford, UK, 2007.
4. Asad, Talal. Genealogies of Religion: Discipline and Reasons of Power in Christianity and Islam. Baltimore, MA: John Hopkins University Press, 1993.
5. McCutcheon, Russell. Manufacturing Religion: The Discourse on Sui Generis Religion and the Politics of Nostalgia. Oxford, UK: Oxford University Press, 1997.

6. Nicholson, Hugh. *Comparative Theology and the Problem of Religious Rivalry*. Oxford, UK: Oxford University Press, 2011.
7. Nicholson, Hugh. "The Reunification of Theology and Comparison in the New Comparative Theology." *Journal of the American Academy of Religion* 77 (2009): 609–46.
8. Clooney, Francis X. *Comparative Theology: Deep Learning Across Religious Borders*. Chichester, UK: Wiley-Blackwell, 2010.
9. Clooney, Francis X. "Comparative Theology: A Review of Recent Books." *Theological Studies* 56 (1995): 521–50.
10. Clooney, Francis X. "Comparative Theology." In *The Oxford Handbook of Systematic Theology*, edited by J.B. Webster, Kathryn Tanner, Iain R. Torrance. Oxford, UK: Oxford University Press, 2007, pp. 653–69.
11. Fredericks, James. Faith Among Faiths: Christian theology and Non-Christian Religions. New York: Paulist Press, 1999.
12. Race, Alan. Christians and Religious Pluralism: Patterns in the Christian Theology of Religions. London: SCM Press, 1983.
13. Hedges, Paul. Controversies in Interreligious Dialogue and the Theology of Religions. London: SCM Press, 2010.
14. Clarke, James F. *Ten Great Religions: An Essay in comparative theology*. Boston: James R. Osgood and Company, 1876.
15. Maurice, Frederick D. *The Religions of the World: and their Relations to Christianity*. London: Macmillan and Co., 1886 [1847].
16. Ward, Keith. *Religion and Creation*. Oxford, UK: Oxford University Press, 1996.
17. Nicholson, Hugh. "Comparative Theology after Liberalism." *Modern Theology* 23 (2007): 229–51.
18. Thatamanil, John. "Comparative Theology after 'Religion'." In *Planetary Loves: Spivak, Postcoloniality and Theology*, edited by Stephen D Moore, Mayra Rivera. New York: Fordham University Press, 2011, pp. 238–57.
19. Knitter, Paul F. *Introducing Theologies of Religion*. Maryknoll: Orbis, 2002.
20. Hedges, Paul. "Particularities: Post-modern Tradition-Specific Approaches." In *Christian Approaches to Other Faiths*, edited by Paul Hedges; Alan Race. London: SCM, 2008, pp. 112–35.
21. Clooney, Francis X. "Reading the World in Christ: From Comparison to Inclusivism." In *Christian Uniqueness Reconsidered: The Myth of a Pluralistic Theology of Religions*, edited by Gavin D'Costa. Maryknoll: Orbis, 1990, pp. 63–80.
22. Cheetham, David. "Inclusivisms: Honouring Faithfulness and Openness." In *Christian Approaches to Other Faiths*, edited by Paul Hedges, Alan Race. London: SCM, 2008, pp. 63–84.
23. Schmidt-Leukel, Perry. Transformation by Integration: How Inter-faith Encounter Changes Christianity. London: SCM, 2009.

24. Kiblinger, Kristin B. "Relating Theology of Religions and Comparative Theology." In *The New Comparative Theology: Interreligious Insights from the Next Generation*, edited by Francis X. Clooney. London: T&T Clark, 2010, pp. 21–42.
25. Nicholson, Hugh. "The New Comparative Theology and the Problem of Theological Hegemonism." In *The New Comparative Theology: Interreligious Insights from the Next Generation*, edited by Francis X. Clooney. London: T&T Clark, 2010, pp. 43–62.
26. Hedges, Paul. "Post-Colonialism, Orientalism, and Understanding: Religious Studies and the Christian Missionary Imperative." *Journal of Religious History* 32 (2008): 55–75.
27. Ford, Margaret. An Evangelical Family Revealed: The Bickersteth and Monier-Williams Letters and Diaries 1880–1918. Layerthorpe: Ford Publishing, 2010.
28. Hedges, Paul. Preparation and Fulfilment: A History and Study of Fulfilment Theology in Modern British Thought in the Indian Context. Bern: Peter Lang, 2001.
29. Farquhar, John N. *The Crown of Hinduism*. London: Humphrey Milford/Oxford University Press, 1930 [1913].
30. O'Connor, Daniel. *The Testimony of C. F. Andrews*. Madras: Christian Literature Society, 1975.
31. Schmidt-Leukel, Perry. "Pluralisms: How to Appreciate Religious Diversity Theologically." In *Christian Approaches to Other Faiths*, edited by Paul Hedges, Alan Race. London: SCM, 2008, pp. 85–110.
32. Troeltsch, Ernst. "The Place of Christianity Among the World Religions." In *Christianity and Other Religions: Selected Readings*, edited by John Hick; Brian Hebblethwaite. London: Fount Paperbacks, 1980 [1923], pp. 11–31.
33. Williams, Rowan. Paraméswara-jnyána-góshthí: A Dialogue of the Knowledge of the Supreme Lord in which are Compared the Claims of Christianity and Hinduism, and Various Questions of Indian Religion and Literature Fairly Discussed. Cambridge, UK: Deighton, Bell and Co., 1856.
34. Badham, Paul. "The Significance of Rowland Williams." *The Welsh Journal of Religious History* 1 (2006): 50–58.
35. Hedges, Paul. "Rowland Williams and Missions to the Hindu." In *Religious Dynamics Under the Impact of Imperialism and Colonialism: A Sourcebook*, edited by Marion Eggert, Hans-Martin Kraemer, Björn Bentlage, Stefan Reichmuth. Leiden: Brill, forthcoming.
36. Griffith, Sydney. The Church in the Shadow of the Mosque: Christians and Muslims in the World of Islam. Princeton: Princeton University Press, 2008.
37. Bhogal, Balbinder S. "Sikh *Dharam* and Postcolonialism: Hegel, Religion and Žižek." *Australian Religion Studies Review* 25 (2012): 185–213.
38. Hedges, Paul. "Can We Still Teach 'Religions'?: Towards an Understanding of Religion as Culture and Orientation in Contemporary Pedagogy and Metatheory." In *International Handbook for Inter-Religious Education*, edited by Kath Engebretson, Marian Souza, Gloria Durka, Liam Gearon. New York: Springer Academic Publishers, 2010, pp. 291–312.
39. Clarke, James J. Oriental Enlightenment: The Encounter between Asia and Western Thought. London: Routledge, 1997.

40. Heelas, Paul. *The New Age Movement*. Oxford, UK: Blackwell, 1996.
41. Maurice, Frederick D. "Letter to R. H. Hutton (8 January 1854)." In *The Life and Letters of Frederick Denison Maurice: Chiefly told in his Own Letters*, edited by Frederick D. Maurice. London: Macmillan and Co., 1884, volume II.
42. Barth, Karl. *Church Dogmatics: A Selection*, edited by Helmut Gollwitzer, translated by Geoffrey William Bromiley. New York: Harper Torchbooks, 1962.
43. Said, Edward. *Orientalism*; New York: Vintage Books, 1979.
44. Olson, Carl. "Orientalism." In *Studying Hinduism: Key Concepts and Methods*, edited by Sushil Mittal, Gene R Thursby. London: Routledge, 2008, pp. 278–88.
45. Kabbani, Rana. *Imperial Fictions: Europe's Myths of Orient*, rev. ed. London: Pandora, 1994.
46. Smith, David. *Hinduism and Modernity*. Oxford: Blackwell Publishing, 2003.
47. Lyon, David. *Postmodernity*. Buckingham: Open University Press, 1994.
48. Dorien, Gary. "American Liberal Theology: Crisis, Irony, Decline, Renewal, Ambiguity." *Crosscurrents* 55 (2006): No 4. www.crosscurrents.org/dorrien200506.htm.
49. Monier-Williams, Monier. *Modern India and the Indians*, 4th ed. London: Trübner and Co., 1887.
50. Mandair, Arvind. "The emergence of modern 'Sikh theology': Reassessing the passage of ideas from Trumpp to Bham i Vir Singh." *Bulletin of SOAS* 68 (2005): 253–275.
51. Mandair, Arvind. Religion and the Specter of the West: Sikhism, India, Postcoloniality, and the Politics of Translation. New York: Columbia University Press, 2009.
52. Thomas, Terrence. "East Comes West." In *The British: Their Religious Beliefs and Practices 1800–1986*, edited by Terrence Thomas. London: Routledge, 1988, pp. 72–100.
53. Cracknell, Kenneth. Justice, Courtesy, Love: Theologians and Missionaries Encountering World Religions, 1846–1914. London: Epworth Press, 1995.
54. Wood, Nicholas. "Confessing Christ in a Plural World: A Missiological Approach to Interfaith Relations with Particular Reference to Kenneth Cragg and Leslie Newbiggin." PhD thesis, University of Oxford, 1996.
55. Sharpe, Eric. *Comparative Religion: A History*, 2nd ed. La Salle: Open Court, 1991.
56. Bouquet, Alan C. *The Christian Faith and Non-Christian Religions*. London: James Nisbet and Co., 1958.
57. Beckford, James, Richard Gale, David Owen, Carl Peach, and Paul Weller. *Review of the Evidence Base on Faith Communities*. London: Office of the Deputy Prime Minister, 2006.

Reprinted from *Religions*. Cite as: Drew, Rose. "Challenging Truths: Reflections on the Theological Dimension of Comparative Theology." *Religions* 3 (2012): 1041-1053.

Article

Challenging Truths: Reflections on the Theological Dimension of Comparative Theology

Rose Drew

523 Shields Road, Glasgow, G41 2RF, UK; E-Mail: rosemdrew@gmail.com

Received: 27 September 2012; in revised form: 27 October 2012 / Accepted: 29 October 2012 / Published: 1 November 2012

Abstract: Given that comparative theology is aimed at learning from the insights of other religious traditions, the comparative theologian's confessional perspective must be engaged and subject to possible transformation through the discovery of truth in those traditions. Despite Francis Clooney's and James Fredericks' attempts to distance comparative theology from the theology of religions, its truth-seeking dimension makes participation in the theology of religions unavoidable. Crucial to integrating what is learned, moreover, is a willingness to allow presuppositions about the other to be challenged and to make revisions if necessary. Keith Ward exhibits this willingness but, on this basis, distinguishes comparative theology from confessional theology, thus obscuring the legitimacy of revision from a committed religious standpoint. Where comparative theologians are willing and able to integrate all that is learned through their study of other traditions, comparative theology can be conceived of as both a confessional enterprise and a contribution to what Wilfred Cantwell Smith called 'World Theology'—that is, the ongoing attempt to give intellectual expression to the faith of us all.

Keywords: comparative theology; confessional theology; theology of religions; world theology; inclusivism; pluralism; identity; Clooney; Fredericks; Ward

Introduction

From the time I first started to study and appreciate Buddhism, I never felt as if I were embarking on a fundamentally different enterprise when I stepped out of a Christian theology seminar and opened an anthology of Buddhist texts; my interest was always in whether or not the ideas I was encountering were true, and how they might relate to what I already believed, as a Christian. In contrast to many of my Buddhist studies peers, whom I'm sure assumed we were doing religious studies, I felt as if I was doing theology. Yet what kind of theology? If the study of a religious tradition other than one's own can be a genuinely theological enterprise, then those engaged in that enterprise must try to carve out a recognised disciplinary space for it, and to explain as best we can what is at stake. This is, perhaps, particularly important in the modern British academic context where the disciplines of theology and religious studies frequently coexist in single academic departments and the nature of the relationship between them is ambiguous and disputed.[1]

Influential in the contemporary attempt to define a theological approach to the study of other religious traditions are advocates of comparative theology. The term 'comparative theology', though long in use, has been popularised by contemporary thinkers such as Francis Clooney, James Fredericks, Robert Neville, and Keith Ward. Not all protagonists understand the discipline in precisely the same way. Initially, I will focus predominantly on Clooney's and—to a lesser extent—Fredericks' understanding. Clooney and Fredericks insist that it is not comparative religion they are recommending, but a genuine form of theology, 'an intellectual discipline grounded in faith' ([2], p. 132). Comparative theology, explains Clooney,

> marks acts of faith seeking understanding which are rooted in a particular faith tradition but which, from that foundation, venture into learning from one or more other faith traditions. This learning is sought for the sake of fresh theological insights that are indebted to the newly encountered tradition/s as well as the home tradition ([3], p. 10).

Ultimately, it is this desire to learn from other traditions that distinguishes comparative theology from attempts to engage theologically with other traditions out of apologetic or missionary motives. And it is also this emphasis on learning *from*—rather than merely *about*—other traditions that distinguishes it from comparative religion, phenomenology of religions, or history of religions, all of which seek to avoid a theological approach. Hence, as Ward explains,

> [c]omparative theology differs from what is often called 'religious studies', in being primarily concerned with the meaning, truth, and rationality of religious beliefs, rather than with the psychological, sociological, or historical elements of religious life and institutions ([4], p. 40).

Similarly, Catherine Cornille asserts that '[w]hat distinguishes comparative theology from the historical or phenomenological study of other religions ... is its commitment to and pursuit of truth' ([5], p. 139). Like phenomenologists, comparative theologians attempt, as far as possible, to gain an insider's perspective on the religious tradition they study so as to better understand it on its own terms. But unlike phenomenologists, they undertake this exercise in order to ascertain whether there might be truth and value in the other's religious perspective from which they might learn; they seek insights which may enhance, enrich, or fruitfully challenge the confessional perspective with which they set out.

---

[1] See [1], p. 8.

In this short essay I would like to draw out some implications of the claim that comparative theology is a truth-seeking enterprise by considering some crucial respects in which the confessional perspective of the theologian is engaged in the process. I begin by exploring the relationship between comparative theology and theology of religions, before honing in on a crucial respect in which the theologian's confessional starting point must be open to being challenged and revised in the process of comparative study. I then consider what such revision would entail, before concluding that comparative theology should be seen as a form of confessional theology, but one which involves the expansion of the theologian's faith perspective to include the truth discovered in the other.

Comparative Theology and Theology of Religions

Clooney and Fredericks are keen to distinguish comparative theology from theology of religions. The latter discipline involves formulating an understanding of other religious traditions that is consistent with one's own theology. Theology of religions is associated by Clooney and Fredericks with abstract, *a priori* theorising about religious diversity. This, they stress, is precisely what comparative theology is not. Clooney, for example, describes theology of religions as involving reflection,

> from the perspective of one's own religion on the meaning of other religions, often considered merely in general terms. By contrast, comparative theology necessarily includes actually learning another religious tradition in significant detail ([3], p. 14).

Comparative theology is, crucially, concerned with the concrete task of studying the specifics—scriptures, rituals, artworks, and so on—of particular traditions, in order to learn from them. It is about 'going deep', says Clooney, not about 'generalizing' ([3], p. 107). While Clooney sees a role for both comparative theology and theology of religions, Fredericks goes as far as to suggest the latter enterprise be abandoned altogether and replaced by the former. To embrace a particular stance in the theology of religions is to make up one's mind about other religions without ever having to find out anything about them, thinks Fredericks; it is to 'escape the necessity of taking other religious believers seriously' ([6], p. 115).

As a number of thinkers have pointed out, however, if comparative theology is a genuinely truth-seeking enterprise, then it cannot be as neatly distinguished from theology of religions as Clooney and Fredericks would like,[2] not least because comparative theology presupposes certain assumptions about the tradition studied. If one studies another tradition with a theological interest in truth, then it is presumably because one's confessional perspective gives one reason to see that tradition as a potential source of truth and value. This locates the starting point of comparative theology with respect to the threefold typology commonly used in the theology of religions, comprising exclusivism, inclusivism, and pluralism. Since exclusivists hold that only their own tradition contains salvific truth and value, comparative theology cannot emerge from exclusivism. Rather, it must proceed from provisional inclusivist or pluralist assumptions; either assuming the

---

[2] See, e.g., [7], pp. 90–104; [8], pp. 235–36. For further references see [9], pp. 24–25.

possibility that the tradition studied may contain salvific truth and value, though in lesser measure than one's own, or assuming that the tradition studied may be equal in salvific truth and value to one's own. In other words, comparative theology depends on a specific theology of religions, even if that theology of religions is not explicitly worked out but only implied by the comparative theologian's confessional starting point. Christians might, for example, assume the Holy Spirit to be active outside the Christian tradition and, hence, potentially responsible for truth and goodness in other traditions, and might therefore engage in comparative theology in the hope of deepening their knowledge of God. Although Clooney has been reluctant to explicitly endorse a particular stance within the theology of religions as a presupposition of his study of Hinduism,[3] he acknowledges that his sympathies are inclusivist—a position he sees as balancing 'claims to Christian uniqueness with a necessary openness to learning from other religions'.[4]

As well as being motivated by an implicit theology of religions, comparative theology must also include explicit reflection on the types of questions addressed in the theology of religions. For, eventually, the theologian must try to determine whether what is encountered in the tradition studied is in fact true and valuable, a process which requires an attempt to relate the claims of that tradition to the claims of one's home tradition.[5] Where the tradition studied *is* judged to contain truth and value, moreover, that discovery must somehow be integrated into the theologian's home tradition. It might be, for example, that the insights identified prompt the rediscovery of lost or obscured strands of thought or practice within one's tradition. We see this, for example, in renewed Christian interest in 'negative theology' as a result of the encounter with the Buddhist doctrine of emptiness, and in Buddhist theologies which seek to promote social engagement and critique as a result of the encounter with Christian social ethics. Or theologians might start to reflect differently on familiar figures within their own tradition by looking at those figures from the perspective of the tradition encountered. Clooney, for example, finds Christian insight into Mary enhanced by reflection on Hindu devotion to Laksmi and Devī ([3], p. 93–99). And theologians such as John Keenan and Joseph O'Leary have experimented with more radical integrations by applying a Buddhist hermeneutical framework to the tenets of Christian faith.[6] But another crucial affect of the discovery of truth in the other, of which proponents of comparative theology do not always take full account, should be reflection on whether the presuppositions about the other which were implicit in their confessional starting points are vindicated or challenged by that discovery. Let us focus on this point.

Clooney speaks of the 'transformative nature of interreligious study' ([3], p. 39) and envisages comparative theology leading to a 'transformed reappropriation of confessional views' ([14], p. 26) and 'a significant change in one's Christian theology' ([10], p. 64). Fredericks reflects, similarly, that '[o]nce Christians begin to take the truths of non-Christian religions seriously, we should not expect

---

[3] Kiblinger ([9]) sees such reluctance on the part of comparative theologians as problematic and urges them to be more explicit about their presuppositions and more forthcoming about the effects on their comparative theology.

[4] Clooney ([3], p. 16). See also [10].

[5] Perry Schmidt-Leukel makes this point persuasively ([7], p. 100).

[6] See e.g. [11–13].

that their faith will be left untouched' ([6], p. 9). Yet neither seems altogether willing to allow their comparative study to challenge their presuppositions about the overall truth and value of the tradition studied. Emphasising the complexity of questions concerning the relative truth of Hindu and Christian claims due to their embeddedness within their distinctive contexts, Clooney recommends 'the patient deferral of issues of truth' until further study has taken place and understanding has deepened ([15], pp. 187–93). In the meantime,

> provisional theological assessments become the norm... Should enquiry support the faith position of one tradition over against others on a specific point, this specific insight will not be decisive regarding which religion is truest or best. Later on, regarding another issue, the other tradition's position may appear more plausible ([3], pp. 112–3).

In this way, says Clooney, comparative theology focuses on 'actual instances of learning' and 'leaves to others the large judgments about religions' ([3], p. 41).

Yet is this an entirely accurate portrayal of Clooney's own approach, given that there are presuppositions about 'which religion is truest or best' implicit in his confessional starting point? Clooney avoids theorising about his presuppositions, and prefers to speak of the *practice* of 'including' when discussing his approach, rather than of 'inclusivism' ([3], p. 16). He also avoids using the language of 'superiority' or 'inferiority' when it comes to Christianity and Hinduism. But if Clooney is—or was—affirmative of expressions of Christian faith which *entail* the superiority of Christianity, then the implication that other traditions are inferior cannot be avoided, even if their inferiority is not explicitly stated. Moreover, Clooney admits inclusivist sympathies and inclusivism *involves* a judgement that Christianity is truest and best. Through comparative theology the insights of Hinduism may be brought to bear in all sorts of beneficial ways on Christian theology, but a world-view which entails that Christianity is superior to all other traditions will never be capable of fully affirming Hinduism's truth and efficacy.[7]

Beginning one's comparative work with the assumption that the tradition one studies is inferior to one's own is defensible, given the assertions of uniqueness found in many traditional expressions of faith. In the Christian case, for example, the assumption of superiority tends to emerge from Christological claims about Jesus Christ's unique divinity and constitutive role in salvation. But if through comparative study one increasingly finds instances of truth and value in the other, would it not be a better expression of the openness towards which comparative theologians aspire to allow the assumption of one's own superiority to be challenged by that discovery? Of course, Clooney's careful avoidance of explicit discussion of questions of superiority and inferiority could be taken as significant in itself, but is silence on this issue enough? I am not recommending that comparative theologians

---

[7] S. Mark Heim [16,17], for example, suggests a Christian inclusivist theory which attempts to affirm the salvific efficacy of Hinduism by accepting that the religious end sought by Hindus is real and obtainable. But insofar as he sees that religious end as less than fully salvific, his theory does not endorse the Hindu claim that Hinduism is efficacious with respect to *ultimate* salvation or liberation. Hence, what is affirmed is not, in the end, the Hinduism in which Hindus place their faith.

relinquish their commitment to the detailed study of other religious traditions, but only that there be greater readiness to integrate all that is learned. Given Clooney's desire to avoid both assertions of definitive truth or falsity ([3], p. 112) and the mere 'restatement of an earlier position, after a brief detour into comparison' ([15], p. 187), any presuppositions about Christian superiority must be subject to revision along with any other theological presuppositions that are challenged by the study of Hinduism. If inclusivist assumptions are treated as non-negotiable, then openness—or willingness to learn—is compromised and comparative theologians fall foul of their own critique of *a priori* theologies of religions which make detailed learning appear unnecessary. As Hugh Nicholson notes, bias and distortion are mitigated not by pursuing an unobtainable neutrality and objectivity, but by acknowledging one's normative commitments and being willing to submit those judgements to possible revision.[8] What would such revision involve?

A Posteriori Pluralism

Renouncing the assumption that one's home tradition is best would mean rejecting one's inclusivist presuppositions in favour of pluralist assumptions. Fredericks denounces pluralism because, as far as he is concerned, it 'effectively allows Christians to pass over the religious differences that distinguish them from their non-Christian neighbours without ever having to respond to them in any depth' ([6], p. 115). But a pluralism which emerges out of a deepening acquaintance and appreciation of another tradition is an *a posteriori* pluralism, not an *a priori* one. Indeed, as Paul Knitter points out,

> [f]or many Christians, it's precisely because they have already engaged in dialogue, ... that they are trying to rearrange their theological baggage and work out new models for understanding other religions. ... What they've seen in the dialogue doesn't quite fit what their theology has been telling them. Before they can explore further in the dialogue, they have to readjust their theological maps ([8], p. 236).

Fredericks, who has been more vocal about—and critical of—theology of religions than has Clooney, argues that pluralism involves a retreat to a meta-religious position outside the traditions in question which diffuses the tension between openness and commitment that is essential to comparative theology. It does this, thinks Fredericks, by claiming that 'all religions are expressions or interpretations of the same transcendent Reality' ([6], p. 170). But the Christian comparative theologian's growing recognition of Hinduism's truth and value comes not from stepping outside a Hindu perspective but from stepping ever more deeply into it, *i.e.* from a deepening experience of and identification with the truth and value discovered therein, without a corresponding rejection of Christianity. Hence, a renunciation of the assumption of superiority, grounded in one's own discovery of truth in the other, requires no retreat to a meta-position. Rather it can be seen as a confessional stance, an expression of one's growing faith in more than one tradition, as one immerses oneself increasingly in two religious worlds, flitting to and fro between them and identifying increasingly with both.

---

[8] Nicholson ([18], p. 59). Similarly, Kristin Kiblinger suggests that the comparative theologian's theological biases about the other be held 'tentatively, not dogmatically' ([9], p. 31).

Cornille claims that although someone belonging to one religious tradition may attempt in dialogue 'to understand the other from within' and, in so doing, gain considerable knowledge of another, those located in one tradition 'lack by definition the element of faith necessary to attain the deepest experience of the other' ([5], p. 144). But is this quite true? If the study of Hinduism has been for Clooney 'an act of religious learning leading to … deeper knowledge of God' ([3], p. 17), then as someone who knows God through both Christianity and Hinduism, can he not now claim some measure of Hindu faith? Over the years, Clooney has increasingly acknowledged the ambiguity that comparative study introduces to the theologian's location, recognising the complication of his own religious identity through his increasing immersion in the Srivaisnava world. He acknowledges that the sustained effort 'to think, imagine, even pray as would an insider' ([19], p. 103) have not left him unchanged. '[O]ne becomes enough of an insider that the tradition's realities work powerfully and invite assent', he reflects ([19], p. 102). As the comparative theologian takes both traditions to heart, 'she will begin to theologize as it were from both sides of the table, reflecting personally on old and new truths in an interior dialogue' ([3], p. 13). Thus, as Clooney says, comparative theology, 'opens the door to a kind of multiple religious belonging', as through this work, theologians find themselves 'having commitments and intuitions pertaining to at least two traditions' ([2], p. 146). Indeed, occasionally, this process can go as far as full-blown dual belonging, where there is roughly equal identification with—and full participation in—both traditions.[9]

Kristin Kiblinger argues that the ideal, championed by Clooney, of trying to see the tradition studied as would an insider is an ideal that is never completely met, since comparative theologians always carry their own religious baggage with them, including their presuppositions about the tradition studied ([3], p. 32). But what if those presuppositions are revised as their experience of the other deepens? As Knitter notes, '[w]hile we have to be aware that we bring our theological baggage to the journey of dialogue, that doesn't mean that during the journey we may not have to rearrange, or even dispose of, some of that baggage' ([8], p. 236). Kiblinger might argue that since one's criteria for discerning truth in the other tradition are derived from one's confessional starting point, a kind of inclusivism always operates in comparative study; one always wears the lenses of one's home tradition, and they prevent one from ever fully gaining an insider's perspective on the other.[10] But this fails to appreciate the capacity of dialogue to change and expand one's very criteria for what counts as truth. Certainly one's confessional starting point affects what one finds in the other, but the influence of the other in turn affects what one looks for. This transformation of one's perspective need not signify an abandonment or distortion of one's tradition. Ninian Smart suggests the following structure for how the expansion of criteria might legitimately occur from the perspective of one's home tradition:

---

[9] See [20].
[10] See [9], p. 32.

If faith F presents C as a criterion of truth, then faith T may turn out to do well or badly by that criterion. If well, then that is a ground for respecting criterion D put forward by T, and so something like an inter-system consensus about criteria cannot be ruled out ([21], p. 68).

Given an increasing immersion in and identification with the tradition studied, pluralism can surely develop, not as an abstract theory about religions in general, but as an expression of the fact that one's own commitments and intuitions now pertain to two traditions. This might lead one to embrace the idea that these traditions somehow express the same transcendent Reality, but this will not be the result of having adopted a supposedly meta-religious stance, as Fredericks claims, but may instead emerge out of reflection on one's own experience, now transformed; for, from one's Christian perspective, how could the truth and value one has discovered in Hinduism bear no relation to the truth and value one knows in Christianity and, from one's Hindu perspective, how could the truth and value one knows in Christianity be unrelated to the truth and value one has discovered in Hinduism?[11] Fredericks suggests that pluralism diffuses the creative tension on which comparative theology thrives. But not only does renouncing the assumption that one's home tradition is best not eradicate tensions between the traditions, it can actually encourage greater attention to them, inasmuch the temptation to simply assume that the other tradition is wrong where it differs is diminished.

Moreover, ceasing to assume that one's home tradition is superior need not entail a *definitive* judgement that the traditions in question are equally true and valuable, but only a relinquishment of the assumption that they are *not* equally true and valuable and a revision of expressions of faith which *entail* that they are not. Perhaps the comparative theologian will never feel able to make a definitive judgement about their equality. But a shift away from a provisional inclusivism to a provisional pluralism is a way of taking theologically seriously the truth discovered in the other. Moreover, each insight discovered in the other's perspective gives one further cause to suspect that pluralism is correct. For, as Perry Schmidt-Leukel points out, '[t]hrough contributing concrete and specific case studies, comparative theology can help to increase or decrease the overall plausibility of an exclusivist, inclusivist or pluralist view' ([7], p. 101). In this way Clooney's 'actual instances of learning' can help inform the 'large judgements about religions' that he would prefer to avoid.

Confessional Theology in Transformation

At times Clooney makes statements that suggest that his comparative studies have indeed challenged his presuppositions about the relationship of Christianity to other traditions. He speaks, for example, of learning to be 'resistant to the grandiose rhetoric of either [the Christian or Hindu tradition] about its uniqueness' ([22], p. 205), and of retaining belief in the efficacy of the Passion of Christ but losing the capacity to claim that knowledge of Brahman does not save ([15], p. 192). And elsewhere he writes: 'I confess that Jesus is Lord, but I cannot now assert that Śiva is not Lord nor that Nārāyaṇa did not

---

[11] Indeed, I have argued elsewhere that when identification with both traditions develops to such a degree that one identifies fully and equally with both traditions, embracing the idea that both are orientating one towards a single ultimate, transcendent reality becomes both a logical and spiritual necessity ([20], pp. 82–85).

graciously undergo embodiment in order to enable humans to encounter their God' ([14], p. 181). But such sentiments are frequently set within the context of the tension he perceives between them and the demands of Christian identity. He reflects, for example, that there may not be space within the Christian community for scholarship which defends the worship of goddesses, and so although he is able to understand and appreciate—and is even inclined to recite—the words 'Devī, may you stand forth before us', he feels 'unable to voice so definite an entreaty' because the 'rules governing insider identity in the Catholic community forbid prayer to Devī' ([19], p. 107). Through honest scholarship faith and reason are occasionally brought into 'acute tension', he reflects ([19], p. 110); and one is left 'caught between faith and understanding' ([19], p. 107).

It would seem at such points that, through his 'acts of faith seeking understanding', Clooney has arrived at an understanding which is at odds with traditional expressions of faith found in his home tradition. But while it may be tempting for committed Christian comparative theologians to throw their hands in the air at this point and return to the less agonising task of deciphering Hindu or Buddhist texts, this may ultimately be to do a disservice to the Christian tradition. Christian theologians surely have a responsibility to interpret the Christian revelation in the light of new historical circumstances, including new knowledge of other religious traditions. If that knowledge calls into question certain expressions of Christian faith, they must be willing to rethink those expressions, in faithfulness to the Christian revelation, even if significant shifts are required.[12] As John Cobb notes, if I am to be genuinely open to learning from another religious tradition, then 'I must be ready to learn even if that threatens my present beliefs' ([23], p. 45). Clooney is no doubt right that there is no place for worship of Devī for those operating within a Christian framework. Worshipping Devī simply would not make sense in the Christian context. But this does not mean that the theologian's experience and appreciation of a context in which worship of Devī *does* make sense—and not only makes sense but relates one transformatively to God—cannot receive recognition in the Christian framework. This recognition can come, in part, through a revision of expressions of Christian faith which entail that the Hindu context is inferior because it is different. No one is in a better position to contribute to this revision than those who have witnessed for themselves the efficacy of both frameworks.

Renouncing the superiority claim implicit in one's theological starting point means finding ways of expressing the truths of one's home tradition that do not entail that claim. Within the Christian tradition this requires controversial Christological revisions. Deeming 'theologizing about Christ and the world religions, the uniqueness of Christ, salvation outside the church, and related issues' to fall within the less urgent remit of theology of religions, Clooney excuses himself from this task ([2], pp. 137–8). But given the flaws they see in *a priori* judgements about such matters, is it not incumbent upon Christian comparative theologians, as people who have learnt deeply from other traditions, to enter the fray, or at least not—as Fredericks does—to criticise those who do? For as Clooney says, '[o]nly when an interreligious theological conversation is actually taking place can there

---

[12] Clooney suggests that careful comparative study 'should rarely make headlines' ([3], p. 112). But is this something that can be known in advance?

be progress in drawing conclusions from it and about it, either to reaffirm or revise established theological positions' ([14], p. 28).

Keith Ward's understanding of comparative theology is rather different from Clooney's and Fredericks' and more accommodating of the potential need for significant theological readjustment. Comparative theologians, argues Ward, should be 'prepared to revise beliefs if and when it comes to seem necessary' ([4], p. 48). He acknowledges that the divine revelation found in the apostolic witness to the life, death, and resurrection of Jesus is at the heart of Christian commitment. But suggests that comparative study must be allowed to influence Christian understanding of these paradigm events ([24], p. 347). Ward supposes, however, that the willingness to revise where necessary is where comparative theology diverges from confessional theology, which he sees as 'a form of apologetics for a particular faith'. Comparative theology he designates, by contrast, 'an intellectual discipline which inquires into ideas of the ultimate value and goal of human life, as they have been perceived and expressed in a variety of religious traditions' ([4], p. 40). Ward wishes to make clear that comparative theology is not merely about expressing the faith of one's own community, exploring its official beliefs, submitting to its authority and defending its views 'even if critical enquiry begins to question its assertions' ([4], pp. 40, 46); it is not restricted to an 'activity from within the believing community' ([4], p. 38), confined to certain 'protected propositions' which are 'exempt from questioning' ([4], p. 41). Ward does not mean by this that comparative theology requires a 'tradition-neutral investigator' ([4], p. 47); he readily acknowledges that the theologian always works 'from a particular perspective' ([4], p. 49). But he is keen to carve out a genuinely theological discipline in which truth is freely pursued, even where that truth calls into question the beliefs of one's community, and to uphold this discipline as also genuinely dialogical, involving co-operation, discussion, argument, and conversation amongst people of differing beliefs.[13]

While I am in accord with Ward's vision of comparative theology as both a genuinely free enquiry, driven by the search for truth, and a genuinely interreligious enterprise, I am not sure that distinguishing it from confessional theology on these grounds is helpful, since to do so detracts from the legitimacy of revision from a committed religious standpoint. Can Christians not be open to pursuing truth wherever it may lead, and to doing so, in part *because* of their Christian commitment? If revisions of the Christian tradition are legitimate, moreover, then that legitimacy must be argued for on Christian grounds and to argue for it on Christian grounds is to be engaged in confessional theology. Hence, in this regard I agree with Clooney's recommendation that we not 'distinguish "the exploration of a given revelation" (in confessional theology) from a broader survey of traditions (in comparative theology)' ([14], pp. 25–6). Ward's notion of confessional theology as mere repetition of traditional understandings is arguably too narrow. I suggest that, insofar as the task of comparative theology is undertaken from a basis of *some* religious perspective or other to which new learning is then related, it should count as a form of confessional theology, broadly construed. Certainly, as the Christian theologian's understanding of Christianity is transformed through immersion in and identification with

---

[13] Ward ([4], p. 45). At times Ward's reflections suggest that he does not take the distinction between confessional and comparative theology to be as clear-cut as he at other times presents it. See, e.g. [4], p. 49.

a second tradition, this *complicates* the sense in which her theology is confessional, since she is no longer drawing on just the resources of her home tradition. After doing comparative theology for a long time, reflects Clooney, one may still be a Catholic in dialogue with Hinduism,

> but one is also deeply influenced by the Hinduism of the Hindu with whom one converses. Ideally, it will no longer be possible to seat people neatly around the table according to neatly separated religions, as if people keep coming to the table without having been influenced by the other tradition ([2], p. 139).

But this enrichment of one's Christian identity does not mean that one's theology is no longer grounded in faith.

Here, Wilfred Cantwell Smith's reflections on the theological project that lies before us may be helpful. He called this project 'World Theology' or 'Global Theology', by which he meant a form of theology concerned with transforming Christianity through non-Christian insights. A transformed Christian theology, thought Smith, 'will interpret the history of our race in a way that will give intellectual expression to our faith, the faith of all of us, and to our modern perception of the world' ([25], p. 125). Christians engaged in the process end up with a theology which is thoroughly Christian but also more than Christian—'Christian, plus', as Smith puts it—because it is penetrated and transformed by insights derived from other traditions. And at the same time as Christians engage in this enterprise, so do theologians in other traditions, as they too attempt to step into the perspectives of others to see what light is thereby shed on the world and on their own traditions. World theology can be understood, then, as a kind of permanent interreligious colloquium, generating theologies which, although Christian or Hindu, say, are also *more than* Christian or Hindu: more comprehensive for the integration of the insights of others and, hence, more genuinely universal.

Conclusions

If comparative theologians are sincere in their intention to take the truths of other traditions seriously, then they must be willing to allow those truths to challenge their confessional presuppositions and to make revisions where necessary. I am not arguing that all comparative theologians must abandon inclusivism in favour of pluralism, but only that inclusivist presuppositions cannot be exempt from the effects of comparative study. I have tried to show, moreover, that revision need not involve making a definitive judgement about the truth and value of the tradition studied in relation to one's own, nor a retreat to a meta-position outside both. Rather it need only involve an acknowledgement that one finds sufficient truth and value in that tradition that one is not able, in good conscience, to hold that one's home tradition is superior and, hence, a willingness to revise expressions of faith which entail that it is.

Being clear about this truth-seeking, constructive dimension of the enterprise is crucial to carving out a disciplinary remit for comparative theology distinct from comparative religion, phenomenology of religions, or history of religions. For if comparative theologians shy away from the theological implications of their growing understanding of other traditions, then their comparative study ceases to bear on their confessional perspectives and their intention to learn from others is compromised. In some cases, this shying away is easy to sympathise with. We must acknowledge the constraints placed upon some theologians by their ecclesial location. Given that Ward is an Anglican, while Clooney is a Roman Catholic and member of the Society of Jesus, it is perhaps unsurprising that Ward is more willing to revise beliefs where necessary. Faced with the threat of Vatican censorship,[14] silence on the question of Christian superiority may be as much as we can reasonably expect from comparative theologians such as Clooney. But where such constraints operate, it is hard to see comparative theology as an entirely free pursuit of truth.

Where comparative theologians are freer—and willing—to follow the dialogue with other traditions wherever it may lead, comparative theology can be conceived of along the lines suggested by Smith: as theology which, working from a particular religious starting point, attempts, through dialogue, to contribute to the task of giving expression to the faith of us all. This kind of theology is not a matter of plundering other traditions for whatever one finds useful and then going on one's way, but of being genuinely open to having one's perspective transformed through dialogue with others; it is a matter of us all, with our diverse commitments, doing theology together. Perhaps we could think of the horizon towards which this kind of interreligious theology reaches as a collaborative alliance of increasingly comprehensive *theologies in dialogue*, theologies which stand in shifting relations of both convergence and creative tension. The alternative is that confessional theology increasingly assumes the role of a reliquary for a faith that is incapable of integrating the understanding that contemporary knowledge of other religious traditions has brought.[15]

Conflicts of Interest

The author declares no conflict of interest.

References

1. Warrier, M., and Oliver, S., eds. *Theology and Religious Studies: An Exploration of Disciplinary Boundaries*. London and New York: T&T Clark, 2008.
2. Clooney S.J., Francis X. "Comparative Theology—As Theology." In *Interreligious Hermeneutics in Pluralistic Europe: Between Texts and People*, edited by David Cheetham, Ulrich Winkler, Oddbjørn Leirvik, and Judith Gruber. Amsterdam and New York: Rodopi, 2011, 131–147.

---

[14] This has been the recent fate of a number of Roman Catholic theologians who have questioned Christian superiority. Roger Haight [26,27], for example, proposes a Christology which interprets Jesus as the Christ 'in a way that does not construe Christianity as the one and only true faith and way of salvation uniquely superior to all others' ([27], p. 151). In 2004, after investigating Haight's work *Jesus—Symbol of God* [26], the Congregation for the Doctrine of the Faith reaffirmed its verdict that the book contains serious doctrinal errors (see [28]). Consequently, Haight was forbidden to teach theology at Catholic universities and, more recently, to write on theology or to teach at any institution, even if unaffiliated with the Catholic Church.

[15] I am grateful to Francis Clooney, John Berthrong, and Magdalen Lambkin for their helpful comments on an earlier draft of this essay.

3. Clooney S.J., Francis X. *Comparative Theology: Deep Learning Across Religious Borders*. Chichester: Wiley-Blackwell, 2010.
4. Ward, Keith. *Religion and Revelation: A Theology of Revelation in the World's Religions*. Oxford: Clarendon, 1994.
5. Cornille, Catherine. "Meaning and Truth in the Dialogue between Religions." In *The Question of Theological Truth: Philosophical and Interreligious Perspectives*, edited by Frederiek Depoortere and Magdalen Lambkin. Amsterdam and New York: Rodopi, 2012, 137–155.
6. Fredericks, James L. *Faith among Faiths: Christian Theology and Non-Christian Religions*. New York: Paulist Press, 1999.
7. Schmidt-Leukel, Perry. *Transformation by Integration*. London: SCM Press, 2009.
8. Knitter, Paul F. *Introducing Theologies of Religions*. Maryknoll: Orbis, 2002.
9. Kiblinger, Kristin Beise. "Relating Theology of Religions and Comparative Theology." In *The New Comparative Theology: Interreligious Insights from the Next Generation*, edited by Francis X. Clooney S. J. New York: T&T Clark, 2010, 21–42.
10. Clooney S.J., Francis X. "Reading the World in Christ: From Comparison to Inclusivism." In *Christian Uniqueness Reconsidered: The Myth of a Pluralistic Theology of Religions*, edited by Gavin D'Costa. Maryknoll: Orbis, 1990, 63–80.
11. Keenan, J. *The Meaning of Christ: A Mahayana Theology*. Maryknoll: Orbis, 1989.
12. Keenan, J. *Grounding our Faith in a Pluralist World—With a Little Help from Nagarjuna*. Eugene: Wipf & Stock, 2009.
13. O'Leary, J. *Religious Pluralism and Christian Truth*. Edinburgh: Edinburgh University Press, 1996.
14. Clooney S.J., Francis X. *Hindu God, Christian God: How Reason Helps Break Down the Boundaries between Religions*. Oxford: Oxford University Press, 2001.
15. Clooney S.J., Francis X. *Theology after Vedanta: An Experiment in Comparative Theology*. Albany, NY: SUNY Press, 1993.
16. Heim, S. Mark. *Salvations: Truth and Difference in Religion*. Maryknoll: Orbis Books, 1995.
17. Heim, S. Mark. "The Depth of the Riches: Trinity and Religious Ends." *Modern Theology* 17:1 (January 2001), 21–55.
18. Nicholson, Hugh. "The New Comparative Theology and the Problem of Theological Hegemonism." In *The New Comparative Theology: Interreligious Insights from the Next Generation*, edited by Francis X. Clooney S. J. New York: T&T Clark, 2010, 43–62.
19. Clooney S.J., Francis X. "Neither Here nor There: Crossing Boundaries, Becoming Insiders, Remaining Catholic." In *Identity and the Politics of Scholarship in the Study of Religion*, edited by José Cabezón and Sheila Greeve Davaney. New York: Routledge, 2004, 99–112.
20. Drew, Rose. *Buddhist and Christian? An Exploration of Dual Belonging*. London and New York: Routledge, 2011.
21. Smart, Ninian. "Truth, Criteria and Dialogue between Religions." In Religious *Pluralism and Truth: Essays on Cross-Cultural Philosophy of Religion*, edited by Thomas Dean. Albany: State University of New York Press, 1995, 67–71.

22. Clooney S.J., Francis X. *Beyond Compare: St. Francis de Sales and Śrī Vedānta Deśika on Loving Surrender to God*. Washington, DC: Georgetown University Press, 2008.
23. Cobb, John B. *Transforming Christianity and the World: A Way beyond Absolutism and Relativism*, edited by Knitter, P. Maryknoll: Orbis, 1999.
24. Ward, Keith. *Religion and Community*. Oxford: Clarendon, 2000.
25. Smith, Wilfred C. *Towards a World Theology: Faith and the Comparative History of Religion*. London and Basingstoke: Macmillan Press Ltd, 1981.
26. Haight, Roger. *Jesus – Symbol of God*. Maryknoll: Orbis Books, 1999.
27. Haight, Roger. "Pluralist Christology as Orthodox." In *The Myth of Religious Superiority: A Multifaith Exploration*, edited by Paul Knitter. Maryknoll: Orbis Books, 2005, 151–61.
28. "Congregation for the Doctrine of the Faith." *Notification on the book 'Jesus Symbol of God' by Father Roger Haight S.J.* Available online: http://www.vatican.va/roman_curia/congregations/cfaith/documents/rc_con_cfaith_doc_20041213_notification-fr-haight_en.html (accessed on 4 October 2012).

Article

The Idea of a Highest Divine Principle—Founding Reason and Spirituality. A Necessary Concept of a Comparative Philosophy?

Claudia Bickmann

Philosophical Seminary of the University of Cologne, University of Cologne, Albertus Magnus Platz, D-50937 Cologne, Germany; E-Mail: Claudia.Bickmann@uni-koeln.de; Tel.: +49-221-2825188

Received: 2 September 2012; in revised form: 26 October 2012 / Accepted: 29 October 2012 / Published: 30 October 2012

Abstract: By reference to the Platonic, Aristotelian, and Neo-Platonic philosophical traditions (and then to German Idealism, including Husserl and Heidegger), I will indicate the way in which the concept of reason—on the one side—depends on the horizon of spirituality (by searching for the ultimate ground within us and the striving for the highest good); and inversely—how far the idea of the divine or our spiritual self may be deepened, understood and transmitted by reference to reason and rationality. But whereas philosophical analysis aims at the universal dimensions of spirituality or the divine (as in Plato's idea of the 'highest good', the Aristotelian 'Absolute substance', the 'Oneness of the One' (Plotinus and the Neo-Platonists) or the Hegelian 'Absolute spirit'),—Comparative Theology may preserve the dimension of spirituality or divinity in its individuality and specifity. Comparative Theology mediates between the universality of the philosophical discourse and the uniqueness of our individual experience (symbolized by a sacred person—such as Jesus, Brahman, Buddha or Mohammed) by reflecting and analyzing our religious experiences and practices. Religion may lose its specificity by comparative conceptual analysis within the field of philosophy, but Comparative Theology may enhance the vital dimensions of the very same spiritual experience by placing them in a comparative perspective.

Keywords: European metaphysics, comparative theology; comparative philosophy; spirituality; reason and rationality; Kant's theory of religion; Heidegger's immanent transcendence

1. Introduction

1. Opening the philosophical horizon for a Comparative Theology and Philosophy, our question, from the onset, leads to the heart of Religion and its role within the different civilizations in our times. Religion, as we argue, is irreducibly bound to our human life—as individuals and social beings. Touching the heart of our existence—religion opens the dimension of the ultimate. Thus, does a Comparative Philosophy and Theology was to face the problematic of how to justify the claim for the absolute truth within different world religions? We will argue:

(a) that the idea of an absolute fundament of being and thinking, of the divine as the originating source of the whole, has been developed in all world-religions;

(b) that Comparative Theology has to take into consideration, that the methods and ways to justify the respective truth-claims are different within most religious, theological and philosophical traditions: While Western traditions from their beginning with the Pre-Socratics stressed the need for a theoretically based approach and awareness of the essence of religion—by reflecting the unifying ground for thinking and being,—the Asian way, as it seems, predominantly bound spiritual awareness to the ethical, the moral dimension of our human nature.

2. And while Comparative Theology refers to the insights of the respective religious traditions, their histories and practices,—and thus remains bound to the horizon of specific religious experiences,—Comparative Philosophy analyzes the methods and principles to justify the specific truth-claims within the different World-religions and Theologies. What Comparative Philosophy loses concerning the concreteness of a specific religion, its practices and histories, it may gain with regard to the explication of the presuppositions of the different religions: Asking in a more general or universal way for the possibilities and limits to develop a coherent concept of God, it analyzes e.g., the relation between truth and revelation, the justification of the Oneness of God, the idea of the origin of the cosmos as a whole, the relation between knowledge and belief, knowledge and science, *etc*. Thus it investigates the essence of religion by asking for the grounding principles in all different World-religions. Its relation to Comparative Theology is close and even intertwined, but both fields of scrutiny are oriented into different directions. The strength of Comparative Theology, as developed e.g., by Francis Clooney, is to open the horizon for a comparative analysis by reference to the specific beliefs, practices and history of a specific religion—taking Christianity as the starting point [1]. Thus starting with a shared religious experience, it may enter a common discourse in a more distinguished and contextually integrated way. Instead of merely concentrating on general principles and grounding relations, Comparative Theology does not lose its specific reference to Christianity: In its comparative

theological perspective the Christian horizon is opened to reflect different World-religions and to help to develop them mutually. Francis Clooney concentrates on Hindu Religion and Theology in a comparative analysis by integrating the rich Hindu traditions of wisdom and spirituality into Christianity [2]. Both traditions are taken from their strongest sides and may develop each other complementarily. Klaus von Stosch develops Comparative Theology with regard to the late Wittgensteinian 'language-game-theory' in order to investigate the common heritage between the Christian and Islamic religion and theology [3]. And while Comparative Theology enables us to improve one's own religious heritage by (re)-integrating essential dimensions into the framework of a respective tradition, Comparative Philosophy abstracts from their specific historical or practical dimensions in order to investigate the possibilities and limits of a general or universal comparative analysis. Thus Comparative Philosophy does not reach the same degree of concreteness as opened by Comparative Theology, which enters the sphere of the distinguished traditions more specifically.

The following theses are developed within the horizon of a Comparative Philosophy. We will take the deep affiliation of the spiritual awareness and concept of God within the predominantly monotheistic religions,—in Judaism, Christianity and Islam,—to the Platonic, Aristotelian and Neo-platonic philosophy as a starting point [4]. Here we find a high degree of theoretical analysis and dogmatic distinctiveness partially correlated with a lack of spirituality and a loss of the vital sources of our belief. Thus the dimension of wisdom and spirituality—necessary for a meaningful life—was less in the center of interest than it had been e.g., in most Asian traditions. But we will argue dialectically: What the monotheistic religions gained by their alliance with philosophy, they simultaneously lost regarding the dimension of spiritual experiences and wisdom as a life-orienting source for human beings. The discovery of the philosophical implications of religion (e.g., search for truth, truthfulness, wisdom, the idea of a unifying ground, justice, *etc.*) leading to the idea of an originating ground of being and acting, was developed complementary within the Platonic-Neo-Platonic insight: The idea of an all-encompassing unifying principle as the ultimate horizon of our theoretical investigation. Thus, with regard to this founding principle, the concepts of God in Judaism, Christianity and Islam became deeply intertwined with the Platonic-Neo-platonic and Aristotelian metaphysics till Heidegger.

Both traditions: The Platonic, Aristotelian and Neo-Platonic philosophy and monotheist religions influenced each other mutually. The philosophical dimensions of religion and the religious implications of philosophy revealed the (in-itself) contradictory nature of reason and spirituality. The Platonic and Neo-Platonic Idea of the 'Oneness of the One' was substantially affiliated with the justification of three monotheistic religions in a specific way: While the Jewish and Islamic monotheism found its fundaments within the negative-theologian horizon, explained within the first hypothesis of the Platonic dialogue 'Parmenides', thematizing the radical 'Oneness of the One' without any predication [5];—the Trinitarian Christian approach stressed the need for an in-itself dynamical God. The unity of God should not be questioned by reference to a principle of differentiation and becoming, but rather be fully understood in its in-itself-dynamic structure. As analyzed by Plotinus and Proclus, theologians found a justification for the in-itself-dynamic principle of a Trinitarian God with regard to the first three hypotheses of this dialogue—whereby the Idea of the

Oneness (1st hypothesis) should sublate and negate itself to being and becoming (2nd hypothesis) and return to its own (3rd hypothesis) by its self-consciousness (the absolute spirit) [6–10].

Thus a comparative philosophical perspective—between European approaches to the relation between religion and philosophy and some Asian traditions—might reveal that within Western civilizations, religion and philosophy shared the demand for a unifying principle of thinking and being, while the ethical and spiritual dimensions prevailed within most Asian traditions.

But we may face a further substantial difference between the respective relations of religion and philosophy in both hemispheres: Within European history religions found their answers long before their questions raised within the sphere of Philosophy: Philosophies from Plato to Heidegger later tried to justify or legitimize the unconditioned Absolute, the idea of a Oneness of the One, within the area of thinking; while we may find an inverse relation between religion and philosophy within some Asian traditions: The Hindu Advaita Vedanta-school e.g., stressed the idea of a predicate-less ultimate ground leading from theoretical abstraction to belief.

A further striking difference between the hemispheres of the European and Asian Civilizations may be found in contemporary history: While the idea of a unifying principle within the horizon of Christianity and its allied metaphysical traditions is abandoned now within the horizon of a skeptical, relativistic and scientific modern Western philosophy, we face an upsurge of the profound and deep questioning of this topic within modern Asian spiritual philosophy An amazement and deep disquiet is now pervading Western Philosophy and Theology, which leads to an irritation about one's own access to a value-based concept of humanity; while in modern Asian, Indian, Chinese and Japanese philosophy we still may find a strong tendency to generate distinguished theoretical concepts to found the spiritual basis of morality and a value-oriented approach to our self- and world-understanding. Comparative Philosophy has to take into account this European shift from metaphysics to post-metaphysics. Not only does philosophy lose its founding principle in post-metaphysical times,—the consequences for the justification of religion as the essential basis of human existence should be still more serious: As reduced to our human needs or merely based on a human sentiment religion should no longer be able to develop an understanding of the relations between man and cosmos, immanence and transcendence within the framework of philosophy.

2. Religion within the Horizon of European Philosophy

Three Models within European History

The predominantly theoretical analysis within European thinking—inheriting the monotheistic demand for an explication of the highest ground of thinking and being, (in one of its mainstreams from the Aristotelian inspired Scholastic medieval ages till modern science oriented Philosophy) and the remaining prevalence of a practical, ethical approach to all life affairs within the Asian traditions might be—it seems—the most striking difference between the two traditions.

A Comparative Theology has to face an even more essential difference between the two hemispheres: Within Western thought development the understanding of the divine being changed according to the theoretical framework of understanding: Thus, we will take Philosophy as the framework to approach the similarities and differences regarding the spiritual ground of reason and morality within Western Philosophy. Taking into consideration, that Comparative Theology takes one specific religion as the horizon for a comparison with other spiritual traditions, we argue, that Theology and Philosophy are deeply intertwined by answering the question of how to understand, describe and interpret the idea of an origin of the cosmic whole and the idea of a meaningful path of our lives within the respective tradition. By reference to Christianity and the main philosophical traditions to explicate the substance of Christianity, three epochs may be named. These Epochs may indicate, to which extend the Idea of God is maintained or even abandoned within the area of Philosophy.

1. The classical European concepts from the Pre-Socratics till the Hegelian System—similar to most Asian traditions—stressed the need to consider a unifying highest principle, grounding the created world: Reaching out from the more sensually based concepts of the Pre-Socratics to the intelligible principle such as the Idea of the 'highest good' from Plato [11] to Kant [12]; or the idea of the absolute spirit from Aristotle [13] to Hegel [14]. The need to ask for an unconditioned absolute as the all-determining principle still seemed to be unquestioned.

2. Since the era of Enlightenment the dimensions of thinking and being, reason and morality, were separated into different spheres or domains: Reason was interpreted as the human capacity of knowledge or thinking and morality as the capacity to act under normative rules or to strive for a good fulfilled life. Both should no longer be united by a common principle, no unifying ground should be valid or unquestioned within the theoretical sphere. Since the deep affinity of all spheres in a cosmic whole, created by a divine being, was lost in post-metaphysical times, religion was either reduced to our needs (Feuerbach [15], Marx [16]) or to our individual religious feelings (Schleiermacher [17], Jacobi [18]).

3. Within a third model of classical German Philosophy from Kant to Heidegger, a unifying ground, a divine principle, was maintained: The task was to explain the compossibility of our free will with the boundaries of our physical nature. Spirituality was interpreted as a part of our human nature striving for the ultimate within the contingency of the ever-changing empirical circumstances. Kant argues as follows: "... if the critique of pure practical reason is to be completed, it must be possible at the same time **to show its identity with speculative reason** *in a common principle*, for it can ultimately be only one and the same reason which has to be distinguished merely in its application" [19]: "Indeed there is properly no other foundation for (morality, C.B.) than the critical examination of a pure practical reason; just as that for metaphysics is the critical examination of the pure speculative reason" ([19], AB XV). Thus for Kant—as well as the concepts of German Idealism, the distinction between our speculative, theoretical and our practical, moral reason was bound to a **horizon of spirituality** expressing one and the same human capacity, called reason, only distinguished between two **different ways to apply** this capacity in the sphere of knowledge or morality, in a theoretical or practical way ([19], AB XV).

Reason, as they argue, should not be identified with rationality: while rationality is limited to the analyzing functions of our understanding, reason integrates intuition, understanding, judgment, the sphere of ideas and spirituality—as the ultimate capacity of our consciousness. Whereby reason simultaneously is not just regarded as a principle of consciousness, but as the grounding principle of being likewise: Nature has to participate in an intelligible principle, if we want to understand its purposiveness from the smallest microbes to our human nature. Thus only by reference to reason as a principle of thinking and being, nature and spirit could be regarded as just two poles of the same sphere of being and becoming. From Kant to Schelling and Hegel, the idea of the integrative horizon, founding reason and morality, presupposes the idea of God as the unifying ground of all existing beings.

3. The Three Irreducible Ideas of an Unconditioned Principle as Heuristic Scheme for a Comparative Philosophy

Within a Comparative Philosophy the question arises: How should one understand this integrative, all-encompassing horizon—uniting the in-itself-contradicting nature of our human reason—within a coherent philosophical theory? We will try to name those universal principles, underlying all different World Religions, in order to find a point of comparison, which might serve as a heuristic scheme, helping to understand the similarities and differences between the different World Religions. Only by reference to such a heuristic schema, as we argue, a comparative discourse may be opened and only by reference to such a point of comparison the differences might be illumined.

From Plato to Hegel, but also within different Asian traditions, a triangular structure of three unconditioned 'quasi-objects' constitute the framework of our investigation:

- The first idea of an unconditioned fundament of being is linked to **the self** as the unconditioned ground within us—leading to an in-itself contradicting concept of a human being: Freedom and necessity are the irreducible dimensions of a person. And since freedom leads to the idea of a super-natural ground within us, a coherent concept of spirituality is based on this in-itself contradicting nature of a person.
- The second concept of the unconditioned ground outside of us is linked to the idea of the phenomenal world, to the **world as a phenomenal whole** and object of our intuition, reason and understanding. Hence the question arises: How freedom may be integrated in a fully determined structure of the given world? Only by presupposing freedom as the unconditioned ground within us, a coherent concept of the phenomenal world is possible, the concept of a contradictory of the cosmos as a whole.
- The third idea of the unconditioned leads us to the idea of an ultimate principle uniting the intelligible and the natural world. This idea is necessary to understand the cosmic whole as the all-encompassing sphere in its internal relation of spirit and nature, of freedom and nature, reason and morality or freedom and necessity.

These three ideas of an unconditioned ground within and outside of us constitute the objects of the self (Psychology), the phenomenal world (Cosmology) and the unity between both (Metaphysics, or, if related to the highest principle of spirituality—to Religion or Theology).

The modern transformation of this triangular structure of the former specific metaphysics ('Metaphysica specialis') divided the idea of a cosmic totality into three separate domains. No longer can we find in post-metaphysical times the former unity between the three spheres: Within the horizon of metaphysics from Plato to Hegel and within most Asian traditions till modern times, the human soul still should be able to mirror the universal law and return to its own—to strive for knowledge and wisdom. This act of reflection constitutes a circular structure of the 'going into the ground' within the horizon of the cosmic whole. 'Re-flection' than may be regarded as a similar circular movement as the act of 're-ligio': Both may be regarded as just two different ways to re-affirm oneself of the all-mighty grounding horizon within and outside of us, within heaven and earth.

And while 're-ligio' is linked to the individual self, the act of 're-flectio' mirrors individuality only in an abstract form—losing the immediacy of our specific life. Thus the very personal dimension of 're-ligio'—as the expression of a universal principle in an individualized form—cannot be substituted by any philosophical or theological reflection. We rather gain in the sphere of religion, what we lose by referring to notions or concepts.

4. The Triangular Structure of our 'Being-in-the-world' between Transcendence and Immanence

A Comparative Philosophy may take into consideration, that this triangular structure, as we hold, finds its religious and theological expressions in all world traditions, as the all-encompassing horizon mediating the two spheres just as the two opposite sides of being as a whole. And since the beginning of human investigation this triangular structure took a different shape: It manifests itself as idea of the ultimate horizon and was named —among others—'Dao', the 'highest good', the concept of 'Ren' or the 'Idea of the absolute substance'. As possible paradigms of an all-integrating, all embedding and embracing principle, they are meant to interpret the compatibility between the poles of nature and spirit, reason and morality, *etc.*

A Comparative Philosophy, asking for the major principles within all different spiritual world traditions, faces the problem of how to define the relation between the integrating horizon and the two opposite dimensions?

1. We presuppose a **radical Immanence of the highest principle** with regard to its all-encompassing function as developed in Panentheism, Daoism or Buddhism.
2. Or else the ultimate horizon is regarded in its **radical Transcendence**—beyond all dichotomies: like in Neo-Platonism, Hinduism and Islam.
3. A third model is a combination of the two: represented by the Christian Trinitarian Exegesis of the threefold existence of god. God should indicate its existence **simultaneously in an immanent and transcendent manner**. He manifests himself as a human being, indicating that he is not an absolutely transcendent being, beyond all knowing and being, but rather represents the essence of being itself. To interpret the Trinitarian approach in this way, bridges are built to Non-European religions: We similarly may interpret the 'Dao' within the first book of Laotse's

Dao-de-Jing, as a principle beyond all dichotomies in a radically transcendent manner and simultaneously as a mediating horizon—*i.e.*, in its ultimate immanence [20].

5. Comparative Philosophy in Post-metaphysical Times

5.1. Western Philosophy Shifting to Practical Reason

Within European philosophy and theology a new epoch started after the system-buildings of Hegel and the German Idealism. With Feuerbach, Nietzsche and Marx practical reason became the new founding horizon: During a long period of time Western Philosophy (under the auspices of the Aristotelian scholastics and until Kant and Hegel) attention was given to the following: to the understanding of the categories, principles and rules guiding the concepts of ourselves and to the ideas of the cosmic whole and God as the uniting, all-encompassing principle. With Kant's critical shift, the application of the categories was restricted to the spatio-temporal world ([12], KrV. B 294). The three major ideas of the former 'Metaphysica specialis' (the self, the freedom of the will and God) were transformed into regulative ideas as functioning horizons in order to schematize our concepts of the empirical world. But the idea of God as the overarching principle still remained unquestioned. The Post-Hegelian left-wing philosophers, Feuerbach and Marx, deeply criticized the idea of a transcendent being as a hypostatical construct of the finitude of our existence: According to Marx, Kant, Fichte, Schelling and Hegel accomplished the theoretical task. Theory now has to be transformed into action. Salvation by a divine being should be replaced by historical liberation. Times demand, as Marx states in his 11th thesis on Feuerbach in 1845, action [21]: Thus "the question, whether objective truth can be attributed to human thinking" should no longer be "a question of theory but (should be) a practical question [15]". No longer should our human nature be understood as embedded in a supra-natural sphere.

The following approach will indicate the necessity to suppose the idea of a highest principle in order to understand ourselves in a theoretical and practical way in post-metaphysical times. By analyzing the presuppositions of the spiritual implications of our thinking and being—the inevitability of the assumption of the idea of the divine may be indicated. Thus philosophically the horizon is opened to enter the sphere of transcendence.

5.1.1. Plato's Allegory of the Cave

Let us imagine ourselves in a situation as the prisoners in a cave, as Plato described at the beginning of the 7th book of his Republic [22]:

Living in an underground den, legs and necks in chains,—unable to move. Relieved and forced to turn around, we will reveal the delusion of our former access to the phenomenal word and the world as a whole. We may conclude from this allegory, that self-knowledge is needed, in order to understand the presupposed cultural, religious, scientific or philosophical concepts, which influence and impregnate our actions—explicitly or not. As Plato argues, without a clear understanding of the major principle of the highest good, which unites knowledge and action or thinking and being, nature and spirit, the political leaders will be unable to organize a morally determined political order according to the idea of a harmony between all spheres.

5.1.2. The Prevalence of Self-reflexion (Confucius, Plato, Kant)

Thus Self-reflexion in the very ancient Platonic sense may serve as the opening path to our mutual understanding:

Self-reflexion according to Kant means: 1. to think through ourselves, 2. to think coherently and 3. trying to think from the point of view of the others [23].

Interrogating and questioning the predominantly reductive approach to the phenomenon of religion by naturalized epistemologies or socially oriented philosophies, a new Comparative Philosophy of religion will open the floor for the necessary enlightening and understanding the premises of our religious nature in a self-critical way. Instead of reducing religion to our practical needs and purposes or interpreting its intentions as merely projections of the finite into the infinity of the divine, we will argue that religion is an irreducible dimension of our human nature. While philosophy touches individuality only in a generalizing attitude, Religion touches the irreducibility of our individuality in its specifity.

5.1.3. Two Extremes Approaching the Integrative Ultimate Principle

However, the question remains within the horizon of a Comparative Philosophy—in post-metaphysical times: how to get access to such an ultimate principle, which may unite all spheres of reality, the natural and the intelligible likewise?

In order to argue in a coherent way, we have to take into consideration, that the idea of a highest divine principle cannot be presupposed in any of our philosophical theories. We rather have to argue for its necessity by analyzing the presuppositions of our highest natural and moral aims: Thus we will consider the following: The idea of an absolute harmony between our highest natural demands for happiness and the highest intelligible demands for morality and justice in all societies seemed to be given in Leibniz's idea of the 'originating monad'. According to Kant—different from Leibniz—the idea of a highest being, presupposed in the idea of a highest ultimate goal is merely an a-priori transcendental object of all we might strive for. Kant names it: the Ideal of pure reason. "As the idea gives the *rule*, so **the ideal** in such a case serves as the *archetype* for the complete determination of the copy; and we have no other standard for our actions than the conduct of this divine man within us, with which we compare and judge ourselves, and so reform ourselves, although we can never attain to the perfection thereby prescribed. Although we cannot concede to these ideals objective reality (existence), they are not therefore to be regarded as figments of the brain; they supply reason with a standard which is indispensable to it, providing it, as they do, with a concept of that which is entirely complete in its kind, and thereby enabling it to estimate and to measure the degree and the defects of the incomplete" ([12], (KrV). AA 04. A 569 B 597). Taking into account, that according to Kant, reason is a creative organism striving for harmony between nature and spirit and thus serving as a constitutive function to create a world under moral rules, it may be regarded as a source of the intelligible world. Kant's central quest of how we may fit into the world can be answered only by reference to the sphere of spirituality. Spirituality as the domain of religion leads to an answer to the question of: "What can we hope? ([12], (KrV) AA 04. A 805 B 833)."

Whereby the highest divine being is not regarded as object of our intentionality, but as its necessary founding principle: Thus we presuppose an ultimate ground within and outside of us, a highest being, in which the contradicting spheres of nature and spirit may find harmony (as similarly presupposed in Daoism and Buddhism)—indifferently in which historical or cultural circumstances we find ourselves. As Kant holds, we would even be unable to understand our human nature without the assumption of the regulative idea of the all-determining highest good as a necessary implication of reason and morality.

5.2. The Opening Horizon of a Common Ground

5.2.1. The Irreducibility of a Concept of Transcendence

This idea of harmony, as Kant holds, presupposes transcendence as the ultimate horizon and spirituality as our attitude towards cosmos and life. According to Kant, spirituality is a guiding force in our human life. But why should spirituality be an implication of reason and morality at all?

Kant argues as follows: If we do what we ought to do, what may we then hope ([12], (KrV). AA 04. A 805 B 833)?

Happiness, as he holds, is the satisfaction of all our desires in an extensive, intensive and protensive way, (...), and "the *practical law*, derived from the motive of *happiness*" ([12], (KrV). AA 04. A 806 B 834) he terms, is a pragmatic rule of prudence).

But the law, which has no other motive than *worthiness of being happy*, is a moral (law of morality). "The former advises us what we have to do if we wish to achieve happiness; the latter dictates to us how we must behave in order to deserve happiness" ([12], (KrV). AA 04. A 806 B 834). The former is based on empirical principles; the latter considers only the "freedom of a rational being in general, and the necessary conditions under which alone this freedom can harmonize with a distribution of happiness" ([12], (KrV). AA 04. A 806 B 834).

Hence, if

1. the contingency of our empirical existence does not guarantee the fulfillment of our highest natural goods and
2. the unconditioned state of morality is incompatible with our sensually bound existence regarding the attainment of happiness,
3. the assumption of an *ideal of a highest good*, entailing the possibility of a harmony among our striving forces, is a necessary ingredient of our free moral actions.

Since the idea of a wanted harmony between our free will and the natural conditions of our existence presupposes a unity between our speculative reason, linked to the question: "What can I know?" and our free moral will to create a world under moral rules, we may ask:

"What, if we act in a moral way, we might hope for? This third question is theoretical and practical at the same time. Inasmuch as we are bound to our sensual nature, we are—simultaneously—free to act in a moral way. But the achievement of happiness—or harmony in a future world,—we might have deserved by the conduct of a moral life, is not attainable by us." ([12], (KrV). AA 04. A 806 B 834).

Thus our ultimate—theoretical and practical—questions are bound to a third one, which might give an answer to the question of the unifying principle between the two spheres: The question of a justified hope, as Kant held, lead us to the idea of the highest good, uniting our highest natural and moral goods and opens a **sphere of spirituality**—as the necessary link between moral actions and our striving for happiness.

Our sense of transcendence and of spirituality, as Kant argues, is an implication of our in-itself-contradictory nature. Bound to the finitude of the natural world, we will ask, how the in-themselves-contradictory dimensions, the natural and the super-natural—in and outside of us—are united?

A Comparative Theology or Philosophy may provide a helpful distinction in order to understand the specifities of the different traditions. Hereby the striving forces of the whole can be presupposed as either forces of the matter or forces of an intelligent principle; so that we may consider its substratum as a lifeless or a vivid being:

1. The **Idealism** assumes—according to Kant ([23], (KU) AA 04. A 319 B 323.) either (a) a living matter (in a pantheistic or hylozoistic way as in *Deism such as Daoism, Buddhism, or Aristotelianism* or (b) an idea of a living highest being as in *Christianity.*

2. or else we presuppose—in a **materialistic way**—(a) an inanimate matter (as done within the realism of a mechanistic causality in the atomism of Democritus or Leucippus or (b) a lifeless God as in a fatalistic conception.

The question arises: How to avoid the one-sidedness with regard to the highest principle, to the idea of God as the almighty being? How to find access to its ultimate transcendence and understand immanence as being founded by the divine being?

Within the horizon of an intercultural philosophy, Martin Heidegger's' analysis of transcendence as the all-embedding horizon with regard to our "Being-in-the-word" [24] gains great importance e.g., for new Chinese Philosophers or the Japanese Kyoto-School [25–26]. Here spirituality is based on the modality of our existence: Existence as a mode of being within ourselves as being beyond ourselves.

Martin Heidegger tried to answer this question by reference to the analysis of our 'Da-sein'—understood as a mode of 'being-in-the-world' ([24], S.113). With Martin Heidegger a horizon of a Comparative Philosophy may be opened, one which paves the way for spirituality and transcendence as the grounding dimension of our existence.

5.2.2. Heidegger: The Ultimate Horizon of Transcendence: A Mode of our Being-in-the-world?

Being-in-the-world in its triangular structure: How to find access to the ultimate horizon, to the sphere of spirituality?

We are—according to Martin Heidegger,—being within ourselves, always beyond ourselves. Self-understanding, as a mode of 'being-in-the-world' and as act of transcending ourselves, grasps the irreducible horizon of the wholeness of being—and integrates both spheres in a non-contradicting way.

However, conceptualized or not, being as 'Dasein' never fails to be completely understood. There are degrees of understanding of ourselves as beings-in-the-world: from the unconceptualized approach, the absorption of the "they" or in the "world", till the authentic "potentiality-for-Being-its-Self" or even the ontological and phenomenological understanding of the totality of the structural whole [27].

We may find different steps of enlightening the horizon, in which we find ourselves by birth and by tradition. An ontological and phenomenological investigation of the different ways, in which our 'Dasein' exists and acts according to moral rules, defines the characters of the disclosure of our being-in-the-world.

Our being-in-the-world, however, is already a mode to understand the world.

World itself, if not understood as the infinite sum of objects, indicates the horizon, in which human beings understand themselves. And while the idea of a whole provides the orientation in the world, we nevertheless may fail to find the adequate path to live according to ourselves or to society, or according to nature as the all-embedding framework of our life or even according to the interdependence of the relations between all these spheres.

This moderate Heideggerian way to interpret transcendence or spirituality (or the ultimate horizon) as 1. a mode of 'Being-in-the-world', 2. as striving for the highest good by acting and enlightening ([27], p. 168 ff.) and 3. finally as rationally understanding and founding our 'Being-in-the-world' in an intelligible way ([27], p. 123–177, S. 153 ff.);—may this Philosophy and Theology serve as an opening comparative horizon to Daoism, Buddhism and Confucianism?

5.3. Preconceptions for a Comparative Philosophy within the Horizon of Modern Western Traditions

5.3.1. Two Major Obstacles

The idea of an integrating horizon as the source of spirituality (articulated similarly in the principle of the 'Dao' or 'Ren' or the European idea of the 'highest good') is questioned in post-metaphysical ages. Two major tendencies of modern thinking may be named as responsible for dismissing the idea of a highest being or a highest good.

(a) The conceptualistic and nominalistic shift. Within the conceptualistic and nominalistic shift—entering European philosophy by William of Ockham,—the given concepts,—such as the idea of the good, of being or truth—should no longer be understood as possible expressions of essential or distinguishable properties or qualities, but should rather be regarded as merely external names or titles for numerically defined units of our conceptualizations.

(b) The scientific approach. The second dominant domain within post-metaphysical thinking follows a naturalized epistemology of our scientific access in nearly all theoretical disciplines from physics to cognitive sciences. Here the idea of a founding principle is questioned likewise.

Hence, searching for an adequate method to approach major Asian topics and concepts by referring to contemporary European philosophy, self-reflection and self-critique is needed: A thorough examination of our concepts is demanded to figure out, whether or not our predominantly prevailing heuristic scheme of a skeptically relativizing or a scientifically naturalizing methodology might at all be prepared for our mutual understanding.

Taking into account these post-metaphysical premises of our contemporary European Philosophy—itineraries will not be easily found to bridge our different traditions in Orient and Occident.

5.3.2. Methodological Questions: The European Fallacy

Entering by translating the respective terms?

The question arises: how to reach an adequate understanding of the idea of the highest good in the different cultures.

Translating the Confucian, Taoist or Buddhist concept of `Ren´ by the idea of Humanity, Benevolence or the Highest good or the Dao as `Way´, ´Reason´, `logos`, both translations might be easily misunderstood as a projection of our Platonic-Kantian understanding of the highest principle of reason and morality.

As Friedrich Schlegel argued in 1797: If we do not want our philological translation to be just a projection of what we want or an indication of our honorable scholarship, and then be astonished in a widely childish manner about the miracle we ourselves have produced, we first have to be aware of the double difficulty we face:

The topic of my contribution, searching for a unifying principle of reason and morality, confronts us with two unbridgeable steps in a vast and empty territory:

a. One step stems from our post-metaphysical modern theories to our own classical heritage from Plato to Hegel. Our thesis: Only within early European philosophy we find an equivalent concept to the Chinese Ren or Dao.
b. The second step might still be higher—leading into the area of the Chinese approach to their own ultimate principles,—which is hardly sufficiently recognized and profoundly studied in European thinking.
c. Hence in modern times of Occidental skeptical Philosophy the heuristic scheme or systematic equivalent to the Chinese principle of ´Ren´ or the ´Dao´ seems to be missing.

5.3.3. The European Fallacy within the Horizon of a Comparative Philosophy

To avoid a possible misunderstanding, we will follow a new route to open our post-metaphysical thinking to the Asian traditions. Just two examples of self-reflection may be named:

First of all we have to take into consideration, that, for an adequate concept of 'Ren' or 'Dao', the itineraries into the different traditions of the Asian Philosophy might not lead us—as it is the case within European traditions—to a definition of a possible object or idea, a definite premise or argument or a subject-centered construction, or even a claim for truth in the sense of consensual, coherence or correspondence-oriented truth-theories. We rather may find forms of philosophizing, which cannot be understood by reference to the concepts of objectivity or subjectivity, by abstract definitions or arguments—but may only be found beyond or apart from such dichotomies like the 'self and the other', 'reason and morality', 'spirit and nature'. We may rather find them in an area of in-difference, the in-between-space of the extremes: between leave off and do, spirit and nature, *etc.*

Secondly: The Asian classical concepts of time are not oriented towards a progress in permanence as in Western Modernity, but rather take a circular shape; so that the rules and laws of behavior might rather be understood as embedded in cosmos and nature, mirroring micro- and the macrocosmic dimensions. Hence it might appear as if human spirit did not remorse inasmuch from its natural homestead.

5.3.4. Creative Designing, Intellectually Condensing or Conceptually Reflecting Approaches

But yet, this self-critical attitude by referring to Asian thinking might be deceiving; examining carefully the different approaches to the ultimate principles within the respective Asian traditions, we may distinguish at least three different lines of interpreting the classical texts:

a. The almost poetically embedded presentations within the different aphoristic concepts of Confucius, Zhuangzi, Mengzi or Laotse or Buddha.
b. The more intellectually condensed elaborations by different Neoconfucian texts, integrating Daoism and Buddhism into Confucianism. (e.g., Zhu Xi and Wang Yang-ming) or the Indian Hindu schools of the Advaita-Vedanta, the Mimancha or the Nyaya-School.
c. And finally within modern Indian, Chinese or Japanese traditions, which tend to conceptually reflect systematically differentiated approaches.

Within a Comparative Philosophy astonishing parallels might be found with regard to these Asian traditions within Western European Philosophy:

However all three types need to be carefully considered with regard to the specific context of their traditions, in order to avoid a projection of what we want onto the respective framework and to avoid a mere appropriation of the other.

Thus the conceptually oriented as well as the deconstructive approach of Western heuristics have to exercise some caution, when being confronted with allegoric, symbolic or poetic forms, inasmuch as the allegorically oriented presentations cannot be hastily transformed into mere concepts of abstract notions.

These methodological problems are similar in both traditions. Thus they are an intra-cultural and inter-cultural challenge of a Comparative Philosophy likewise.

6. Conclusions

If Religion, as we argued, is irreducibly bound to our human life, touching the heart of our existence, Comparative Philosophy may develop the idea of the divine as the originating source of being as a whole within the different spiritual traditions.

While Comparative Theology, as developed by Francis Clooney, refers to the insights of the respective religious traditions, their histories and practices, it takes the specific religious experiences of Christianity and the Hindu traditions as a starting point to prepare for a mutual learning. Hereby, the spiritual dimension of our human consciousness is not only maintained, it is even enriched by the searching for a mutual understanding. Comparative Philosophy, endangered to either reduce spirituality to the concepts of the divine, or to ignore the spiritual needs of our human lives at all, has to regain the horizon of transcendence in modern times: Since only by reference to the horizon of transcendence our Being-in-the-world may be explained. And only by reference to the area of transcendence we may find the ultimate spiritual horizon to understand the finitude of our existence. Thus philosophy in post-metaphysical times has to reconsider the grounding principle of being and thinking, in order to bridge the gap to theology. Sharing the same horizon, as Hegel already holds, Philosophy, theology and religion are nonetheless oriented in different directions.

But since Comparative Philosophy argues primarily within the framework of the different philosophical post-metaphysical traditions, we face the situation, that modern European Philosophies became independent from any dimensions of religion or spirituality. In our article we tried to indicate that, in order to enter the field of a Comparative Philosophy, we have to take into account, that most non-European traditions still cling to the idea of a highest metaphysical entity or a highest divine being,—as it was prevailing in early European philosophy till the area of Enlightenment and, within the horizon of contemporary Non-European traditions inter alia in Daoism, Buddhism or Hinduism. In order to be prepared for a comparative analysis, philosophy has to open up again towards the respective spiritual traditions in all different world-religions. Here Comparative Theology, as developed by Francis Clooney, plays an important role to transmit, to translate and to transform the respective religious traditions for a common mutual understanding and learning. For only by a deep acquaintance with the respective experiences and practices of the religious traditions, may we shed a light on the specific subject of a religious faith. And only by reference to the specifity and concreteness of religious experience and practice,—explained and translated within the horizon of a Comparative Theology,—philosophy may we find our way back to the horizon of the ultimate principle, to the all-embracing horizon of thinking and being. Only then may Philosophy proceed by asking for the possibilities and limits of a coherent concept of God, the relation between truth and revelation, the justification of the Oneness of God, *etc.*, and investigate the grounding principles of the different World-religions in a comparative analysis.

We end up by stating, that Comparative Philosophy, reflecting the ultimate, has to take the methods, the object and the themes of Comparative Theology as a starting point to investigate similarities and differences between the different world religions. And vice versa: Comparative Theology may enter the field of Philosophy, in order to analyze the presuppositions and principles of its own theoretical premises.

Conflicts of Interest

The author declares no conflict of interest.

References

1. Francis X. Clooney, S.J. *Comparative Theology. Deep Lerning Across Religious Borders*. Oxford: John Willey and Sons Ltd., 2010.
2. Francis X. Clooney, S.J. *Seeing Through Texts: Doing Theology Among the Srivaisnavas of South India*. New York: St. Univ. of New York, 1966.
3. Reinhold Bernhardt, and Klaus von Stosch, eds. *Komparative Theologie*: *Beiträge zu einer Theologie der Religionen,* Band 7. Zürich: Theologischer Verlag Ag, 2009.
4. Werner Beierwaltes. *Platonismus im Christentum*, Bd. 73. Frankfurt/M.: Klostermann, 2001.
5. Plato. *Parmenides*, 137 c ff.
6. Egil A. Wyller. *Einheit und Andersheit. Eine historische und systematische Studie zur Henologie (I-III)*. Würzburg: Königshausen und Neumann, 2000.
7. Luc Brisson. "The reception of the Parmenides before Proclus." In *Zeitschrift für antikes Christentum*. Edited by Hanns Cristoph v. Brennecke, *et al.* Berlin, New York: Walter de Gruyter, 2008, pp. 99–113.
8. Werner Beierwaltes. *Platonismus und Idealismus*. Philosophische Abhandlungen, Bd. 40. Frankfurt: Klostermann, 2004.
9. Gudrun von Düffel. *Hegels Methode als Darstellungsform der christlichen Idee Gottes*. Würzburg: Königshausen & Neumann, 2000.
10. Werner Beierwaltes. *Denken des Einen. Studien zur Neuplatonischen Philosophie und ihrer Wirkungsgeschichte*. Frankfurt/M.: Klostermann, 1985.
11. Plato. *Politeia*, 514 a ff.
12. Immanuel Kant. *Kritik der reinen Vernunft* (KrV). AA 04, A 804 B 832 ff. Kant, Immanuel: Gesammelte Schriften Hrsg.: Bd. 1–22 Preussische Akademie der Wissenschaften (AA), Bd. 23 Deutsche Akademie der Wissenschaften zu Berlin, ab Bd. 24 Akademie der Wissenschaften zu Göttingen. Berlin, 1900ff.
13. Aristoteles. *Metaphysics, Lambda*, 1069 a ff.
14. G.W.F. Hegel. *Wissenschaft der Logik*. Hg. Karl Markus Michel. Frankfurt/M.: Suhrkamp, 1971 ff., Bd. 5.
15. Ludwig Feuerbach. *Das Wesen des Christentums*. Gesammelte Werke von Feuerbach, Ludwig; Bd.5. Bearbeitet von Werner Schuffenhauer u. Wolfgang Harich. Berlin: Akademie-Verlag, 2006.
16. Karl Marx. *Kritik des Hegelschen Staatsrechts.*" In Marx-Engels-Werke, Bd. 1, S. 236. H.A. zitiert nach der (alten) Marx-Engels-Gesamtausgabe. Berlin: Aufbau-Verlag, 1975ff.
17. Friedrich Schleiermacher. *Über die Religion. Reden an die Gebildeten unter ihren Verächtern*. Hamburg: Meiner-Verlag Bd. 255, 1970.
18. Friedrich Heinrich Jacobi. *Von den göttlichen Dingen und ihrer Offenbarung*. Leipzig: Gerhard Fleischer, 1911.

19. Immanuel Kant. *Groundwork for the Metaphysics of Morals*. Kant, Immanuel: Gesammelte Schriften Hrsg.: Bd. 1–22 Preussische Akademie der Wissenschaften (AA), Bd. 23 Deutsche Akademie der Wissenschaften zu Berlin, ab Bd. 24 Akademie der Wissenschaften zu Göttingen. Berlin, 1900ff. GMS AA 04. BA XV.
20. Laotse. *Tao te King*. Texte und Kommentar. Hg. v. Richard Wilhelm. München: Diederichs Verlag. 1998, S. 41.
21. Karl Marx, and Friedrich Engels. *Thesen zu Feuerbach*, II. These, Marx-Engels Werke, Bd.3.
22. Platon. *Politeia*. 514 ff.
23. Immanuel Kant. *Kritik der Urteilskraft*. AA 05. A 156 B 158.
24. Martin Heidegger. *Sein und Zeit* (Being and Time). Tübingen: Niemeyer, 1979, S. 52.
25. Lik Kuen Tong. "Dao and Logos: Prolegomena to a Quintessential Hermeutics – With Specific Reference to its Implications for Intercultural Philosophy." In *Tradition und Traditionsbruch zwischen Skepsis und Dogmatik*, hg. v. Claudia Bickmann and Markus Wirtz. Amsterdam/New York: Rodopi, 2006, S. 461–469.
26. Ryosuke Ohashi. "Die frühe Heidegger-Rezeption in Japan." In *Japan und Heidegger*, edited by H. Buchner. Sigmaringen: Thorbecke, 1989, S. 23–38.
27. Martin Heidegger. "Vom Wesen des Grundes." In *Wegmarken*. Frankfurt/M.: Klostermann, 1967, S. 123–177, S. 168 ff.

Reprinted from *Religions*. Cite as: Moyaert, Marianne. "On Vulnerability: Probing the Ethical Dimensions of Comparative Theology." *Religions* 3 (2012): 1144-1161.

Article

On Vulnerability: Probing the Ethical Dimensions of Comparative Theology

Marianne Moyaert [1,2]

[1] Faculty of Theology, VU Amsterdam, De Boelelaan 1105, Amsterdam 1081 HV, The Netherlands; E-Mail: m.moyaert@vu.nl

[2] Faculty of Theology and Religious Studies, KU Leuven, St. Michielstraat 4, Leuven 3000, Belgium; E-Mail: marianne.moyaert@theo.kuleuven.be

Received: 3 November 2012; in revised form: 4 December 2012 / Accepted: 11 December 2012 / Published: 12 December 2012

Abstract: Though the notion of vulnerability regularly pops up in Clooney's reflections on comparative theology, he does not develop a systematic account of it. What precisely vulnerability is and how it influences interreligious dialog do not receive enough theoretical grounding. In this article I will probe the complexity of this notion and how it plays out in comparative theology. This will not only enable us to grasp the true originality of Clooney's project, it will also allow us to uncover its deeper ethical dynamics. For, as I will seek to show, at its core, comparative theology is moved by an ethical concern to enable a just relation between the *one's own* tradition and the *foreign* one. It is my intention to unfold the deep moral dynamics of this particular interreligious approach and to conceptualize the ethical conditions for interreligious learning as present in comparative theology.

Keywords: comparative theology; vulnerability; ethics of interreligious reading

1. Introduction

Vulnerability is one of the key words in Francis Clooney's comparative theology project. By placing this notion at the center of his approach, he wants to propose an alternative to the classic theology of religions, which he criticizes for putting up a wall between believers belonging to various religious traditions. Unlike both liberal and postliberal theologies, Clooney wants to question defense mechanisms that obstruct the possibility of being touched and affected by the other tradition. If both liberal pluralism and postliberal particularism can be seen as exponents of a desire for control, comparative theology can be regarded as a form of vulnerable theology. Clooney refrains from the (perhaps typical Western) desire to stand above the action and replace the real diversity with neat schematic interpretations of religious plurality. Instead of searching for some philosophical and/or theological vantage point above that messy reality, he operates within a fragile hermeneutical and theological space in the midst of the complexities of interreligious encounter. His engagement with the religious other begins with reading and comparing "non-Christian religious texts" whose wisdom he appropriates through submission. New theological insights emerge from this practice of "inter-texting" that can challenge, interrupt, and transform the home tradition. Becoming vulnerable is the crux of this theological approach. According to Clooney:

> [This] reading practice ... should make it more difficult for us to enjoy the securities that oddly envelop people who talk about surrender to God *within* their own tradition and yet continue to cherish their tradition's intellectual and affective safety net. Here, instead [the two texts] work powerfully together, even as the relevant communities may be disturbed by these texts' being read together and their being taken to heart ... and all without letting new affinities shatter original commitments and loyalties ([1], p. 204).

Though the notion of vulnerability regularly pops up in Clooney's reflections on comparative theology, he does not develop a systematic account of it. What vulnerability is, precisely, and how it influences interreligious dialog do not receive enough theoretical grounding. In this article I will probe the complexity of this notion and how it plays out in comparative theology. This will not only enable us to grasp the true originality of Clooney's project but will also allow us to uncover its deeper ethical dynamics. For, as I will seek to show, at its core, comparative theology is moved by an ethical concern to enable a just relation between both *one's own tradition* and the *foreign* one. It is my intention to disclose the deep-lying moral dynamics of this particular interreligious approach and to conceptualize the ethical conditions for deep interreligious learning present in comparative theology.

In order to fully understand the novelty of comparative theology as vulnerable theology and how this notion of vulnerability points to a web of moral concerns, the concept needs further theoretical elaboration. What precisely is vulnerability? How does it relate to its opposite, invulnerability? How do both notions affect the ethical relation between *one's own* tradition and the *foreign* one?

2. The Complexity of Vulnerability: Some Preliminary Theoretical Reflections

Vulnerability is usually connected to notions such as fragility and frailty. Something that is vulnerable is not strong or powerful but is weak and breakable. This notion recalls the always present possibility of harm, hurt, fracture, and pain and also evokes ideas such as loss, grief, distress, and even discomfort. As Erinn Gilson remarks in her article 'Vulnerability, Ignorance and Oppression', "the conventional and tacitly assumed understanding holds that to be vulnerable is simply to be susceptible, exposed, at risk, in danger. In short, it is to be somehow weaker, defenseless and dependent, open to harm and injury" ([2], pp. 309–10). Vulnerable people are needy people who require aid or care. They are dependent on others.

In this reading, vulnerability is understood as a privative term: it is a shortcoming. In the classical sense, it is a *privatio boni*, *i.e.*, the lack of something that ought to be there. The "good" is *invulnerability*, which is connected to the ideals of being strong, independent, and in control. The invulnerable person dominates every situation he finds himself in; he does not get thrown off-balance when confronted with unforeseen events, nor does he waver when questioned, challenged, or criticized by others. He knows who he is, where he comes from, and where he is heading. There is no stopping him. Invulnerability is seen as a desirable character trait, and vulnerability is projected onto others with whom he cannot identify ([2], p. 312). This rather negative understanding of vulnerability tends to function as an unquestioned prejudice in both everyday discussions of ethical dilemmas as well as in more theoretical approaches to questions of ethical relevance, such as the encounter between people belonging to various social, cultural, and ethnic groups.

In the context of interreligious encounters as well, this understanding of (in-)vulnerability can be seen to be operative when believers are warned to engage in dialog only if they are absolutely certain about their faith. The fear is that believers who are preoccupied with questions and wrestle with certain tenets of their own tradition can begin to doubt their own faith commitment when engaging religious others in dialog. Therefore, steadfastness and certainty are seen as preconditions for interreligious dialog. Only when one believes unwaveringly, is absolutely committed, has incontestable convictions, and accepts certain religious truth claims as non-negotiable does it become interesting to participate in interreligious dialog [3]. Believers who are vulnerable in their religious identity are cautioned to refrain from becoming engaged in the complexities of religious diversity.

This ideal of invulnerability is also implied in the difficulty experienced in recognizing the interdependency between religions. A propensity towards affirming and reaffirming religious traditions as homogenous matrices and impermeable worlds that constitute their own meaning clearly exists ([4], p. 250). The contribution of other religions to one's own tradition is downplayed or denied. Intended or unintended forms of interreligious "borrowing" and "sharing" are rarely looked upon positively [5]. In extreme cases, this may even lead to an ideology of purification ([6], p. 4).

Still, the idealization of *invulnerability* is nourished by a somewhat oversimplified and unilateral understanding of vulnerability. A more nuanced definition that does justice to its complexity and to its commonality is needed. First, vulnerability is the common human *capacity* to be affected and affect in turn. It is akin to receptivity, which points to the *ability* to be touched, interrupted, challenged, and even changed and transformed. It is a capacity that marks the human condition: all human beings are vulnerable. Because of this primary ability, we are physical and social beings capable of interaction and responsibility. In this reading, vulnerability becomes the basic condition of reciprocity. From this perspective, we can imagine that to be *invulnerable* is to be *indifferent, irresponsible, inaccessible, inapproachable*. There is something inhuman about being invulnerable.

Second, vulnerability is an ambivalent notion: it is the condition of potential that makes both positive and negative experiences possible. It can bring about loss and pain, but it also points to the possibility of creativity. In this sense it is an ambiguous term: "Being vulnerable makes it possible for us to suffer, to fall prey to violence and be harmed, but also to fall in love, to learn, to take pleasure and find comfort in the presence of others, and to experience the simultaneity of these feelings. Vuln*erability* is not just a condition that limits us but one that can *enable* us. As potential, vulnerability is a condition of openness, openness to being affected and affecting in turn" ([2], p. 310). From this perspective, we can understand vulnerability as the basic condition to any real encounter, an encounter that can be experienced both positively and negatively and sometimes both at the same time.

This also holds true for interreligious encounters. Postcolonial theology especially has shown that religious traditions are vulnerable: they are receptive to what comes from strange religious traditions. The interdependency of religious traditions is an undeniable reality: religions are affected, interrupted and challenged by symbols, rituals, prayers, and religious meanings belonging to other religions. Meaning from one religious tradition can and does penetrate another and plays havoc with everything there. It can bring about a shift in meaning, even to the extent that the original intention becomes lost ([7], p. 5). However, it is also possible that this play of religious interpenetration brings about a gain in meaning. Vulnerability can bring about innovation, which is so necessary for a tradition to remain a living one, but it can also undermine age-old customs.[1] This explains (in part) why the course of interreligious encounters is not self-evident.

As expounded above, the problem with focusing unilaterally on the negative is that vulnerability then becomes a condition that affects some people (e.g., people with weak and feeble faith convictions), and this is a condition that is to be avoided by all means. To avoid *vulnerability* and the possible pain, discomfort, and distress involved, various defense strategies are activated, the first of which is that of ignoring vulnerability as a common human condition. Indeed, people who empathically claim to be strong, certain, and stable are actually *in denial* ([9], p. 146). Behind the invulnerability that they claim to possess lies a deeper incapacity to deal with the fundamental human condition of vulnerability (see also [10]).

> The denial of vulnerability can be understood to be motivated by the desire conscious or not—to maintain a ... the prototypical, arrogantly self-sufficient, independent, invulnerable master subject. Invulnerability is a central feature of masterful subjectivity because it solidifies a sense of control, indeed an illusion of control. The achievement of full mastery, complete control, utter impenetrability, is an impossibility (one would have to be a god) ([2], pp. 312–13).

Whereas vulnerability, understood as the openness to being affected and affecting in turn, implies the willingness to refrain from domination, people claim that invulnerability points to a desire for

---

[1] I have explained this elsewhere via the metaphor of the body, which symbolizes human vulnerability, understood as receptivity. The body feeds on "strange meanings" to stay alive. But that does not mean that all meanings are equally nourishing and compatible. Some meanings are easily digested whereas others are indigestible. Some meanings go down easily, while others lie heavily on the stomach. Some meanings hurt, cut deep into the skin, leave traces. Some meanings are nourishing, breathe life into one's "own cells," and give strength, but other meanings make one ill. The body develops a resistance to some meanings and the immune systems kicks in. What comes from outside is sometimes rejected, discharged, and spit out. See ([8], pp. 282–83).

control and command, resulting in a closure to interruption, change, and transformation. The latter not only inhibits authentic encounter, but it can also give way to doing real harm. People who are unable to bear their own vulnerability and deny this human condition can seek to compensate their discomfort by claiming to be in charge. This clearly also affects the relation between religious traditions and their adherents:

> People wrestle with the question as to how their age-old traditions can survive in a context of secularization and pluralization. In the midst of change, they may look for something that is permanent, unchanging and ahistorical. They may search for a cultural essence, a core of values that must remain untouched or something that is indisputable and non-negotiable. ... As a result to their insecurity, believers act as "security guards who stand at the door of their religion to make sure that its identity and integrity are not violated by another religion." Because of this fear, many people find it particularly appealing to withdraw behind the closed doors of their own symbolic community ([11], p. 102).

If vulnerability points to openness to the unexpected, invulnerability points to being closed to change and challenge, thereby also inhibiting innovation. Creativity and responsibility originate in the courage to accept our vulnerability as that condition of potential from which both the positive and the negative emerges. Only those who learn to live with the possibility of loss and pain can learn to appreciate the enrichment of being interrupted and challenged. From this perspective, we can understand that not only is vulnerability a *human condition*, it is also a *choice that exhales power and courage*.

In what follows, I will first analyze how this desire for control works in theological approaches to religious diversity and the dialog between religions. The second section analyzes how comparative theology moves beyond the classic theologies of religions towards a specific form of vulnerable theology, thereby also highlighting the originality of this project. In the last section I seek to show how Clooney's cultivation of vulnerability actually points to the ethics of comparative theology.

3. Theology of Religions and the Domination of the In-Between Space

Much reflection on the possibilities and difficulties of interreligious dialog happens in the so-called theology of religions. Alan Race defines it as "the attempt, on the part of Christian theologians, to account theologically for the diversity of the world's religious quest and commitment" ([12], p. 3). How can the challenge of religious diversity be understood in light of the Christian tradition, and how can the Christian tradition be recontextualized in light of the experiences of believers in the context of religious plurality? It is up to theological reflection to clarify why Christians must or, conversely, should not be open to those of other religions. It is theology that sets out how far that openness extends and if there should be limits to the openness for the religious other. The questions of if Christians should open themselves up, *why* this openness is appropriate (or not), and how this openness for the faith of another is related to one's own faith commitment are answered, one by one, through theological reflection on and the interpretation of religious diversity.

The fundamental issue in the theology of religions today is the ongoing discussion between liberal pluralism and postliberal particularism on both the possibility and desirability of interreligious dialog.

This debate in which understandings of other religions under the tropes of respectively, "similarity" or "difference" are contrasted has reached an impasse ([13], p. 9). Pluralists ground their argument for interreligious dialog in a philosophy of religion that traces all religions back to a common ground: there is one ultimate Reality and many historico-cultural expressions. Or, as the British philosopher John Hick puts it, the different religious traditions "constitute different ways of experiencing, conceiving and living in relation to an ultimate divine Reality which transcends all our varied visions of it" ([14], pp. 235–36). The other religions are not rivals but "fellow travelers to the Ultimate" ([15], p. 165). From this perspective, pluralism claims to be the natural partner of interreligious dialog.

The main criticism of the pluralist model is that its focus on commonalities brings about the undermining and removal of the specificity of particular religious traditions in general and of Christianity especially. Pluralists are so eager to promote dialog that they tend to forget the irreducible differences that exist between the religious traditions. Michael Barnes sums up this criticism in a very sharp way by stating that particularity is "all too easily subsumed under an ethic of openness which quickly becomes rigidly ideological" ([16], p. 13). From this perspective, we can understand why pluralism is associated with the mistake of reductionism. David Tracy explains this as follows:

> The official pluralist too often finds ways to reduce real otherness and genuine differences to some homogenized sense of what we (who is this "we"?) already know.... [S]ome pluralists, the vaunted defenders of difference, can become great reductionists—reducing differences to mere similarity, reducing otherness to the same, and reducing plurality to my community of right-thinking competent critics. In this light, there is truth in Simone de Beauvoir's bitter charge that "pluralism is the perfect ideology for the bourgeois mind" [17].

The reaction to this homogenizing tendency is a growing emphasis on the particular nature of religious commitments and on the tradition-specific character of religious meanings and practices. Postliberal theologians especially have resisted the universally colored theological agenda of pluralism. Under their lead, the theological pendulum swings from the virtue of openness to the value of commitment. Their basic assumption seems to be that Christians have to be rooted firmly in their own tradition before embarking on a dialogical journey. Religions are viewed as particular, untranslatable and incommensurable language games. The whole idea of a common ground to which all religions refer is rejected. As Douglas Pratt puts it, "[T]here is no reasonable ground to assume a link across religions: their individual, or particular, identities militate against any such linkage. The difference between them is of such a nature that, strictly speaking, it is illicit even to consider that there is any point of meaningful conceptual contact among the religions" ([18], p. 8). The question is whether this postliberal particularistic approach still allows for interreligious dialog and does not, in the end, lead to a retreat in symbolically closed communities.

The debate between pluralists and postliberal particularism remains too easily at the level of "isms", thereby also downplaying the complexities and dynamics of interreligious relations and inhibiting profound reflection on the dialogical space between the self and the other. Jeanine Hill Fletcher especially has criticized the oversimplified nature of both approaches. Whereas pluralism upholds a logic of sameness that, pushes troublesome, changeable religious realities into a procrustean bed of unrestricted homogeneity, postliberalism affirms a logic of difference that presents religions as "indissolubly distinct entities that thoroughly shape adherents to a radically different understanding of the world, reality and ultimate reality" ([19], pp. 9–10). In both approaches the religious other is seen as a problem that can and should be solved, either by retreating to the security of sameness (pluralism) or by distancing otherness (particularism). The pluralistic discourse on openness turns out to be a "strategy": it constitutes order and thus gives a sentiment of comfort, because it takes away the interruptive and confrontational, even discomforting, character of the encounter with the religious other. The outcome of postliberal particularism is a dichotomy between insiders and outsiders. In recognizing the other in his irreducible otherness and in "granting the other his homeland; [the postliberal particularist] can rest assured and turn his back on him" ([20], p. 91). In any case, the problem of the other is "solved" as "controlled, categorized, schematized…" However different these theological approaches may be, both seem to be marked by a temptation to counteract the *vulnerability* of interreligious encounters as to calm our fears ([21], p. 9).

When vulnerability is counteracted, receptivity for what comes from elsewhere diminishes and interreligious dialog loses its religious significance. The neutralization of vulnerability impacts on the relation to the religious other in a negative way: the religious other is either *harmonized* into the overarching pluralist scheme or the religious other becomes *so strange* that she disappears from our radar. Once the other has been "understood and categorized," it is no longer as necessary to demand a deep knowledge of the other in her particularity. The neutralization of vulnerability also affects the way believers relate to the divine and especially the way revelation is understood. By counteracting vulnerability, receptivity for (O)therness is also ruled out: postliberal theology on the one hand seems to confuse faithfulness to tradition with faithfulness to the divine, thereby forgetting the *Deus semper maior* dictum. The pluralist hypothesis on the other hand situates the encounter with the divine in the private sphere of personal religious experiences, which become the criteria for judging traditions. This hypothesis actually conceals a turn to the self that sets the norm and is in control. Excluded is the possibility that the encounter with the religious other is recognized as an interruptive, disruptive event that may actually put us on God's way.

The question is: Can there be a theology that testifies to the fragile space in which authentic interreligious dialog occurs? Is there a way to theologize about religious diversity that does not neutralize vulnerability from the outset? Can we formulate a theological response to the religious other that resists the all too human desire to construct and control her, thereby limiting the conversation from its very start? Can we make room for surprise, for the unexpected, for the unfamiliar? Are we prepared to change in light of what we learn from other religious traditions? Can there be a fragile space rather than a space controlling the other.

4. Comparative Theology as Vulnerable Theology

In my reading, these questions form the leitmotiv of *comparative theology*. According to Francis Clooney, the project of comparative theology is an original form of faith seeking understanding directed at a deep learning from other religious traditions. Continuing the theological tradition of

Anselm, Clooney (along with other comparative theologians) emphasizes the *seeking* dimension of faith, rather than focusing on faith in terms of what is *certain, non-negotiable*, and *absolute*. Though faith can be simple and stark, the truth all believers long for is never a possession that believers can appropriate for themselves. Believers are, in a sense, pilgrims on the way to truth, knowing it will always elude them to a certain extent. As comparative theologian Scott Steinkerchner puts it, "[t]his side of heaven, the seeking never ends. None of us individually, nor all of us collectively, possess a complete understanding of our faith. That fullness of truth lies forever in the future" ([22], p. 149). The only way to move forward is to ask questions, to study and learn, to seek understanding, and to gain insights that only evoke new questions in a search for more nuanced answers.

In the search for understanding, comparative theology turns to religious texts belonging to different traditions. Its focal point is reading and comparing strange and familiar texts in order to understand the other so that new theological insights will emerge, those which can challenge, interrupt, and transform one's own tradition. Texts from other religious traditions are recognized and appreciated as rich sources for imaginative and possibly constructive theology. This constructive element is realized when the meaning, value, and truth of the similarities and differences discovered through *inter-texting* are assessed ([23], pp. 170–71). In summary, in the *classical* understanding of theology as *fides quaerens intellectum*, the comparative theologian aims at "knowing a loving God more completely and intelligently," ([24], p. 7) but she does so in a *non-classical way* by pondering the truths of other traditions as resources for deepening her faith understanding [25]. In this sense, comparative theology derives its particular nature not from its object but from its sources and methodology ([26], p. 522).

Comparative theology took root in a certain dissatisfaction with theologies of religions that erect unnecessary walls between religious traditions and their adherents and thereby also inhibit real and authentic interreligious encounter. The theological process of constructing religious others is, in the end, a process of suppressing otherness. *A priori* theologies of religions—both liberal and postliberal—are regarded as especially problematic, since they tend to set the interreligious agenda beforehand, thereby immunizing Christians against the otherness of the (o)ther and diminishing the chance of *surprise, interruption*, and *unsettlement*. Here, theology becomes fixated on traditional Christian meanings handed down from the past instead of welcoming what comes from elsewhere as food for thought and as a possible source for semantic innovation. Comparative theologian James Fredericks has expressed his dissatisfaction with the "classic candidates for Christian theologies" in a particular sharp way, saying that they "usually lead to systemic distortions in the reception of the Other. Moreover, these distortions succeed in ... the 'domestication of difference', in which the threat of the Other, as well as its transformative power, are muted" ([27], p. xiv). If we want to attend to the religious other and his traditions we must, so Clooney claims, "deny ourselves the easy confidences that keep the other at a distance" ([28], p. 7).

Instead of trying to "solve the problem of religious diversity" in a theological meta-narrative, comparative theologians engage in crossing borders, moving back and forth between one's own tradition, and the strange religious tradition, allowing themselves to be truly immersed in both. Instead of circling around the doctrinal heart of Christian tradition, trying to find definite answers to the theological meaning of religious diversity, comparative theologians practice theology in a marginal area. Instead of trying to protect the tradition from the possibility of contamination that goes together with encounter, comparative theologians intentionally move to the borderland of tradition. As go-betweens, they invest in learning from the other, accepting that this also entails disturbing experiences of alienation, disenchantment, and friction ([24], p. 165). In this sense, comparative theology seems to be all about leaving the theological *comfort zone* of the centralist approach to theology.

Comparative theologians will sometimes argue that what they propose is not all that new. As Clooney puts it: "Interreligious and comparative learning has always been an inescapable dimension in the life of every community" ([28], p. 24). From this perspective, what they are proposing is *merely* making more explicit, more visible what is in a sense the fundamental vulnerability of religious traditions. Religious traditions are not constituted by sharp boundaries but are rather marked by a certain fluidity, permeability, and hybridity from the outset. Religious traditions were never pure in the first place: they have always been affected and influenced by other religions. Because their boundaries are much more porous than is often acknowledged, religious realities are "messy," they simply cannot be contained in neat categories and boxes [29]. In other words, religious traditions are *vulnerable*, whether they "like" it or not. From this perspective, the whole idea of erecting walls around our "tradition" and investing in "defense mechanisms" is an illusory undertaking. It always comes too late. There is no such thing as a pure tradition nor does there exist some "religious" core, common to all religious traditions, that remains unaffected by the messiness of interreligious encounters. In his article *Comparative Theology after Religion*, John Thatamanil remarks that,

> It would be possible to craft a history of Christian thought and practice written as a series of interactions and transmutations of movements and traditions that Christians have come to demarcate as non-Christian. Such a history would demonstrate not only that many of the central categories, practices and symbols of Christian life are borrowed from Hellenistic philosophical schools, mystery religions, and, of course, most vitally from what we now call "Judaism," but that for long stretches of history, no clearly defined and rigid boundaries existed between "Christianity" and those traditions we now take to be Christianity's others. … Alongside such a history, a companion work could be written that would take note of tremors within (especially Western) Christian self-awareness when such profound entanglements come to surface. I suspect that such a companion history would unearth moments of widespread anxiety among custodians of tradition at just those junctures when "the unbearable proximity" of those whom Christians customarily regard as other is most keenly felt [4].

However, comparative theology is not *just* about noting that traditions—whether they like it or not, whether they know it or not, whether they intend it or not—are from the outset always also constituted by other religious traditions and thus inherently vulnerable. This project aims at a *cultivation* of vulnerability as the crux of doing theology. That is why Clooney not only records that crossing borders has always been part of the history of religious traditions, but he actually creates a liminal space in the form of scriptural intertextuality. Indeed, Clooney emphasizes especially the experimental, creative, and constructive nature of this work, acknowledging thereby the role of the comparativist "who forges a link which was not previously there, a link which (usually) cannot be justified on the basis of historical connections or of similarities so striking that they compel comparison" ([30], p. 154). Placed, studied, and read together, these texts begin to interact, influence, and affect one another (which also has an effect on the reader). These texts begin to move and shift, losing their familiar (perhaps sometimes even predictable and stale) meaning. The underlying assumption is that theologians who are able to sustain experiences of alienation, disenchantment, and friction brought about by this textual juxtaposition can also learn to enjoy the pleasure of discovering new hermeneutical and theological possibilities.

Comparative theology is a never-ending conversational process: particular comparisons yield particular insights, insights that might be revised in the future under the influence of other particular comparisons. The theological reflections that follow from detailed comparisons "can only be tentative and should not be taken as precluding what will be learned in further experiments" ([24], p. 164). In this way, comparative theology remains "pre-systematic and pre-dogmatic." It does not aspire to lead to a "definite theology of religions" ([31], p. 176). On the contrary, those who are looking for clear-cut answers to clear-cut questions are likely to be disappointed by this approach, for many questions will be left open after in-depth study, until "more commentarial work has been done, by more theologians, over a much longer period of time" ([31], p. 184).[2]

5. On the Ethics of Comparative Theology

> The careful reader engaging the two texts in their own two traditions comes to know more than expected, and in a way that cannot be predictably controlled by either tradition.... As we learn more about religious traditions in their depth than has been possible before, we know more deeply the possibilities of several traditions and where they lead us, while yet we also lose the intensity and devotion possible for those who know only their own tradition. We are then left in a vulnerable, fruitful learning state, engaging these powerful works on multiple levels and paradoxically, learning more, while mastering less; we have more teachers and fewer masters ([1], p. 209).

Clooney's plea for *vulnerable theology* is not self-evident. It requires us to withstand the (all too human) inclination to flee from vulnerability; it asks us to abandon the (natural) desire for purity, calls for a renouncement of the strong wish for a stable and seamless identity, demands that we give up the ideal of a clearly delineated identity that can be placed in a binary scheme with otherness, and asks us to refrain from grand theories that solve the problem of the religious other and the implied discomfort ([27], p. xiii). In brief, the belief in the fecundity of interreligious co-reading has to compete with the ideology of invulnerability.

But what motivates Clooney? Why travel via such unusual paths from which inconvenient, unsettling truth may stem? In a first response, Clooney would probably say "why not?" All these texts

---

[2] In his article "Comparative Theology: Between Identity and Alterity," Bagus Laksana refers to the metaphor of pilgrimage to evoke the wandering journey of the comparative theologian. He regards pilgrimage as a "privileged *locus* in which a creative negotiation of religious identity in the proximity and intimacy with God, the Other, as well as with the religious other, occurs in all its complexity" ([6], p. 2).

are readily available, translated or otherwise. They are public classics, sold in bookshops, on the Internet, or in the market. Anyone can read these texts. He even makes the claim that "it is hard to justify not reading the theologies of other traditions when they are pertinent and available" ([32], p. 14). A great curiosity and intellectualist desire to study and learn is without doubt one of the driving motivations behind this project. The human desire to know *more*, he points out, does not stop at the borders of one's own religious traditions.

At a deeper level, of course, Clooney's desire to understand is faith-driven. Comparative theologians believe that their practice of deep learning across religious borders is theologically valuable since it allows them not only to learn from the religious other but also to hear God speak anew and to receive his truth in a different way so that they can learn to know God better ([28], p. 8). Learning from other religious traditions is a theological responsibility: understanding religious others better in all their complexity will allow us to understand our relationship with God better. The detailed study of other traditions follows from a commitment to God. Comparative theologians believe that in opening up to the religious other in and through a detailed study of his texts one realizes a fuller knowledge of God ([24], p. 7). This imaginative appropriation of the strange or different text can be a creative theological source that warns the faith community that God cannot be fixed or reduced to the familiar—just as, by way of a humbler analogy, the text cannot be fixed or reduced to the familiar. It is a way of giving form to the notion that it is not up to theology to determine the limits of God's activity *a priori*. Or, as Clooney would put it, being taught by a strange text entails undergoing a spiritual process that changes the reader and perhaps reveals God in an unexpected way.

> While it would be a bit dramatic to say that God desires that theology be comparative—just as it would be to way that God desires more or less of any particular theological discipline—we do well to see our effort to learn across religious borders as in harmony with God's plan. To suggest that God has not envisioned the actual world in which we live, where neither faith nor religious diversity will vanish at any time soon, would also be a strange thing for a theologian to propose. Knowing God today requires a retrieval of faith, tradition, scripture and practice—precisely as we open ourselves to learning other traditions, in their own comparable complexities ([28], p. 37).

However, next to his intellectual and theological investment, comparative theology creates also an ethical problem since it affects the relation between what is familiar and foreign. A deep moral dynamic underlies Clooney's project, which finds its expression in an *ethic* of interreligious reading: reading understood as an intrinsically relational, and thus reciprocal, act. The foreign religious text is an *other* and to engage in a practice of interreligious reading is to engage in a relationship with something that is other to us. Hence, interreligious reading is analogous to a *conversational* act and comparable to a face-to-face encounter.[3]

---

[3] For his understanding of *reading religious texts*, Clooney is inspired by Paul Griffiths, who dedicated one of his books to the theme of religious reading, even though Griffiths did not concern himself with the specific challenge of interreligious reading, According to Clooney, his project "seeks to exemplify the dynamic that Griffiths has in mind but to do so in the practice of an (inter)religious reading, one that demands vulnerability to both texts, a practice that is

Approximating a foreign religious text appeals to a form of reader-responsibility, intended to avoid falling into the twofold trap of (1) making generalizing and stereotyping claims pushing recalcitrant religious phenomena in a neat scheme of commonality (cf. liberal pluralism) (2) or of making the other so other that he becomes completely alien and thus he disappears from our radar and becomes utterly meaningless (cf. postliberal particularism). The challenge is to respect a certain degree of irreducibility inherent in the foreign religious text, while at the same time refraining from succumbing to the idea of a radical and absolute otherness ([6], p. 3).

In the last part of this article, I want to point to three ethical "conditions" proper to comparative theology: (1) encountering otherness, (2) reticence and hermeneutical openness, and (3) appropriation through disappropriation. These three ethical conditions lead to the concluding section, in which I elaborate on comparative theology as a specific form of interreligious hospitality.

5.1. Encountering Otherness

Comparative theology, understood as religious *inter-texting*, begins with engaging a strange religious text, which is of course part of a larger religious tradition. According to Clooney, reading a "non-Christian" text "initiates an encounter of religions, and involves the reader in hearing and understanding a specific other voice, not just the generic "world religions" ([33], p. 35). The religious text is the other who does not fit into our familiar religious framework and transcends what is known.

A strange text is an exponent of an entire religious tradition, rich in wisdom. A tradition that is practiced in a religious community via a prayerful, ritual, and moral way of life, which molds the identity of its religious believers in a way very different from ours. In this tradition, believers find inspiration, wisdom, and truth. The strange religious text, even though it is only a minor part of a larger religious whole, nevertheless evokes the beauty, vitality, complexity, and richness of the religious life of another. It has the strength to catch our eye, precisely because what it expresses, symbolizes, and enacts is so different from the way we try to live our (religious) life. There is something fascinating, perhaps even beguiling and seductive about a religious other, also when she takes the form of a strange text.

This attractiveness has its root in its recalcitrance: The textual other resists, interrupts, and questions the obviousness of what fully commits us and challenges the naturalness by which we regard our own perspective as the measure of all. The textual other reveals and challenges our natural inclination to control and domination. We are brought out of balance, we become unsettled. This is not necessarily a *pleasant* experience. One should recall the ambiguous nature of *vulnerability*: being affected can be experienced as positive *and* negative. Indeed, there is no need to romanticize being interrupted by the other—the other brings about a disturbance of order. That is why the other is not always the welcome other, especially not when he approaches us in all his beauty, radiance, and brilliance. Put differently,

---

intensified by the spiritual power generated in reading them together repeatedly and that refuses to reduce either to a component of some later and settled 'higher' viewpoint." ([28], p. 63)

the other's beguilement can also become his destruction: the fear is that what is fascinating, tempting and alluring can lead to a loss of faith. Clooney acknowledges this risk:

> [T]he first problem always to be faced in such an encounter is fear: a fear of the loss of God, of Christ; a fear of the dangerous 'other' and of a future one cannot fully predict; a fear of a God who is completely free. To experience another religion, however one meets it, is to awaken at a double twilight of dusk and dawn where God comes but also goes. We should not be surprised if we are vulnerable, afraid, in love-and also alone, angry, annoyed ([33], p. 37).

This unease, brought about by being vulnerable, is where the ethical structure of interreligious dialog takes root. In a Levinasian way, we could say that the textual other makes an appeal, asking to be recognized in its otherness. This is the basic ethical condition for any interreligious encounter: to recognize the "intractable otherness of other religions" ([34], p. 254). The textual other "expects" us to be willing to be addressed and interrupted by an unfamiliarity that does not meet our prejudiced patterns of expectation ([35], p. 64). But the textual other can do no more than make an appeal, asking to be recognized in her otherness, demanding not to be reduced to "sameness". It is always possible to ignore this appeal since the other does not have the force to compel recognition. It is always possible to put aside the appeal of the other and resort to "violence," which can take two forms: either we distance ourselves from the other, turning him into a complete and utter stranger or we reduce him to our own familiar categories. In the end, the religious other depends on our responsibility.

5.2. Reticence and Hermeneutical Openness

What is required is not an enthusiastic embrace of the other but a form of "hesitation" that expresses the fear of inflicting violence on the other.

> [R]eal dialogue begins with the inclination or the temptation to exclude the other than ourselves ... or to reduce the other to ourselves *and* at the same time—at the same origin—realizing that this exclusion or reduction is not allowed.... The ethical '*faith primitif*' of the dialogue is neither magnanimity nor sympathy or empathy, but a dynamism of "restraint" and "shuddering,", namely utter cautiousness and carefulness, fearful in all our advancing self-certainty of doing injustice to the other ([36], p. 236).

In comparative theology, this ethical reticence is expressed in the rejection of *a priori* theologies of religions (either liberal or postliberal) that are too quick, too hasty in categorizing the other. An authentic encounter with the textual other begins with holding back out of fear that one could inflict violence on the other. This restraint enables the other to speak for itself, to become other, to become a subject with a proper voice.

This reticence is the basic condition for becoming vulnerable and receptive to the other. If both liberal and postliberal theologies of religions tend to control the space in-between because they are too quick either with "filling up" the space between the different religions with presupposed commonalities or inflating the in-between space with the presumption of incommensurability, comparative theology is patient, willing to wait, and to listen and learn. Instead of seeking a grand narrative in which the religious other is grasped and contained, comparative theologians allow themselves to be challenged by the often unsettling religious reality and belief of the other. Instead of "solving the problem of religious diversity" in a theological meta-narrative, comparative theology accepts that learning from the other entails experiences of alienation, disenchantment, and friction ([24], p. 165). There is no haste to come up with definite answers. Clooney emphasises time and again the importance of not jumping to conclusions because theology should avoid over-hasty theological judgments. It requires a long and patient engagement with the textual world of the other. Before judging, before assessing, before appreciating—either positively or negatively—the religious other deserves to be heard and understood.[4] The search for truth is preceded by a pledge to justice ([38], p. 62).

> *After* one has read and re-read, thought back and forth from text to context—one can *then* review the questions posed in the theology of religions. "What are we to make of these religions?" "Is Christ unique?", "Are Hindus save by Christ alone?", "Is there revelation outside Christianity?"... The Christian who *first* reads and *then* asks the theology of religions questions will not be asking about what is entirely strange or alien, as if she or he were a gate-keeper who has to decide about whether to let the other in at all; nor will she or he be dealing with what is entirely predictable, once inside. Rather, the basic question will be about how to make sense, as a Christian, of a set of Christian experiences and texts and theologies that now includes certain non-Christian texts that remain vital and creative ([33], p. 36).

This pledge to justice is expressed positively in what I have elsewhere termed hermeneutical openness, *i.e.*, the responsibility to understand the other in the most objective and fair-minded manner possible. As Clooney puts it comparative theology ideally gives way to "a viable understanding of the 'other' in which the encountered 'other' is not manufactured to the comparativist's prejudices and expectations" ([30], p. 7). Its intention is to *understand* the other in his or her otherness and to avoid reading one's own presuppositions into the religious world of the other. This turns interreligious dialog into a hermeneutical challenge, involving the question of mutual understanding or the degree to which individuals belonging to one religion can grasp the meaning of symbols, teachings, and practices of another.

5.3. Appropriation Through Disappropriation

Moving beyond the requirement of hermeneutical openness, Clooney's ethics of reader responsibility also entails the cultivation of certain humility as the appropriate attitude by which to approach a religious text. Clooney sees the religious text more as a subject speaking to the reader and challenging him. It is a poetic whole, constructed by its author to address, challenge, and interrupt the reader ([39], p. 368). Gifted with an "excess of meaning," it has the capacity of intruding on the world of the reader that it intends to transform. To do justice to the specific nature of religious texts and their inherent purpose to bring about transformation, the religious nature of reading these texts should prevail. Religious reading revolves around giving up control and surrendering to the domination of the text.

---

[4] On the criteria of judgment in interreligious dialogue see [37].

From this perspective Clooney reacts against a "consumerist... mining of texts in service of a preconceived agenda neglectful of the text's own purposes" ([31], p. 8). The interruptive and transformative power is immunized from the grasping approach of the master reader. But he also criticizes readers who limit their role to that of the neutral investigator, examining the texts from a distance as objectively and impartially as possible. The text is not an object to be analyzed or even dissected. It is not a carrier of information to be discussed or a depository of interesting ideas to debate. Here too, Clooney objects that, by placing the text at a distance as an object to be analyzed and dissected by the reader, the reader becomes immune to its message. "[Religious] texts expect and invite a humbler, less self-confident reasoning, even off-balance, that draws the mind into a situation it cannot control and that illumines and ignites the heart" ([1], p. 79). Submission rather than control is the appropriate attitude by which a *responsible reader* approaches religious texts.

The possibility of transformation requires an attentive reading, the crux of which is that the reader surrenders to the influence of the text and thereby becomes vulnerable to the possibilities projected before the text, even to the extent of inspiring a radical life change ([1], p. 208). This implies that the reader places herself under the authority of the text: the text takes on the role of teacher; the reader, that of student. The text asks of the interpreter to take a distance from the known and the familiar and to walk into the world of the unknown. Drawing on the reflections of Paul Griffiths, who wrote a book on the habit of religious reading, Clooney claims the following:

> To learn, we must... be vulnerable to possibilities we can probe only to a modest extent, and ready to surrender ourselves to the mysteries latent in what we read... This humble practice changes readers, as they are inevitably drawn into the worlds brought to life in their reading. Readers who are willing to take the risk become competent to read religiously and, upon receiving the riches of the great texts, they also become able to speak, act, and write with spiritual insight and power ([28], p. 59).

This reminds me of what the French philosopher Paul Ricoeur, known especially for his textual hermeneutics, calls the dynamic play between appropriation and disappropriation. According to Ricoeur, a responsible reader can appropriate the world of the text only to the extent that he disappropriates himself. Appropriation is thus inextricably linked to disappropriation. Appropriation is not a matter of imposing our finite capacity for understanding on the text but of exposing ourselves to the imaginative possibilities projected by the text. In this way, hermeneutical appropriation is not the expression of imperialism or colonization but an expression of detachment and of letting go. Thus, understanding is quite different from a constitution whose key the subject possesses; on the contrary, it is the process by which the reader is constituted by the text. Ricoeur puts it as follows, "as a reader I find myself by losing myself. The movement toward listening requires giving up (*désaissement*) the human self in its will to mastery, sufficiency, and autonomy" ([40], p. 224). Ricoeur also speaks about "la dépossession du soi narcissique." Understanding means to understand oneself before the text and in submission to it as reader and student.

6. Conclusion: Reciprocal Hospitality in Response to Invulnerability

In my reading, the comparative theology project embodies the virtue of hospitality, which reaffirms and strengthens its ethical dynamics. It does this in a very specific way, since the comparative theologian wants to be both host and guest at the same time. In this reciprocal form of text-oriented interreligious hospitality "the pleasure of dwelling in the other's language is balanced by the pleasure of receiving the foreign word at home, in one's own welcoming home" ([41], p. 10). Over against reducing the other to sameness (cf. pluralism) on the one hand and alienating the other (particularism), comparative theology seeks to build bridges between two text traditions while always recognizing that both are irreducible to one another. It concerns an attitude of "active receptivity: it is making room for the stranger in one's own space—it is the strange other received into one's home in a way that does justice to the otherness of the other." Comparative theology actually teaches that interreligious relations are not exhausted in attempts to defend one's identity against the unfamiliar, nor is it appropriate to try and reduce what is other to sameness. This intertextual hospitality refuses, on the one hand, to distance the other—this would lead to indifference—and, on the other, to attempt to dominate the other. The other is received in its otherness. What we learn from this intertextual practice is that happiness can also be found precisely in reciprocal hospitality, in becoming vulnerable to each other.

Dwelling in the realm of the other and returning home to one's own religious community with meanings received from another tradition, Clooney argued and illustrates how Christian believers can enrich their understanding of Christian texts and doctrines by re-reading them after deep learning from non-Christians texts. It is a learning in the proximity of the other. This practice of reciprocal hospitality is a form of reaching out to the other, rather than keeping her at a distance, as well as returning home with fresh, challenging, and interrupting insights. Here one values the other for leaving his trace in "our" identity.

The main challenge confronting comparative theology is not merely theoretical in nature, but ethical. The challenge is to overcome all sorts of resistance emerging from a certain fear of otherness that leads to desire to control the in-between space (the ideal of invulnerability). These resistances come from both the "home" and the foreign tradition (see [42]). The resistance on the side of the home community is related to a strong desire to sacralize the mother tradition out of fear of contamination. Hence the empathic claim is that one's tradition is incommensurable, untranslatable and incomparable. But the refusal of comparison equals the refusal to recognize what is foreign as a challenge and source of nourishment for one's own religious identity. One sets out to keep one's own language pure, though this self-sufficiency has secretly nourished "numerous linguistic ethnocentrisms, and more seriously, numerous pretensions to the same cultural hegemony" ([43], p. 4).

The resistance on the side of other tradition flows especially from a certain conceitedness: the foreign religious text is so exceptional that it is beyond comparison. But the recognition that traditions cannot be reduced to one another, the affirmation that religious texts are always also *beyond comparison*, with reference to their uniqueness and the acknowledgment that their meaning can never be exhausted in comparison, does not amount to a denial of the possibility of comparison. Rather, it points to the continuing *asymmetry* between traditions that cannot be removed by comparison. But this is no reason to dismiss the validity of comparison. Speaking about the *incomparability of religious texts* expresses the irreducible value and uniqueness of texts. This is a precondition to comparison rather than an insurmountable obstacle.

Reciprocal hospitality, which implies mutual affection, contradicts the ideal of invulnerability and the illusion of self-sufficiency, and uncovers its underlying xenophobic dynamics. Beyond the fear of contamination and loss of meaning, the textual other is no longer seen as a problem to be solved but as a possibility given to us ([33], p. 38). Here, the genuine attitude of hospitality is realized: recognizing that another tradition may be a source of enrichment for one's own. Comparison is, indeed, always and inevitably a matter of balancing between fidelity and betrayal. To compare and interpret religious texts belonging to different traditions is not possible without loss of meaning. But it is a one-sided view of comparison to focus solely on the loss of meaning. Comparing texts is also a way of giving new life to one's own religious tradition and uncovering new truth dimensions. Comparing seemingly incomparable texts is also an opportunity, for it opens up the possibility of creativity and innovation. From this perspective, we can conclude by paraphrasing a saying from 2 Corinthians 12:9: "Power is made perfect in weakness."

Conflicts of Interest

The author declares no conflict of interest.

References

1. Francis X. Clooney. *Beyond Compare: St. Francis de Sales and Sri Vedanta Desika on Loving Surrender to God.* Washington, DC: Georgetown University Press, 2008.
2. Erinn Gilson. "Vulnerability, Ignorance and Oppression." *Hypatia* 26 (2011): 308–32.
3. Craig M. Gay. "Plurality, Ambiguity and Despair in Contemporary Theology." *Journal of the Evangelical Theological Society* 36 (1993): 209–27.
4. John J. Thatamanil. "Comparative Theology After 'Religion'." In *Planetary Loves: Spivak, Postcoloniality, and Theology*, edited by Stephen D. Moore and Mayra Rivera. New York: Fordham University Press, 2011, 238–57.
5. Charles Burack. "Overcoming the Fear of Mixing Faiths." *Interreligious Insight*, July 2007. http://www.interreligiousinsight.org/July2007/July07Burack.html.
6. A. Bagus Laksana. "Comparative Theology: Between Identity and Alterity." In *The New Comparative Theology*, edited by Francis X. Clooney. New York: T&T Clark, 2010, 1–20.
7. Paul Courtois. *Contraminaties: Cultuur/wetenschap.* Tertium Datur 9. Louvain: Peeters, 2002.
8. Marianne Moyaert. *Fragile Identities: Towards a Theology of Interreligious Hospitality.* Amsterdam/New York: Rodopi, 2011.
9. Richard Kearney, and Paul Ricoeur. "Universality and the Power of Difference." In *On Paul Ricoeur: The Owl of Minerva*, edited by Richard Kearney. Aldershot: Ashgate, 2004, 145–50.

10. Marianne Moyaert. "Facing up to our Own Egypt." In *Paul Ricoeur: Poetics and Religion*. Bibliotheca Ephemeridum Theologicarum Lovaniensium 240, edited by Jozef Verheyden and Theo Hettema. Louvain/Paris/Walpole, MA: Peeters, 2010, 243–61.
11. Marianne Moyaert. "Biblical, Ethical and Hermeneutical Reflections on Narrative Hospitality." In *Hosting the Stranger between Religions*, edited by Richard Kearney & James Taylor. New York: Continuum, 2011, 95–108.
12. Alan Race. *Christians and Religious Pluralism: Patterns in the Christian Theology of Religions*. London: SCM Press, 1983.
13. Paul Hedges. *Controversies in Interreligious Dialogue and the Theology of Religions*. London: SCM Press, 2010.
14. John Hick. *An Interpretation of Religion: Human Responses to the Transcendent*. New Haven: Yale University Press, 1989.
15. David Cheetham. *John Hick: A Critical Introduction*. Aldershot: Ashgate, 2003.
16. Michael Barnes. *Theology and the Dialogue of Religion*. Cambridge: Cambridge University Press, 2002.
17. David Tracy. "Christianity in the Wider Context: Demands and Transformations." In *Religion and Intellectual Life* 4 (Summer 1987): 7–20, 12. Quoted in Marty, M.E. *When Faiths Collide*. Malden, MA: Blackwell Publishing, 2005, 125.
18. Douglas Pratt. "Contextual Paradigms for Interfaith Relations." In *Current Dialogue* 42 (2003): 3–9.
19. Jeannine Hill Fletcher. "Shifting Identity: The Contribution of Feminist Thought to Theologies of Religious Pluralism." *Journal of Feminist Studies in Religion* 19:2 (2003): 5–24.
20. Rudi Visker. "Transcultural Vibrations." *Ethical Perspectives* 1:2 (1994): 89–100.
21. Stephen Duffy. "The Stranger Within Our Gates: Interreligious Dialogue and the Normativeness of Jesus." In *The Myriad Christ: Plurality and the Quest for Unity in Contemporary Christology*. Bibliotheca Ephemeridum theologicarum Lovaniensium 152, edited by Terrence Merrigan and Jacques Haers. Louvain: Peeters, 2000, 3–30.
22. Scott Steinkerchner. *Beyond Agreement. Interreligious Dialogue and Persistent Differences*. Lanham: Rowman & Littlefield, 2011.
23. John J Thatamanil. *The Immanent Divine: God, Creation, and the Human Predicament. An East-West Conversation*. Minneapolis, MN: Fortress Press, 2006.
24. Francis X. Clooney. *Hindu God, Christian God: How Reason Helps to Break Down Boundaries Between Religions*. Oxford: Oxford University Press, 2001.
25. Richard Hanson. "The Hermeneutics of Comparative Theology." Conference paper presented at Engaging Particularities IV: New Directions in Comparative Theology, Interreligious Dialogue, Theology of Religions and Missiology, Boston College, 17–19 March 2006.
26. Francis X. Clooney. "Current Theology: Comparative Theology: A Review of Recent Books (1989–1995)." *Theological Studies* 56 (1995): 521–50.

27. James L Fredericks. *Introduction to The New Comparative Theology*, edited by Francis X. Clooney. New York: T&T Clark, 2010, ix–xix.
28. Francis X. Clooney. *Comparative Theology: Deep Learning Across Religious Borders*. Malden, MA: Wiley-Blackwell, 2010.
29. Helene Egnell. *Other Voices: A Study of Christian Feminist Approaches to Religious Plurality in East and West*. Studia Missionalia Svecana 100. Uppsala: Swedish Institute of Mission Research, 2006.
30. Francis X. Clooney. *Theology after Vedanta: An Experiment in Comparative Theology*. Albany, NY: State University of New York Press, 1993.
31. Francis X. Clooney. *The Truth, the Way and the Life: Christian Commentary on the Three Holy Mantras of the Srivaisnava Hindus*. Louvain: Peeters, 2008.
32. Francis X. Clooney. *Divine Mother, Blessed Mother: Hindu Goddesses and the Virgin Mary*. Oxford: Oxford University Press, 2005.
33. Francis X. Clooney. "When Religions Become Context." *Theology Today* 47 (1990): 30–38.
34. Joseph A DiNoia. "Varieties of Religious Aims: Beyond Exclusivism, Inclusivism, and Pluralism." In *Theology and Dialogue: Essays in Conversation with George Lindbeck*, edited by Bruce D. Marshal. Notre Dame, IN: University of Notre Dame Press, 1990, 249–72.
35. Bart Van Leeuwen. *Erkenning, identiteit en verschil: Multiculturalisme en leven met culturele diversiteit*. Louvain: Acco, 2003.
36. Roger Burggraeve. "Alterity Makes the Difference: Ethical and Metaphysical Conditions of Interreligious Dialogue and Learning." In *Interreligious Learning*, edited by Didier Pollefeyt. Louvain: Peeters, 2007, 231–56.
37. Catherine Cornille, ed. *Criteria of Discernment in Interreligious Dialogue*. Eugene, OR: Wipf and Stock, 2009.
38. Emmanuel Levinas. *Totalité et Infini*. The Hague: Nijhoff, 1961.
39. Francis X. Clooney. "Passionate Comparison: the Intensification of Affect in Interreligious Reading of Hindu and Christian Texts." *Harvard Theological Review* 98 (2005): 367–90.
40. Paul Ricoeur. "Naming God." In *Figuring the Sacred: Religion, Narrative and Imagination*, edited by Paul Ricoeur. Minneapolis, MN: Fortress Press, 1995, 217–36.
41. Paul Ricoeur. *From Text to Action: Essays in Hermeneutics II*. Translated by Kathleen Blamey. London: Athlone, 1991.
42. Marianne Moyaert. "*The (Un-)Translatability of Religions? Ricoeur's Linguistic Hospitality as Model for Interreligious Dialogue*." *Exchange: Journal of Missiological and Ecumenical Research* 37 (2008): 337–64.
43. Paul Ricoeur. *On Translation*. London: Routledge, 2006.

Reprinted from *Religions*. Cite as: Scheuer, Jacques. "Comparative Theology and Religious Studies in a Non-religious Environment." *Religions* 3 (2012): 973-982.

Article

Comparative Theology and Religious Studies in a Non-religious Environment

Jacques Scheuer

Faculté de théologie, Université catholique de Louvain, Grand Place 45, bte L3.01.02, Louvain-la-Neuve B-1348, Belgium; E-Mail: jacques.scheuer@uclouvain.be

Received: 22 August 2012; in revised form: 9 October 2012 / Accepted: 12 October 2012 / Published: 17 October 2012

Abstract: The intellectual landscape of Europe bears the marks of a long history of cultural perceptions of, and scientific approaches to, religions. The sciences of religions had to establish their autonomy from churches and theologies. However, the cultural context and the institutional set-up of 'laïcité' did not foster the development of comparative religion, much less comparative theology. However, this situation may have an advantage: it should discourage the exercise of comparative theology as a sectarian endeavour apart from broader anthropological perspectives and concerns. Comparative theology should not become the last refuge for religious nostalgia. In Europe, interreligious relationships (and hence comparative theologies) should not be isolated from simple or more sophisticated forms of indifference, agnosticism, or atheism. The active presence of a non-religious environment as well as the growing interest in Buddhism, are challenges to comparative theology: its contents, its approach, its intended audience.

Keywords: comparative theology; Europe; *religio*; comparative method; historicity; intra-religious dialogue; Buddhism; non-belief; authority; Western reception

1. A Lack of Experience and a Lack of Expertise

Through many, long centuries Europe experienced the rather homogeneous society and culture of Christendom. From the Mediterranean shores up to Scandinavia, the indigenous religious traditions had been pushed back or somehow integrated into the dominant Christian universe. Willy-nilly, Jewish communities were to be more and more contained within the walls of their ghettos. From southern

Spain to Turkey and the Caucasus, the Muslim dominions cut off Europe from the rest of the world. Most Europeans however had little contact with and scant knowledge about Islam: indeed, it was widely considered as a sort of Christian heresy rather than a distinct religion in its own right.

Children growing up in the Near East or in India, for instance, soon become aware of the presence of other communities in their neighborhoods. They may know little about the beliefs and practices of those others. They may not care to know. But they are aware of other calendars and feast-days, of different dietary rules and perhaps dress-styles, of other places of worship. From their parents and elders they learn the subtle art of avoiding interference and preserving communal peace. For many, long centuries most Europeans had little or no experience in this field. No wonder if upon the arrival, after World War II, of other believers, with their customs and mores, Europeans were unprepared: 'Muslim scarves' and other such items soon generated endless controversies. This lack of experience and the resulting lack of expertise could be quite understandable, were it not for the Europeans' itch to act as teachers to the rest of the world.

2. Europe's Religious Landscape

The age of homogeneous Christendom now belongs to the past: the quiet birth of comparative theologies may be just one indication of this development. In this perspective, it may be useful to provide a rough sketch of the new religious landscape and the promises it holds for comparative reflection.

The religious traditions of pre-Christian Europe ceased long ago to play any active part, except perhaps for the Greek or Greco-Roman heritage. Its influence however is felt at the level of philosophical thought rather than religious beliefs, indeed of philosophies that have been duly pruned and divested of any living religious inspiration. Of late, though, there has been a surprising (or perhaps not so surprising) revival of interest in the wisdom and ethical traditions of the Stoa and other ancient schools, including a new appreciation of their 'spiritual exercises'.

From the very start, from New Testament times, Christian-Jewish relations have been a special case, indeed a unique instance of some sort of 'theology of religions' and also of 'comparative theology'. After a long history of contempt and aggressive apologetics, the post-World War II generations have seen significant improvements in dialogue and theology. Selected areas of Jewish thought and spirituality have become a source of inspiration to many Christians[1].

Sadly enough, the contribution of Islam to Christian thinking appears to have lost since ages much of its potential. On issues where agreement or convergence seems possible, the similarities or greater proximity may have dulled theological interest. On issues where disagreements loom large (for example, christology, the Trinity), a negative type of both defensive and offensive apologetics led into a dead end. In a paradoxical way, the fact that Christian faith in Europe does not thrive anymore under the regime of Christendom may prove a hindrance to mutual understanding, due to the lack of correspondence or parallelism between the respective social and political situations of the Christian

---

[1] The relevance of Christian-Jewish relations for a Christian theology of religions and even for comparative theology may be illustrated by the 10-volume *Dogmatique* of Gérard Siegwalt [1], esp. vol. I/2.

and the Muslim communities. However, the rapid pace of change in these fields may open new avenues to fruitful encounter.

Except for a short period of romantic enthusiasm at the beginning of the 19th century, Hinduism has not evoked much response in Europe. To be more accurate, it did not strike roots in coherent and structured ways among the European populations; it actually never earnestly attempted to do so. This did not prevent more diffuse influences on Western thought and values.

While the European 18th century witnessed a wonderful appreciation for Chinese teachings in the fields of ethics and polity, it remains to be seen whether our century, with growing freedom inside China and a more assertive presence abroad, will develop an interest in traditional Chinese wisdom and spiritual practices.

For the last fifty years or so, Buddhism, more than any other tradition, has attracted the attention of a growing and significant minority of Europeans. It is at the intersection of Buddhism and Christianity that much interreligious dialogue, philosophical debate and comparative theology develop and are likely to further develop across our continent. In the European context at least, it is not insignificant that a number of sketches or essays in comparative theology resort to the resources of a tradition to which, in the eyes of many, labels such as 'religion' and 'theology' are rather ill-fitting[2]. It is meaningful as well that Buddhism, in the West and particularly in Europe, is present at the levels of philosophy and psychology as much as theology. European philosophers, not all of them Buddhists, include Buddhist thought in the making of what may be called 'comparative philosophy'; and Buddhist philosophers, both Japanese and Western, deal with European thought. In all likelihood, the philosophical dimension of the encounter will impact comparative theologies as well.

3. Towards New Types of Religion?

Each religion or tradition exhibits distinctive characteristics. In several respects, Buddhism, including its several branches or 'Vehicles' and numerous schools, may be seen as furthest away from Christianity (and other forms of revelation monotheism); yet, the universal claim of its wisdom, as well as an ancient history of adaptation to very different cultures and languages, single it out, if not as *the* spirituality of tomorrow, at least as one of the major spiritual paths for the next generations. When taking into account its appeal to quite a number of Westerners, we are invited to consider, from the perspective of a Christian practice of comparative theology, some characteristics which are not usually included in our understanding of 'religion'. Among those that appear more significant in the Western reception of Buddhism, let us mention briefly:

---

[2] Some Buddhist authors however do not hesitate to use 'theology' in an analogical way. See the volume of essays edited by R.R. Jackson and J.J. Makransky [2].

its individual *and* global or cosmic dimension, while less attention is paid to intermediate rungs of the ladder, such as family or state: this suits rather well the individualism and the political 'weightlessness' of many Europeans today;[3]

its pragmatic approach rooted in the experience of the (phenomenological) subject, with relatively little concern for metaphysical problems;

a rather horizontal or 'immanent' type of transcendance or realization;

a measure of affinity with several philosophical and spiritual schools of the Western (Greco-Roman) Antiquity (before or apart from the Jewish or the Christian heritage);

a mobility and fluidity allowing individuals to break free from religious bonds to space (Jerusalem, Bethlehem, Rome…) and to chronological time or salvation history. If not ignored altogether, such religious bonds to space and time are played down: they become mere 'skillful means' or optional ways divested of any authoritative or compulsory nature. The essential core is the 'here-and-now', in other words, whatever happens to be, to any mobile and autonomous individual subject (but not a self, not a Self!), always and everywhere available and so to say, 'portable'. An apt illustration of this is the usually strong emphasis on meditation, for lay as well as monastic disciples.

4. The Comparative Study of Religions

'Comparative theology', as the label of a recent development and a fledgling discipline, may look a little awkward, especially if one remembers how, about 150 years ago, the young comparative study of religions struggled to break free from denominational theologies considered as static, dogmatic and parochial. No need to go here into the details of a rather complex intellectual and institutional history. One should remember however that the comparative method in the History of religions, particularly in its phenomenological school, attempted to include, in the documentation to be gathered and analyzed, if not all religions past and present, at least a representative sample of the empirical diversity of religions or, to be more accurate, of the diversity of religious types and forms: a rather ambitious program, but a necessary condition if one intends, through the comparison of empirical data and perhaps the method of 'free variation' or the simulation of models, to bring to the light general patterns and deeper structures, distinct and contrasting types of religions and even, in the case of scholars with a more speculative bend of mind, some 'essence' of religion.

As a matter of fact, the available documentation, from prehistorical times up till now, in spite of its gaps and silences, keeps growing day by day. It exceeds by far the strength and resources of any single scholar or team of scholars. Besides, the scientific disciplines and methods which claim to make significant contributions to those ambitious programs of inquiry and analysis, have multiplied and become more differentiated. Even disregarding a number of short-lived and superficial fashions, the intellectual history of rival schools and trends through some 150 years leaves us with a bewildering, sometimes chaotic landscape. Each school or discipline, while offering some new or not so new light,

---

[3] See several contributions to the special issue of the French journal *Esprit* [3]. For insightful commentaries and interpretations from a sociological angle, see for instance Le Quéau [4].

questions or at least relativizes by its very existence the promises and achievements of the others. More than any other, the sociology of knowledge considers all interpretations and conclusions with suspicion or at least with critical caution.

The built-in limitations of any research in the field of social sciences or humanities, as well as the growing awareness of the historicity of both data and scientific tools and theories, contributed to the flowering of various postmodern (or 'late modern') philosophies and ideologies. Even scholars little concerned with such theories came to acknowledge the virtues of prudence and modesty. Most dedicate themselves to monographic studies of a well-demarcated field. Others apply some comparative method to a few items which they feel confident to study with some mastery. These modest approaches usually evoke little response from the public, while more ambitious theories and bold syntheses are welcomed by a broader readership but meet with the skepticism of most scholars.

5. Comparative Theology—Personal Engagement—Intra-religious Dialogue

The present intellectual landscape in the scientific studies of religion may to a certain extent explain the modest style, indeed the spirit of craftsmanship of several pioneering contributions to the new field of 'comparative theology'. While individual factors remain significant, the contrast is impressive between, for instance, the ample syntheses and the synoptic tables of Jacques-Albert Cuttat's *Expérience chrétienne et spiritualité orientale* (1967) [5] and, some thirty years later, the explorations published by Francis X. Clooney [6].

However, other, more specific, factors have played their part.

As was pointed out several times already, the exercise of comparative theology may have provided a welcome opportunity to scholars tired of or puzzled by and somewhat skeptical about the current state of the (mostly Christian) theologies of religions: their global approach, the vague tone of their discourse, their a priori methodology, the absence of concrete data. Tackling limited, discrete issues could be a way to start afresh, to proceed from the bottom up. It would also remind one how important and fruitful it is to build on personal relationships of encounter and dialogue. The in-depth study of the data and (whenever possible) the courteous meeting with other believers require a patient, modest and rather selective or sectorial approach.

Comparative theology, more so than the comparative or other methods in use among historians of religions, requires personal commitment. The believer-cum-theologian, rooted in a particular tradition and community, is expected to go through a process of 'crossing over' and 'coming back' (or 'coming home'), a process of discernment and integration, which demands more time and maturing than the 'mere' comparison undertaken by an external, detached and 'objective' observer. One might even consider comparative theology, at least in the last stage of its process, as a form of '*intra*-religious dialogue' if, following Raimon Panikkar's suggestion [7], one understands this as the quiet echo and the continuation or further maturing and elaboration, in the heart and mind of each believer, of her experience of *inter*-religious encounter and dialogue.

6. Comparative Theology: Too Narrow?

If practiced on the narrow base of familiar concepts of religion, comparative theology is liable to suffer from several defects or shortcomings. These would affect its contents, their perception, and the intended audience.

6.1. Contents

Comparative theologians should remain alert to the risk of developing their reflection against the background of some vague 'religious' anthropology or some ideology of the 'sacred'. The danger or temptation, which is sometimes allowed to remain unattended, would be to pay exclusive attention to items that are common or alleged to be common to all religious cultures, thereby ignoring other dimensions and potentialities of human beings and societies. In order to avoid or reduce the danger of too narrow a base, it may be advisable to use some broader categories, such as Tillich's 'ultimate concern'. But such devices will have a merely cosmetic effect unless they call our attention to concrete manifestations of this ultimate concern outside the area of what is spontaneously and traditionally considered as 'religious' or 'sacred'. All sorts of anthropological issues, themes, values and symbols are likely to fall through the 'religious' sieve and get lost or be discarded as irrelevant to the comparative theologian's endeavor.

It may be useful, in this context, to remind briefly that the very word and concept 'religion' are far from being universal: several scholars called our attention to the genesis and development of *'religio'* in the Latin language and the Roman culture, as well as to the impact, somewhat later, of Jewish and above all of Christian thought upon its further evolution [8,9]. There is no adequate correspondence between 'religion' and axial terms and concepts in use in other civilizations, for instance *dîn, dharma* or *jiao* [10]. Even if some clear and precise standard definition of 'religion' or 'sacred' could be coined and adopted by convention, one should not expect that a particular phenomenon considered as 'religious' in the ambit of a given tradition would necessarily be interpreted as such in other contexts. Even within the boundaries of a single cultural world, phenomena which for centuries have been deemed 'religious' or 'sacred' may come to lose this qualification.

6.2. Perception

The point at issue is not the mere fact that items (notions and images, patterns of behavior, norms and values) may fail to appear under our searching 'religious' light. It will not be a simple case of absence or of incomplete documentation. Whatever their relationships may have been in past centuries, religion and the absence or denial of religion nowadays are correlative. Belief grows and thrives or decays in a context of non-belief; in other words, belief appears against a background of (at least, possible) non-belief; indeed, in a number of present-day societies and in many social, professional and other circles, belief is less plausible than its opposite.

The non-religious backdrop against which particular religious traditions appear is not neutral or innocuous. It affects every religious aspiration, its exercise and its manifestations. It questions what religion and religions are likely to claim as obvious, as a matter of course: for instance, the links between cosmology and religious narrative, between political power and its religious foundations, between cure and prayer or atonement. The non-religious background or the non-religious dominant culture impacts, often in unsuspected ways, the perception religions shape of themselves. Is it (was it ever? is it still?) possible for them to offer keys opening an access to reality as a whole, to the whole of reality?

Actually, when atheism, agnosticism, absence of God or silence about God are taken into consideration as the context in which discourses on religion (including comparative theologies) may, at the dawn of the third millennium, take shape in Europe, it will soon become evident that versions of atheism or agnosticism are as numerous and diverse as the forms of religious conviction and confession. The growing interest in Buddhism and other Far Eastern teachings, as well as the rediscovery of some wisdom schools of Western Antiquity, add diversity to the landscape; these traditions may also function as bridges or open new perspectives beyond the familiar binary confrontation between Christian faith and modern Western types of atheism. The exercise of comparative theology becomes more complex but also more promising. It remains however to be seen whether and how representatives of these atheistic or agnostic traditions will join the conversation.

Buddhism, once more, may have here a particular role to play. Monotheistic religions built upon a revelation do experience a weakening or decline of the monopoly they at one time claimed on the European populations. This is already clearly the case for Judaism and Christianity; European Islam or Islam in Europe may not remain forever immune to that trend. Certain forms of 'scientific' atheism and materialism do not fare much better. On the ground left free by the ebb tide, there is plenty of space for other images of the world, new types of interiority, new forms of spiritual quest. A selective interest in Buddhist teachings helps fill the gap. In turn, as in a spiral movement, a growing familiarity with Buddhism and a few other schools opens our eyes to neglected dimensions or underexploited resources of culture and spirituality. While the range of options is fast growing, the temptation to monopolize the history of religions or comparative theologies as an exercise in apologetics should recede.

6.3. *Audience*

If 'religious' matters, in the usual sense of the word, constitute the exclusive basis of comparative theologies, if the denial or absence of religion is not acknowledged as possible, plausible, indeed probable in large sections of the public, comparative theologians may have to lecture in front of empty seats. Comparative theology will lose or never regain much of its audience. It is hard to see how it could be of interest to persons and even circles where religion, especially religious—and even more Christian—doctrines and theological debates seem irrelevant.

In countries such as France and most of Central and Eastern Europe, the spirit of *laïcité* or a historical heritage of state atheism reduced the place of religion in most universities to almost nil. Even such disciplines as history of religions or comparative religion are rather underdeveloped. There is a lingering suspicion that they do not meet scientific standards or, worse, that they may cover up some sort of religious, confessional and parochial apologetics. Theology as a matter of course has been relegated to private, denominational institutions outside the University. No wonder comparative theology is almost unheard of, with the rare exception of a few Church faculties. While the general public is unaware of its existence, even most believers do not realize its relevance and potential, not to mention those who are afraid of syncretistic drift. As a consequence, believers are left without resources in the face of a growing pluralism at the philosophical and religious level. A broader, more inclusive approach to comparative theology may meet the interest of a larger public. And addressing new audiences may in turn foster new ways of doing comparative theology.

6.4. Authority—Creativity—Reception

The weakening hold of religion on large sectors of the European population makes it all the more urgent to tackle the question of authority in comparative theology. The authority of a text (or a practice, a norm, a model figure…) is at stake both on the side of the 'lending' tradition and of the 'borrowing' one. The weight of authority of a borrowed element has to be ascertained. To put it less forcefully, determining its level and mode of authority should help understand the meaning and significance of that element in the context of its own tradition. But that weight of authority will not necessarily dictate its value or importance in the eyes of the borrowing or receiving tradition. It all depends on the main objective aimed at. If the comparative theologian values lasting and global relations of exchange and dialogue, she will give priority to elements acknowledged by the lending tradition as important and authoritative. And she will take seriously the ways of reading indigenous to that tradition.

This concern, however, may have to do with interreligious relations rather than comparative theology as such, where interests and priorities are to a larger extent determined from the point of view of the borrowing tradition. To the 'borrower', a religious item (text, teaching, ritual, symbol) may appear significant and worthy of interest in spite of the fact that the lending tradition considers it less important, marginal, or even unorthodox and unacceptable. In many cases, its value will depend on its capacity to give expression to and transmit a spiritual experience or a wise teaching. From the point of view of the borrowing tradition, even elements that cannot be integrated or assimilated may be appreciated for their potential to surprise, stimulate, and renew: they give food for thought. This happens frequently, for instance, in exchanges between Christianity and Buddhism.

Now, when we come to the second stage of the comparative theology process, the constructive phase where elements discovered in the lending tradition are welcomed by the theologian intending to use them in a creative way as a resource to deepen and further elaborate her own reflection, the weight of authority granted to these new developments does not remain a purely individual issue but becomes the concern of a believing community. The 'reception' by the community—in ways that differ in accordance with the principles of each religious tradition—plays a decisive part. This reception may well undergo evolutions and revisions, but it is one essential condition of the theological value and validity of the whole enterprise.

Our present postmodern or late modern situation, however, bears the mark of a great fluidity and of the individual nature of initiatives, encounters, experiences, and reflection. It is then to be expected that reception by a community will be deemed less important or even negligible. The interest, value and fruitfulness of a reflective and spiritual process involving 'foreign' resources will rather be measured against personal aspirations and changing expectations. This fluidity and weightlessness make it ever more difficult to foresee the outcome of contacts and exchanges between religions or wisdom traditions, between communities.

Mobility and fluidity impact the style and method of theological work: they lead either in the direction of extreme porosity and eventual dilution or in the line of defensive assertions of identity, culminating in traditionalist or fundamentalist postures. It remains to be seen how each particular tradition (Hinduism, Buddhism, Christianity) will muster the necessary intellectual and spiritual resources to avoid both pitfalls. Wisdom teachings based on personal experience are likely to be less disturbed, while monotheistic faiths based on some form of divine revelation may experience more destabilizing jolts.

7. Is Comparison Outdated?

In other words, does comparative work have a future? The following pessimistic hypothesis could be formulated: the 'comparative age' is (has been?) but a brief intermezzo, a transitional phase in the history of culture. According to such a scenario, the story unfolds in three stages:

First, the age of identities, of cultural, religious and other forms of ethnocentrism, usually accompanied by a feeling of superiority—whether naive, quietly unassuming or full of contempt. As we know from experience, even a message claiming universal validity and aiming at reducing discriminations, may consciously or unconsciously carry some imperialistic urge to spread an exclusive model, one single reference, till the ends of the world. This is sometimes the impression left, for instance, by Western or Western-inspired manifestos on behalf of the 'human rights'. Far from being open to difference, to the different 'other', such moves tend to reduce and assimilate the other to the self. The model advocated, sometimes under the guise of some utopia, may be but the extension of my (our) own identity, an identity brandished as the secret key of history or the basic law of reason.

After the long era of identities, humankind entered the age of difference, the discovery and appreciation of otherness. This may be illustrated by intellectual and cultural ventures such as ethnology, anthropology, the comparative history of religions; that is also where interreligious dialogue draws inspiration from. Comparative study may manifest a genuine openness to the other as such, to her difference and singularity. But it also happens that the image of the other is used as a device at the service of the self: the representation of the other is then nothing but a tool for the critique and improvement of one's own society. This was probably the main objective of 18th-century French writings such as *Lettres persanes* or *Lettres chinoises*; a number of Utopian novels and even 'science fiction' stories have similar aims.

In the age of difference, contrary to the French saying "*Comparaison n'est pas raison*", comparison puts reason to work: it gives food for thought or challenges entrenched forms of reason. When long-distance travel and trade are common fare, when planet Earth seems to be shrinking, knowledge about the other(s) becomes unavoidable: comparison belongs to reason.

The comparative age, however, seems to lead, by some iron law, beyond stable identities, into a mobile and fluid world. We have come under the spell of some postmodern subtle mood suggesting that identities and differences are elusive and rather irrelevant. When pushed to the extreme(s), individualism and the worship of the singular (values which paradoxically may be shared by a large majority of the population…) make comparison almost an impossible task. More importantly, comparison becomes useless and meaningless: why on earth take the trouble to compare autonomous singularities which may prefer not to expect anything from one another?

Yet it is to be feared that the lack of interest in the other, even if laced at the beginning with polite, non-aggressive benevolence, may eventually lead to violent confrontation. In our globalized, crowded and complex world, the art of living together demands the patient practice of conversation and the readiness to learn from our differences. In our world, comparative theologies have a role to play, even at the level of culture, society and polity.

Conflicts of Interest

The author declares no conflict of interest.

References

1. Siegwalt, Gérard. *Dogmatique pour la catholicité évangélique*. Paris: Cerf, 1986–2007, 5 vols. in 10 parts.
2. Jackson, Roger R., and John J. Makransky, Ed. *Buddhist Theology: Critical Reflections by Contemporary Buddhist Scholars*. London: Routledge Curzon, 2000.
3. "L'avenir des religions sans Dieu." *Esprit* 233 (June 1997): 1–328.
4. Le Quéau, Pierre. *La tentation bouddhiste*. Paris: Desclée de Brouwer, 1998.
5. Scheuer, J. "'Effectuer en nous-mêmes le geste intérieur…': la contribution de J.-A. Cuttat à la rencontre des religions." *Nouvelle Revue Théologique* 129 (2007): 64–86.
6. Scheuer, J. "Interreligieuse, dialogale, confessionnelle: la théologie comparative de Fr.X. Clooney." *Revue théologique de Louvain* 36 (2005): 42–71.
7. Panikkar, Raimundo. *The Intrareligious Dialogue*. New York: Paulist Press, 1999.
8. Despland, Michel. *La religion en Occident: évolution des idées et du vécu*. Paris: Cerf, 1979.
9. Feil, Ernst *Religio. Die Geschichte eines neuzeitlichen Grundbegriffs*. Göttingen: Vandenhoeck und Ruprecht, 3 vols., 1986, 1997, 2001.
10. Bianchi, Ugo, ed. *The Notion of 'Religion' in Comparative Research*. Rome: L'Erma di Bretschneider, 1994.

Reprinted from *Religions*. Cite as: Ganeri, Martin. "Tradition with a New Identity: Thomist Engagement with Non-Christian Thought as a Model for the New Comparative Theology in Europe." *Religions* 3 (2012): 1054-1074.

Article

Tradition with a New Identity: Thomist Engagement with Non-Christian Thought as a Model for the New Comparative Theology in Europe

Martin Ganeri

Heythrop College, University of London, Kensington Square, London W8 5HQ, UK;
E-Mail: m.ganeri@heythrop.ac.uk

Received: 26 September 2012; in revised form: 13 October 2012 / Accepted: 16 October 2012 / Published: 6 November 2012

Abstract: British theologians have criticised contemporary comparative theology for privileging learning from other religions to the exclusion of challenge and transformation in the Christian encounter with the thought of other religions. Moreover, a wider concern in Britain about contemporary expressions of theology in the academy, including comparative theology, is about their accountability to the ecclesial communities to which theologians belong. This paper aims to retrieve the Thomist engagement with non-Christian thought as a model for contemporary comparative theology that also addresses these concerns. The paper outlines Aquinas' understanding of Christian theology's engagement with non-Christian thought as being one of transformation, using the Biblical image of water changing into wine to illustrate what is involved. The paper points to historical examples of Thomist encounters with Indian thought and suggests some new applications. Using the Thomist model for contemporary comparative theology is a case of tradition coming to have a new identity, one that balances learning with challenge and transformation, one that bridges the divide between the academic and the ecclesial exercise of theology.

Keywords: comparative theology; Thomas Aquinas; Catholic Church

1. Introduction

This article emerges out of my own experience as a British Catholic theologian and Dominican friar of the Province of England, who is engaged in the exercise of comparative theology in the university and seminary contexts and concerned to explore what form of comparative theology might bridge the gap that often exists between what is possible to do in the university and what is acceptable and attractive to the wider Catholic community. Within the English speaking Catholic community in Europe there are a number of attitudes that are becoming increasingly widely and strongly held among the younger generation and which Catholic theologians have to address: first, a suspicion of contemporary theologies of religions and of interreligious dialogue as supporting a doctrinal position that does not hold clearly enough to traditional and official Catholic teaching; second, a concern over the degree to which the theology done in the modern university context is still carried as a confessional discipline that has a clear connection with and is accountable to the ecclesial community and faith traditions to which the theologian belongs; and third, a re-emphasis on the classical theological traditions of Catholic Christianity as found in the Fathers of the Church and Scholastic theology as providing the theological account necessary for sustaining the present and next generation of Catholics, along with an affirmation of Pope Benedict's teaching that the documents of the Second Vatican Council, including those dealing with other religions, should be read within a 'hermeneutic of reform' marked by renewal in continuity with these earlier theological and doctrinal traditions of the Church [1]. All three attitudes reflect concerns over what is felt necessary for the Church to continue in the highly secularised context in which the European Catholic community finds itself.

The new comparative theology has as yet gained little acceptance in Britain among Catholic theologians, or by those in theological or seminary training, or within the wider Catholic community. Getting beyond this is very difficult, not least because comparative theology is easily taken as epitomising what is objected to by those who hold the three attitudes I have outlined above: comparative theology's emphasis on respectful openness to and learning from other religious traditions seems very close to an affirmation of pluralist and relativist theology of religions; the different forms of comparative theology developed in the academic context often have no clear connection to the norms of ecclesial traditions and are often perceived to be indistinguishable from the more secular disciplines of comparative religion or religious studies; moreover, the very 'newness' of the new comparative theology seems to make it very much one of those forms of Catholic theology emergent since the Second Vatican Council which are characterised by a 'hermeneutic of discontinuity and rupture,' breaking with the classical traditions of patristic and Scholastic theology and with traditional doctrinal teaching.

For such reasons comparative theology is seen as being on the edge of mainstream Catholic theology. This is unfortunate, when the pioneers of Catholic comparative theologians, such as Francis Clooney and James Fredericks, themselves both Catholic priests, have taken pains to assert that comparative theology is distinct from religious studies precisely by being confessional in character, as something done by believers and for believers, as 'faith seeking understanding' (*fides quaerens intellectum*) in the classical Western formulation of theology. Moreover, considerable space is given by such theologians to reading classical Christian texts alongside those of other religious traditions. However, there is a gap between such claims and the actual perception and reception comparative theology has had.

In such a situation, in order for comparative theology to gain greater acceptance and credibility within the wider Catholic community, those engaged in it would do well to show clearly that it can address the concerns and expectations of that community. With this aim in mind, in the years in which I have myself been engaged in comparative theology, it has seemed to me necessary to return to and to retrieve the classical models within Christian theology for engagement with non-Christian traditions and to demonstrate that comparative theology is in continuity with them, that it is *tradition with a new identity*. My own work has centred on a comparative encounter between the Scholastic theology of the 13th century Dominican theologian Thomas Aquinas (1224/5–74), the most influential of all the Scholastics, and the Hindu tradition of Vedānta and so it has been natural for me to revisit the model Aquinas himself gives for engaging with non-Christian thought. Comparative theologians working with the Church Fathers or other Scholastic thinkers might want to consider how well the different models of engagement found in those other thinks might work as forms of comparative theology.

In this article, then, I would like to consider the approach taken by Thomas Aquinas as a form of comparative theology that is thoroughly traditional, but also capable of being thoroughly contemporary. It is one that helps bridge the gap between the exercise of comparative theology within an academic context and the expectations of the ecclesial community to which that theologian belongs, in this case the Catholic community. Moreover, Aquinas's account is instructive in itself as a model of how do comparative theology in that he sets out a number of general principles that show why and how Christian theology can engage constructively with non-Christian thought and he gives us a very clear analysis of the actual process involved in Christian theological engagement with non-Christian thought, what happens to that thought as it is assimilated into Christian theology. As a pattern for engagement, then, it remains very helpful.

At first sight, however, it might seem an odd thing to look to Thomas Aquinas for a form of comparative theology. Was not Aquinas rather more against the Gentiles than for them, as the title of one of his major works, the *Summa Contra Gentiles*, suggests? Yet, if we read his works what is remarkable is the extent to which he does engage with non-Christian thinkers, whether Greek, Jewish or Muslim, as he explores and constructs his own Christian theology. Aquinas takes them seriously and he takes pains to argue that Christian theology can engage with and learn from their thought without the integrity of Christian faith being undermined. His resultant theology is in fact profoundly shaped by non-Christian thought.

In the Catholic tradition Thomism has enjoyed very considerable prestige and has impeccable credentials as a normative model for any theology to follow. There is also currently a revival of Thomist studies, finding new ways of reading and applying the thought of Aquinas to the current concerns of theology and the Catholic community. Contemporary Thomists have themselves increasingly come to characterise the work of Aquinas and other Scholastics as interreligious and comparative in nature, as they relate their work to contemporary disciplines of study, including comparative theology ([2–4]; and other essays in [5]). The continuing importance of the Thomist tradition for Catholic theological engagement with non-Christian thought within official Catholic Church teaching can be seen in the fact that as recently as 1998, in *Fides et Ratio*, Blessed John Paul II commends Thomas Aquinas as a model for doing theology in the contemporary world because of his 'dialogical' engagement with Jewish and Arab teaching as well as with Greek philosophy (*FR 43*). The Pope also encourages further contemporary engagement with non-Christian cultures and their traditions (*FR 72*).

In order to expand on the initial points I have made about the context and perception of comparative theology, I shall first consider the work of Gavin D'Costa as the British theologian who has responded most fully to comparative theology. I then outline the model Aquinas himself gives, with examples of how it has been used by later Catholic theologians and of how it might be applied to new engagements with non-Christian thought. The retrieval of such a classical model does not have to mean that a contemporary comparative theologian is unable to change and adapt it and so find a new identity for it and in the final section of this article I indicate ways in which the model should be developed to incorporate shifts in contemporary Catholic reflection on other religions as well as the methods and concerns found in the new comparative theology.

2. A British Theologian Reflects on the Context and Exercise of the New Comparative Theology

Professor Gavin D'Costa, who holds a chair in Christian Theology at Bristol University is one of the UK's leading Catholic theologians. D'Costa's perspectives are important for those interested in the reception of the new comparative theology in English speaking Europe, because he is a theologian who represents the three attitudes I noted in the introduction, but also one very interested in a sustained and positive engagement with other religious traditions. D'Costa is not a comparative theologian as such, but has been very much concerned with Christian theology of religions and with the exercise of such theology in the contemporary English-speaking academy [6–9]. D'Costa is sympathetic to the aims and approaches of the new comparative theology, but also critical of many of its manifestations as failing to be sufficiently theological and doctrinal in character. Central to D'Costa's position is the affirmation of the tradition-specific nature of any theology of religions, so that other religions are inevitably approached from within the theologian's own perspectives and evaluative criteria. D'Costa's positive vision for the future of academic theology of any kind also involves a retrieval of classical and specifically Thomist models of theology.

D'Costa's wider concerns about and programme for theology as a discipline in the modern academy, as set out in his study, *Theology in the Public Square: Church, Academy and Nation* (2005). D'Costa does not deal explicitly with comparative theology in this book, but his arguments provide a wider context for understanding and appraising his critical affirmation of comparative theology. D'Costa argues that contemporary universities in the English-speaking world have become increasingly secularised. The discipline of theology in these institutions is likewise losing its tradition-specific and confessional character and becoming increasingly replaced by, or translated into, religious studies, the modern discipline held ideally to operate as the phenomenological study of a variety of religious traditions determined by the application of neutral reasoning. Examining accounts of how the shift from theology to religious studies has taken place in academic institutions, D'Costa finds a key element to be the separation of theology done in the academy from the ecclesial community, whether it be it through loss of Church control over the institution, diminished employment of practising members of that ecclesial community to be governors and teaching staff within the university, or the decline of a clear relationship between the shape and practice of theology and the faith traditions of the ecclesial community ([10], pp. 40ff). The greater such separation becomes, the more difficult it has been for confessional theology to maintain a place in the university context.

The alternative to, or remedy for, the demise of theology in academic institutions lies in a retrieval and explicit reaffirmation of the connection with the ecclesial community to which the theologian belongs. As modern examples of what form such a connection looks like from a perspective of official Catholic teaching, D'Costa points to two recent official documents of Catholic Church: *Ex Corde Ecclesia* (On Catholic Universities), issued in 1990 by Blessed John Paul II and on the *Ecclesial Vocation of the Theologian*, published by the Congregation of the Doctrine of the Faith also in 1990, documents which emphasise the intellectual connections that should exist with the doctrinal and moral traditions the Catholic Church, as well as the spiritual and ethical dimensions of doing theology, with God himself the ultimate object of all theology and of human life. Far from resulting in a sectarian retreat from interest in and engagement with other religious traditions, such documents promote a positive engagement with other academic disciplines, including the study of other religions. As D'Costa puts it, quoting from *ex Corde Ecclesiae*:

[t]he theological understanding suggested here, although not unpacked in minute detail, envisages mutual conversations and enrichment with theology as the initiator, as it is able to straddle the disciplinary boundaries of each subject. Theology:

serves other disciplines in their search for meaning, not only by helping them to investigate how their discoveries will affect individuals and society but also by bringing a perspective and an orientation not contained within their own methodologies. In turn, interaction with these other disciplines and their discoveries enriches theology, offering it a better understanding of the world today, and making theological research more relevant to current needs. Because of its specific importance among the academic disciplines, every Catholic university should have a faculty, or at least a chair, of theology ([10], pp. 95–96).

D'Costa looks to Patristic and Scholastic views about Christian theological engagement with philosophy, the non-Christian learning available at the time, as models for understanding how to do theology in the present ([10], pp. 7ff). In the Patristic period he identifies three attitudes towards engagement with philosophy: first, the position which shunned engagement, often associated with Tertullian (c.160–225), that since all truth and salvation were to be found in the Bible such philosophy was of no value; second, the critical encounter and accommodation of Justin Martyr (c.100–165) and many following him:

The second, containing rich diversity, sees the Greek philosophical heritage as *preparatio* (preparation) and *paidagogus* (an education finally aiming at Christ). Origen (c.185–254) uses the metaphor of the ransack of the Egyptians for the future of Israel, so that all leaning could in principle be turned to the service of God ([10], p. 7).

And third, opposition to uncritical adoption of philosophical concepts in such a way that they shape and determine the Christian message rather are shaped and transformed by it.

It is the second approach that D'Costa favours as the right way for the present and for his vision of how theology should operate in the contemporary academy. D'Costa points to the flowering of this approach in the Medieval period, which saw the emergence both of the institution of the Western university and of Scholastic theology within it, manifest in the work of such Scholastic theologians as Albert the Great (1079–1142) and Thomas Aquinas:

> [d]ialectics becomes firmly established as part of Christian education, giving an important role to *ratio*, thereby providing a bridge between all forms of knowledge and learning and Christian revelation. This was embodied in the Aquinas's great synthesis of the Aristotelian and Augustinian traditions in Thomism, providing an important role for philosophy, adequately Christianized, to expound doctrine. It also allowed Aquinas to relate the different disciplines and show the role of the virtues (both intellectual and moral) in education. It also showed in practice how all knowledge can be integrated, critically, into the Christian vision. Aristotle, Islamic appropriation of Aristotle, and Greek philosophy are all brought to the aid of Christian theology in Aquinas. My own book flows out of this tradition. ([10], p. 12)

Fundamental to D'Costa's position is to defend the place of confessional theology in the modern academy against the argument that religious studies is preferable, because it is a neutral discipline. Here he follows closely the influential position put forward by the moral philosopher Alisdair MacIntyre, who argues that all reasoning and practice is tradition-specific and who rejects modernity's claim to be able to advance neutral disciplines ([10], pp. 13, 26, 88ff). Any intellectual system or rationality is formed within a particular system and this conditions the reasoning of those within that tradition and hence their perspectives on other cultures. There is thus no neutral vantage point from which to view different religious traditions.

What D'Costa is proposing here about theological engagement with other religious traditions turns out to have a great deal in common with the stance taken by new comparative theologians, when they insist that comparative theology is different from religious studies, precisely because it is confessional theology. The convergence between what D'Costa proposes and comparative theology, *qua* theology, can be seen later in the book when D'Costa draws together his arguments and explores how such a confessional theology is able to produce a 'theological religious studies' ([10], p. 144). Here he considers two cases of women from different religious traditions who are revered for the manner of their deaths, understood to be acts of atonement for their own sins and those of others: the Hindu Sati Roop Kanwar and the Christian martyr, Edith Stein. D'Costa aims to 'to show how a theological reading is often able to understand what modernity cannot: religious self-sacrifice as a means of winning merit through grace ([10], p. 145). Rather than establishing a neutral common concept of holiness or sanctity as a cross-cultural category, which tends to downplay and hence distort the irreducible difference of traditions, he argues that a Christian theologian can study another religion in its integrity, but will also view it from within Christian categories of sanctity. Thereby, the theologian may come to recognise in Roop Kanwar both the presence of a self-sacrificing sanctity of the sort present in the case of Edith Stein and the work of divine grace in her actions ([10], chapter 5).

D'Costa's final goal, it has to be said, is to have separate institutions where Catholic theology can function with integrity ([10], pp. 216–7). Even without this, however, he can still see a place for theologians within the wider modern academy insofar as they can maintain the distinctive character of their discipline, sustained by explicit connections with the ecclesial community and its traditions of faith and theology. D'Costa's arguments, it seems to me, are true of the wider context in which theology is being done in contemporary British universities and hence true of the context in which comparative theology is done as well. For this reason, I want to concretise D'Costa's suggestions and explore what it means to do comparative theology within the frame developed by Thomas Aquinas, as a theological approach that does have a very strong connection with the Catholic ecclesial community and its traditions, while also engaging with non-Christian thought from within the interpretive criteria of Christian faith, evaluating and transforming the thought it encounters so that this thought serves to enrich the expression of Christian faith.

D'Costa also comments explicitly on the new comparative theology and how well it fits his own understanding of what is necessary in Christian theological engagement with other religions. In *Christianity and World Religions: Disputed Questions in the Theology of Religions* (2009) D'Costa recognises comparative theology as an approach to Christian engagement with other religions that wants to do something different from earlier forms of theology of religions concerned with general theories of other religions, especially their salvific status. D'Costa agrees with central features of the new comparative theology, such as its insistence on particular engagements with texts and on the potential for such encounters to transform Christian self-understanding. However, he disagrees with the position taken by Fredericks that separates dialogical encounter from theology of religions, since, in D'Costa's view, some kind of theological perspective is always present in any encounter. Moreover, he criticises the fact that, despite the confessional stance of comparative theologians and their insistence on the evaluative nature of the approach, what is stressed is learning from other religions (what he otherwise calls inculturation), whereas judgements from the perspective of one's one tradition about the truth of what is encountered (what he otherwise refers to as missiology) tend not to be raised. Here comparative theology is not being true to itself as a tradition-specific confessional theology:

> I would prefer to see theology of religions and comparative theology as complementary, as aspects of dogma on the one hand, and missiology and inculturation on the other. In the latter, the reality of other religions must be confronted and its exact contours responded to in terms of apologetics, proclamation, dialogue, and learning from, and one must be attentive to the ways in which some of the new findings might generate fresh dogmatic questions ([7], p. 45).

D'Costa picks out the approach taken by Raimon Panikkar (1918–2010) in the first edition of the *Unknown Christ of Hinduism* (1964)[1] as model for the kind of comparative theology he would like to see more of. In the third part of the book, Panikkar develops what he calls a Christological *bhāṣya*, or commentary, on a Hindu Vedāntic text. Panikkar, as a Christian theologian, identifies the *Īśvara*, the creative Lord, in Vedānta with Christ and thus reads Vedānta in the light of Christian faith in the Trinity. This, Panikkar argues, helps resolve a genuine difficulty within Vedānta about how to relate the Absolute (*Brahman*) to the world. Panikkar is thus engaged, like contemporary comparative theologians, in a serious engagement with particular aspects of a text and tradition within Hinduism. However, Panikkar is also looking at this from a Christian theological perspective and makes a judgement about the truth of what he studies in terms of the presence of Christ ([7], pp. 40–45). This is an approach very similar to what D'Costa does in his own 'theological religious studies.' As D'Costa comments:

> This too is comparative theology, but in a mode that is not at all present in the work of the comparative theologians I have examined. It exhibits all the positive characteristics of the present movement, but in contrast is also able to really engage with the other, asking penetrating questions, putting challenges, engaging in mission at the very same time as really trying to understand the other in its own terms ([7], p. 43).

D'Costa, then, is very much in favour of the kind of encounter with other religions found in comparative theology, but wants to keep the two aspects of theological appraisal of and learning from other religions together. This, he argues is the mark of classical Christian theologians, including Aquinas:

> As with any area of theology, it is demanding, and it requires learning beyond the traditional boundaries of the theological discipline. Nevertheless, historically, the greatest theologians have often done this: Aquinas, for instance, in his immersion in the Aristotelian heritage transmitted through the Arabs, injected into theology both new vigour and a profound critique of alternative traditions. Dialogue and mission are indeed part of the same activity ([7], p. 54).

D'Costa's concern to integrate theology of religions with comparative theology and to balance doctrinal evaluation and transformation with learning is representative of responses by other theologians to the new comparative theology, as well as of internal debates among comparative theologians themselves.[2] Again, it is the Thomist approach that provides a good model for doing a form of comparative theology that meets these concerns. Panikkar, likewise, describes what he is doing as like Aquinas' creative use of Greek thought ([13], pp. 134–7).

---

[1] In the second edition of this work (1981) Panikkar's theological position has shifted somewhat more towards a pluralist theology and hence does not serve to illustrate what D'Costa has in mind.

[2] See, for instance, the review by Daniel Keating of Clooney's book, *The Truth, the Way, the Life: Christian Commentary on the Three Holy Mantras of the Śrīvaiṣnava Hindus* ([11], pp. 283–6). For a sustained examination of this issue within the new comparative theology and argument for the role of theology of religions by a comparative theologian, see Kristin Beise Kiblinger, ([12], pp. 21–42).

3. Theology and non-Christian Thought in the Work of Thomas Aquinas

I would now like to consider what kind of model Aquinas himself gives us for theological engagement with non-Christian thought, in the hope that it can both meet the concerns expressed by D'Costa and serve as a positive support for the type of engagements developed in modern comparative theology. For his part, Aquinas does not use the English terms 'theology' or 'non-Christian thought.' Instead he uses the Latin terms *sacra doctrina* and *philosophia*. *Sacra doctrina* (sacred teaching) is more narrowly used to mean divine revelation, the revealed truths of faith, but also by extension means the reflection on this revelation that Christian thinkers undertake, what the modern academy would call 'Christian theology.'[3] On the other hand, *philosophia* is used to refer to the disciplined exercise of natural reason, to the natural truths discovered through the exercise of natural reason, and to the works of non-Christian thinkers, be they ancient Greek or medieval Jewish and Islamic, in which these are contained. I shall generally translate *sacra doctrina* as 'Christian theology,' reserving the term 'revelation' for cases where the narrower term is more appropriate, using the term *sacra doctrina* when both senses are to be understood. I shall likewise translate *philosophia* as 'philosophical work' or 'natural reasoning' as appropriate, using the term 'philosophy' when both are meant. Aquinas' account of how Christian theology can make positive use of non-Christian philosophical works is the basis for identifying his work as a version of comparative theology.

In Aquinas' most influential work, the *Summa Theologiae*, Christian theology is depicted as a *scientia*, a 'science' in the sense of a systematic body of knowledge, developed by reasoning from a set of first principles to further conclusions (*Summa Theologiae* (henceforth S.T.) 1.1.8).[4] While the labelling of *sacra doctrina* as a *scientia* is not new to Aquinas, Aquinas was the first to treat theology as a true *scientia* in the Aristotelian sense of the term. And in so doing Aquinas thus consciously adopts a non-Christian methodology for structuring his account of Christian revelation and Christian theology.

Within this theological science, the first principles are the articles of faith taken from divine revelation, which are then explored and explained through the resources of philosophical works and the exercise of human reasoning. Philosophical works are accepted as 'authorities,' which in different ways further the exploration of revelation. Aquinas argues that such authorities serve, 'not indeed to prove faith...but to make manifest certain things which are handed down in revelation (*hac doctrina*).' (S.T.1.1.8 ad 2). For Aquinas the authority of non-Christian philosophical works cannot be placed on an equal footing with either the authority of divine revelation found in the cannon of Scripture or with the authority of the doctors of the Church, but nonetheless they have a legitimate and indeed very important role to play in the construction of Christian theology (S.T.1.1.8 ad 2).

In the *Summa Theologiae* and other works Aquinas uses a number of scriptural images to characterise what happens when Christian theology engages with philosophy. The most striking of

---

[3] Which sense Aquinas means in the opening question of his mature work, the *Summa Theologiae*, has been subject to considerable debate. In this and his other works taken as a whole, however, both senses would seem to be implied.

[4] For the *Summa Theologiae* see [14].

these is the more Johannine image of changing water into wine and it is this image which best conveys what kind of comparative theology we find in his work. Aquinas' approach is one of engaged, constructive theology, one that appropriates and transforms the non-Christian thought it encounters. Such an image of the encounter also accords quite well with contemporary appraisals of what is involved in cross-cultural engagements: that any attempt to assimilate the concepts and practices of one culture into another or involves some degree of rupture and change. Another aspect of MacIntyre's position about the tradition-specific nature of all rationality is that, because terms and concepts are embedded in their own traditions, any attempt to translate or use them by another tradition will involve a process of change of what they meant in their own tradition as they become integrated into one's own tradition ([15], pp. 370–88).

Aquinas develops the image of water into wine in his commentary on Boethius' *De Trinitate* [16]. Although this is an early and relatively minor text of Aquinas, it is here that he gives his fullest treatment of the way Christian theology engages with philosophy, the fundamental features of which are then re-affirmed and further articulated in other works, according to the particular concerns of those works. The *de Trinitate* has thus remained a primary text for understanding the way Aquinas conceives of the relation between Christian theology and philosophy.[5]

3.1. Watering Wine Down or Changing Water into Wine

One recurrent objection to Christian theology engaging with philosophy is the idea that this introduces something foreign into Christian theology and hence that it dilutes Christian faith. This is the first and third attitudes D'Costa identifies that Christian theologians took in the Patristic period and which remained as newer forms of philosophy were encountered. In contemporary Catholic theology it is reflected in a general reluctance to study the thought of other religious traditions. The image of water and wine occurs a number of times in Scholastic works in the context of just such a concern.[6] In the 13th century there was considerable controversy over the use of the thought of Aristotle communicated via the Arab translations and commentaries of Avicenna and Averroes, both over particular points where this thought seemed to contradict revelation, such as the eternity of the world, and also over the desire on the part of some Christian scholars to make philosophy the sole criterion and means for knowing truth.[7] This is very much the third approach D'Costa identifies in the Patristic

---

[5] For good discussions of the importance of the water in wine image in Aquinas and its relation to his use of philosophy, see ([17], pp. 253–69, [18], pp. 154–69).

[6] The image of water and wine is used for the same theme, but in different ways, by other Scholastics. So, for example, Bonaventure uses the image when he warns of the dangers of the use of philosophy in the exposition of Scripture: 'Indeed, not so much of the water of philosophy should be mixed with the wine of Sacred Scripture that it turn from wine into water ([19], Volume 5, p. 291).

[7] Especially promoted by members of the Arts faculty in the university of Paris, and exemplified by so-called Latin Averroism of Siger of Brabant and Boetius of Dacia. This led to the condemnations of 1277. See ([20], pp. 387–409 and [21], pp. 32–6).

period and which he sees reflected in the contemporary academy when theology does become assimilated to the methods and values of religious studies.

In the *de Trinitate* Aquinas introduces the scriptural image of water and wine in the form of just such an objection to Christian theology making use of philosophical arguments and authorities:

> Besides, secular wisdom is frequently represented in Scripture by water, but divine wisdom through wine. But, in Isaiah Chapter 1, innkeepers are censured for mixing water with wine. Therefore, teachers are to be censured who mix philosophical doctrines with revelation (Boethius De Trinitate (henceforth B.D.T.) 1.2.3.arg.5).[8]

In reply to this objection, Aquinas argues that what happens when Christian theology makes use of philosophy is not so much the dilution of the one by the other, but the transformation of the water of philosophy into the wine of an enriched Christian theology:

> It can, however, also be said that when one of two things passes over into the domain (*dominium*) of another, it is not reckoned to be a mixture, except when the nature of both is changed. Whence, those who use philosophical doctrines in theology by bringing them into the service of faith, do not mix water with wine, but change water into wine (B.D.T. 1.2.3. ad.5).

In support of this, Aquinas makes two general points about the relationship between natural and revealed truth (and hence between philosophy and Christian theology), before setting out three ways in which the water of philosophy is turned into the wine of Christian theology.

3.2. Nature and Grace

The first general point Aquinas makes is to argue that the relationship between philosophy and theology is part of a wider one between nature and grace. Just as grace does not do away with nature, but presupposes and perfects it, so revealed truth perfects natural truth and Christian theology's systematic exploration of revelation perfects philosophy:

> It must be said that the gifts of grace are added to nature in this manner that it does do away with it, but rather perfects it; whence also the light of faith, which is infused into us by grace, does not destroy the light of the natural reason divinely placed in us (B.D.T. 1.2.3.co.1).[9]

So, just as human nature more generally is elevated by divine grace into a higher dignity of life whereby human beings come to share in the divine life itself in beatitude, so the water of philosophy is turned into the wine of theology rather than the two simply mixed together, because natural truths are elevated and transfigured as they serve to make revealed truth manifest in Christian theology.

---

[8] All passages are my own translations of the Latin edition [16].
[9] Likewise, ST 1.1.8

3.3. The Unity of Truth

The second general point Aquinas makes is that the truths discovered by natural reason cannot be in opposition to the truth given in revelation:

> And although the natural light of the human mind is insufficient to make manifest those things which are made manifest through faith, it is however impossible that those things which are handed down to us divinely through faith be contrary to those things which are placed within us through nature. For it is necessary that one be false, and since both are placed within us from God, God would be the author of falsity, which is impossible (B.D.T. 1.2.3. co.1).

For Aquinas, then, there is a unity and harmony within truth, even though that truth is made known to us in two different ways.

These two general points, then, validate the legitimate use of philosophy by Christian theology. The truths found in philosophy are not in opposition to revelation, nor separate from it and unrelated to it, but capable of being drawn into Christian theology's own exploration of truth. The water of philosophy can be made into the wine of theology.

3.4. Turning the Water of Philosophy is Turned into the Wine of Theology

Having set out these general points Aquinas moves on specify three ways in which Christian theology engages with philosophy:

> Therefore we can use philosophy in sacred teaching in three ways: first, to demonstrate those things which are preambles of faith, which it is necessary to know in faith, those things which are proven by natural reasons about God, such as that God exists, that God be one and other such things proven either about God or about creatures in philosophy, which faith supposes; second, to make known through certain likenesses those things which are matters of faith, just as Augustine in the book about the Trinity uses many likenesses taken from philosophical doctrines to make manifest the Trinity; third, to resist those things that are said against the faith whether by showing them to be false or by showing them to be not necessary (B.D.T. 1.2.3 co.3).

The first way is where philosophy is able to demonstrate truths by the exercise of natural reason, which Christian theology already knows by the light of faith. We can know by natural reason some things about God and the world, such as that God exists certain features about God, and we can know that the world is created by God. Here on one level there is simple continuity, since it is the same truths that are being made known. Natural reason fulfils a very valuable role in that it serves to make what we accept on the basis of faith more intelligible to us human beings, whose intellects are more easily led to accept and understand something when it is made known by natural reason. At the same time, the water of such philosophy is transformed into the wine of Christian theology since it is placed in the new context of theology and the truths it discovers are located within the richer knowledge about God and the world that is made known through revelation.

The second way is where theology makes use of what Aquinas calls 'likenesses,' (*similitudine*s), philosophical concepts about ourselves and our world, which resemble the truths known through revelation. In the *de Trinitate* Aquinas gives the example of the way Augustine uses many 'likenessnes' taken from philosophical teachings to make manifest the Trinity. Here Christian theology finds in philosophical concepts about the human mind a 'likeness' for understanding the revealed truth about the Persons of the Trinity. Thus, the account of the mind in terms of understanding and love present within it is a 'likeness' for the relationship of the Son, as the Word of God, and the Spirit, as the Love of God, within in the Trinity.[10] Theology takes such 'likenesses' and uses them to help us again make manifest the things of faith. As with the first way there is here a form of continuity. However, the concepts are also radically reconfigured, since they are applied to a very different case. The inner life of the Trinity is not of the same order as the elements that make up human psychology and the way understanding and love arise and relate in the workings of the human mind is a very different thing to the way the Persons of the Trinity relate to each other within the Godhead.[11] Moreover, and in reverse, the water of human psychology becomes wine of theology in that now the workings of the human mind become seen more clearly as made in the image of God as Trinity.

The third way, finally, is where theology argues against philosophy when it advances something contrary to faith. It corrects error, showing the way reason can go wrong. Here, we might say, there is discontinuity and challenge. In keeping with the affirmation of the unity of truth, a line of reasoning or a philosophical work that contradicts what is known by revelation must be in error in some way. Here the transformation is certainly a radical one, since it is fundamentally one of dissolution. However, again a positive role is given to reasoning, in that, in the light of revelation a Christian theologian is encouraged to find reasons against such arguments brought against what is known by faith, in the certainly that these arguments must be defective.

In all these three ways, then, philosophy is placed in a new context and given a new application. And such transformation is what we actually find in Aquinas' works when theology engages with philosophy, with all the philosophical texts or 'authorities' he draws upon, be they the Greek philosophy of Aristotle or the Arabic philosophy of Avicenna and Averroes or the Jewish philosophy of Maimonides. In the three ways outlined, Aquinas confirms, challenges and radically transforms the concepts and schemes he finds in these sources in the light of what is revealed about God, the world and about human nature and destiny. In this encounter, however, philosophy is of immense importance and value and does lead to a better understanding of revelation. The water of Aristotle or of Avicenna may well become the wine of Christian theology, but the water of their thought still remains the material out of which the theology is made and without it we could not have the resultant theology in the form we have it.

---

[10] As Augustine puts it, 'We found a similar trinity in man, namely the mind, and the knowledge it knows itself with, and the love it loves itself with.' ([22], pp. 402–3).

[11] Other examples include the way Aquinas uses and transforms Aristotelian virtue ethics or causality in the light of order of Christian language of infused natural and supernatural virtues or sacramental causality. For a discussion of these see ([18], pp. 154–69).

It is especially Aquinas' second way that has an immediate resonance with the approach taken in comparative theology. Here we see the aspect of learning that is emphasised by comparative theologians, as Christian theology is enriched through the encounter with non-Christian philosophy, finding new ways of expressing and understanding Christian faith. Indeed, when we consider just how profoundly Aquinas' theology is actually shaped through this encounter, we would seem to find here a powerful affirmation of comparative theology as a legitimate and worthy successor of Aquinas' science of theology. At the same time, we also see the aspect of transformation that D'Costa and McIntyre stress as an important and necessary part of any such encounter. Taken with the other two ways, we thus find here a classical model of theology that is accepted and promoted by the wider community of Catholic theologians for the reasons considered in the previous section, and yet one that encourages the kind of further engagements that are found in comparative theology.

3.5. The Thomist Approach after Thomas

In the centuries since Aquinas there continued to be a sustained interaction between Thomist Christian theologians and the intellectual traditions of other religions, with newer engagements developing with the religious traditions of the East. Aquinas' approach was a model for later Catholic missionaries, theologians and contemplatives, whose theology was formed by the Thomist tradition and who worked out their own encounters with the thought and spirituality of other religions in ways similar to those set out by Aquinas between theology and philosophy.

In the case of India, for example, this lead to a number of sustained engagements with Hindu thought, especially in the 20th century. Thus, for example, Pierre Johanns S.J. (1885–1955), in a series of articles published in the journal, *The Light of the East* (1922–1934), subsequently gathered together in *To Christ Through the Vedānta* (1996), engages with the thought of the various schools of Vedānta, so that he might construct from them a Vedāntic version of the Thomist account of God, creation and of human nature and destiny, accepting some elements as compatible, rejecting others as incompatible, but reconfiguring everything in the light of Aquinas' teaching. Henri Le Saux (otherwise known as Swāmi Abhishiktānanda) (1910–73), in a deep theological and contemplative engagement with Hindu spirituality set out in his book, *Sagesse Hindu, Mystique Chrétienne: du la Védanta à la Trinité* (1965, later translated into English with the title *Saccidānanda: A Christian Approach to Advaitic Experience* (1974), finds in the Vedāntic description of the ultimate reality as *saccidānanda*, 'truth, consciousness and bliss,' a 'likeness' for the Trinity, exploring how the Vedāntic experience becomes transformed in the light of the Christian experience of God as Trinity. We have already noted the work of Raimon Panikkar in the first edition of *The Unknown Christ of Hinduism* (1964). Panikkar describes his Christological reading of Vedānta as discerning the *sensus plenior* (the fuller sense) of the Vedānta text, a process he depicts not as the transformation of water into wine, but with the equally powerful image of death and resurrection.[12]

---

[12] For a fuller account of these and other such engagements see Martin Ganeri ([23], pp. 410–32 and [9], pp. 106–40).

I would like, however, to finish this section by briefly creating a new example of what a detailed application of the model set out by Aquinas might look like in an encounter with Hindu thought, drawing on my own work exploring an encounter between Aquinas's doctrine of creation and the embodiment cosmology found in the Vedāntic theology of Rāmānuja (1017–1137). For Rāmānuja the world is the body of God and this is meant be to be taken literally. In his major work, the *Śrī Bhāsya*, his commentary on the Vedāntic *Brahma Sūtra*s, he defines what it is means to be a body as 'any substance which a conscious entity can completely control and support for its own purposes and whose nature is solely to be accessory of that entity is the body of that entity' (Ś.Bh.2.19) ([24], vol. III, pp. 26–7). A body, then, is any entity that has these fundamental relationships of dependence on a conscious self. In the case of a finite embodied being, like a human being, this accords with the two-substance dualism that is commonplace in classical Hindu anthropology: a human being is a non-material, conscious, self, which has an integral existence of its own, but which comes to take on a certain type of material body, which is dependent on it. In the case of the world, each entity within the world, whether a material entity or one of the finite selves, is the body of God. God is not dependent on the world nor does God form a single composite substance with the entities that make the world up. Rather the world is the body of God just because each entity is wholly dependent at all times in the ways specified in the definition.

What would it mean within Aquinas' scheme for Christian theology to use of this Vedāntic embodiment cosmology? In keeping with the first way Aquinas specifies, theology will affirm the details of the definition as true of the creational relationship itself as known by revelation and as otherwise explored by reason (S.T. 1.44–5, 103–5). For Aquinas creation is 'the emanation of all being from the universal cause, which is God' (S.T. 1.45.1). God is the first and universal cause of all things, in the sense that, as their efficient cause, he bestows on them the entirely of their being and sustains them in being at all times. He governs all things by his providence and is the end of all things. In keeping with the third way, however, Christian theology could not accept that the world is literally the body of God, since the understanding of embodiment that Aquinas upholds is that an embodied being is a substantial unity or composite of soul and body (S.T. 1.75–6). Aquinas rejects the idea that God can be in composition with the world (S.T. 1.3,8). Thus, such a view of embodiment would have to be metaphorical. So, in accordance with the second way, theology could make use of Rāmānuja's embodiment cosmology as a 'likeness,' in the sense that it expresses metaphorically what the creational relationship is and helps us understand what it means in ways that accord with our human intellects and imaginations and with our own immediate experience of embodiment. In the same way Thomas sees the relationship of the soul to its body as expressing what the existence of God in creation is like (S.T. 1.8, 2 ad 3).

4. Tradition with a New Identity

In this final section I now want to consider how this model might be developed further to be more like the kind of approaches taken in the new comparative theology. As I mentioned in the introduction, adopting such a classical model does not mean that newer insights and emphases cannot also be incorporated. Here I think some of the key characteristics of contemporary Catholic reflection on other religions, as well as those of the new comparative theology, can inform the Thomist model so that it does become fully tradition with a new identity.

4.1. Contemporary Church Teaching and the Thomist Approach

In terms of wider Catholic approaches to other religions, it might seem that Aquinas' conception of philosophy as the exercise of natural human reason and of the natural truths that emerge from it is too limiting. Elsewhere in his works Aquinas does affirm that a different type of engagement can take place with Jewish thinkers, since Christians and Jews commonly hold the Old Testament to be revelation. However, where there is no such common revelation, for Aquinas it is human reason alone that provides the point of encounter.

A contemporary Catholic approach to this question would also want to include the new perspectives that are to be found in the modern official teaching, especially that found in the documents of the Second Vatican Council (1962–5) and subsequent Papal statements, especially those of Blessed John Paul II (1978–2005). Thus, with the Council's Declaration on the Relations of Church with Non-Christian Religions (*Nostra Aetate*) it would affirm that the Church 'rejects nothing that is true and holy' in other religious traditions (*N.A. 2*). It would also want to affirm the teaching of the Council, further articulated by Blessed John Paul II, on the universal presence and action of the Holy Spirit. This teaching, with the expectations and possibilities it raises in any theological encounter with other religions, is part of the any contemporary Catholic hermeneutic of religions and needs therefore to be integrated into any contemporary application of the Thomist model. At the same time, contemporary official Catholic Church teaching would affirm with Aquinas that theology accepts as public revelation only that 'made to the apostles and prophets who have written the canonical scriptures' (S.T. 1.1.8 ad 2). In other words, the Church has no mandate for affirming the existence of other forms of revelation on a par with that traditionally accepted by Christian tradition.

So, a contemporary application of Aquinas' approach might not want simply to equate 'non-Christian thought' with 'natural human reason,' but also to be genuinely open to the presence of the 'holy' as the expression of the universal action of the Spirit, while also keeping Aquinas' understanding of what counts as public supernatural revelation. These new perspectives are important if Aquinas' approach is to be a good model for a contemporary Catholic Christian form of comparative theology. We are clearly now in the area of theology of religions, thinking about what the Church's official teaching and what a Catholic theologian can say can say about other religions and their traditions. Here is another reason for wanting to keep theology of religions integral to the exercise of comparative theology, as D'Costa and others have urged. For the contemporary Catholic theology of religions expands the Thomist approach in ways that are conducive to the aims and methods of the new comparative theology. Much the same observation will be true with any retrieval of a classical Patristic or Scholastic model.

4.2. Characteristics of Comparative Theology

Classical models can also be expanded and reconfigured by the characteristic emphases developed within the new comparative theology: its emphasis on deep study of other religions in their integrity; its concern to locate theological engagement in particular encounters with individual texts or in a theological dialogue on particular themes of common interest; its enthusiasm for the richness and sophistication of other religious traditions, with the expectation that there is much to be learnt in the encounter and that there is the real possibility of knowing God better by widening the horizons of theology to include other religions.

It is helpful here to recall some of the main distinctive characteristics of comparative theology as set by Francis Clooney. As Clooney put it:

Comparative theology—comparative and *theological* beginning to end—marks acts of faith seeing understanding which are rooted in a particular faith but which, from that foundation, venture into learning from one or more faith traditions. This learning is sought for the sake of fresh theological insights that are indebted to the newly encountered tradition/s as well as the home tradition ([25], p. 10).

As Clooney goes on to say, comparative theology is a:

[r]eflective and contemplative endeavour by which we see the other in the light of our own and our own in the light of the other. It ordinarily starts with the intuition of an intriguing resemblance that prompts us to place two realities –texts, images, practices, doctrines, persons – near one another, so that they may be seen over and over again, side by side. In this necessarily arbitrary and intuitive practice we understand each other differently because the other is near, and by cumulative insight also begin to comprehend related matters differently. Finally, we see ourselves differently, intuitively uncovering dimensions of ourselves that would not otherwise, by a non-comparative logic, come to the fore ([25], p. 11).

As we have seen, the Thomist approach is one that is more emphatically evaluative than the portrayal of comparative theology here. However, what is equally evident about both the theory and the actual practice of the Thomist approach is that it is open to learning from other religious traditions. The emphasis on learning in new comparative theology in fact allows us to see afresh and to retrieve more clearly something that is already there, but perhaps neglected in some applications of Thomism, where the content of Thomist account as it stands becomes fixed and simply something to be repeated in different ways, rather than a model of theological openness to the true and holy wherever that may be found and of the ever present possibility of new forms of theological expression that can arise from engagement with the thought of other religions.

Moreover, the emphasis Clooney puts on 'reflective and contemplative' and 'intuitive' character of this learning has been a very important contribution of the new comparative theology to all interreligious engagement. Such learning is 'dialogical' in the sense of a theological conversation where an emphasis is placed on the process of listening itself to what another tradition is saying and to a gradual transformation of one's own understanding through reasoning, intuition and the imagination. What this amounts to is a way of understanding the encounter that is less dialectical than that articulated in Aquinas' disputational works and more akin to the contemplative and imaginative reading tradition of *lectio divina* and of traditional Biblical exegesis within the Western Christian tradition, something which has also given rise to rich theological and spiritual insights. Where a number of religious traditions are involved this is reconfigured as under the practice of *collectio* (reading together) promoted in Clooney's own form of comparative theology.

4.3. Contemporary Examples of Thomist Comparative Theology

We have noted that contemporary Thomists have now started increasingly to use the modern terminology of interreligious encounter for what Thomas was doing. To some extent this is simply a matter of labelling, but, along with this, Thomist encounter has also come to adopt more creatively the approaches found in the new comparative theology.

A pioneering figure in this was the Scottish Sacred Heart Sister, Sara Grant RSCJ (1922–2000), who spent many years studying and teaching Hindu traditions in India, as well as engaged in a deep contemplative encounter with them as the head of a Christian ashram in Pune, as she recounts in her Teape lectures, gathered later in *Towards an Alternative Theology: Confessions of a Non-Dualist Christian* (2002). In these lectures and in her other published work, especially her book, *Śaṅkarācarya's Concept of Relation* (1999), which is a detailed study of the relation between ultimate being and finite being in the non-dualist tradition of Advaita Vedānta against the backdrop of Aquinas' account of the relation between uncreated and created being, Grant argues that there are areas of fundamental convergence between the thought of Śaṅkara and Aquinas. Going further, she concludes that Advaita Vedānta is the best conceptual resource Christian theologians can have to express the unique creational relationship of inseparable dependence. In her opinion Śaṅkara is even more successful than Aquinas in expressing what is fundamental and unique in the relation between the world and God. Thus, she argues that his account has something of unique value to offer to all people in relating the 'realm of the spirit and the realm of ordinary life':

> The radical non-dualism of Śaṅkarācarya, understood as I have interpreted it, could be of greatest assistance here, for of all the metaphysical ventures of man, it alone, it seems to me, does full justice to both the immanence of the creator and his absolute transcendence, to the creature's utter contingency and its paradoxical autonomy ([26], p. 192).

For Grant this overcomes a dualism often present in Western theology and spirituality where God is depicted as outside of all things, the 'God up there' or 'out there,' as she would put it ([27], p. 56). Grant finds Śaṅkara's Vedāntic description of Brahman as the Supreme Self, the Supreme Subject within all things and intimately present in all, far better a way of expressing the reality of God immanence in all things as the creator.

In part, in Grant's work we simply see the first and the second ways Aquinas identifies for the use theology can make of philosophy. Śaṅkara's thought is taken up and transformed as it is put to work expressing the Christian doctrine of creation. Grant's own position that there is straightforward convergence between the account of Śaṅkara and that of Aquinas is somewhat questionable. Rather, to some extent at least, she is re-reading Śaṅkara in the light of Aquinas, re-configuring Śaṅkara's thought so that is comes to express the doctrine of a positive creation. However, the encounter with the thought of Śaṅkara and with contemporary manifestations of Advaitic practice is far more than simply an exercise in conceptual theology for Grant. Her encounter with Advaita solves the deepest tensions at the heart of her own spiritual quest, as she recounts so vividly in *Towards an Alternative Theology: Confessions of a Non-Dualist Christian*. Advaita works on her imagination and her contemplative experience as much as her reasoning. Her encounter with Advaita is also a dialogical one, in which the holiness of Advaita practitioners was fully recognised and appreciated.

A second important example is the work of the American Thomist and Catholic priest, David Burrell C.S.C, who in his considerable scholarly studies of Medieval theology has explored and emphasised how important Jewish and Islamic thinkers are for the shaping of Aquinas' own theology, taken as fellow enquirers into issues of God, creation and human life common to all three religions. While Burrell accepts that Aquinas is not interested in other religious traditions as such in the manner of contemporary interreligious dialogue and theology, nonetheless Aquinas' serious engagement with Jewish and Muslim thinkers can rightly be labelled an interfaith and intercultural achievement. For Burrell Aquinas can also function as an important model for contemporary engagement. As he puts it:

> Ours is a very different world from Aquinas,' yet his ability to see the presence of interlocutors from other faiths as a spur to understanding of his own tradition offers us a model which deftly eschews intellectual colonizing and displays the way in which every living tradition grows by carefully responding to challenges from without ([2], pp. 86–7).

More recently, Burrell has started to use the resources of the Medieval tradition to carry out his own exercise in contemporary comparative theology, one which reflects the developments in Catholic approaches to interreligious relations. In *Towards a Jewish-Christian-Muslim Theology* (2011), he considers how contemporary members of these traditions can advance in their theological understanding of a range of topics such as creation, providence, grace and eschatology through an ongoing theological conversation with thinkers from all the three traditions. As Burrell himself states, this is a comparative theology, which takes the form of 'creative hermeneutics':

> I have suggested calling this inquiry an exercise in 'creative hermeneutics,' whereby conceptual patters, often developed separately, can illuminate one another once we see them as executing cognate explorations. This approach reflects the fresh face of interfaith inquiry often associated with the liberating document of Vatican II, *Nostra Aetate*, yet more pertinently part of the air we have come to breathe ([28], p. xii).

In my own work I have also tried to create a theological dialogue between Aquinas and the Hindu Vedāntin, Rāmānuja, that is rooted in a comparison of their texts, but also allows a creative conversation to take place that illumines each other and the theological themes they deal with in such a manner that it can enrich contemporary theologising. In *Two Pedagogies for Happiness* (2010) [29], building on the seminal work by Clooney in *Theology After Vedānta* (1993), for instance, I take Aquinas' *Summa Theologiae* and Rāmānuja's *Śrī Bhāṣya* as textual wholes and explore how they serve as pedagogies, leading their readers to understand why the final human goal is a happiness that lies in the knowledge of God, and, though engagement with the text, actually enabling readers to advance some way towards that goal.

Likewise, going back to the examples I gave in the previous section of how Thomas' model of engagement might be applied to Rāmānuja's embodiment cosmology, I would also want to develop such an engagement further to reflect both contemporary Catholic teaching on other religions and the emphases of the new comparative theology. Rāmānuja's theology is not just an exercise in exegetical skills and clever reasoning. The concepts he develops serve the spiritual goals of the Śrī Vaiṣṇava tradition to which he belonged and for which he undertook his rigorous intellectual work, the goals of realising human happiness as the body of God, with God the support and end of human existence and fulfilment. This is encapsulated in the teaching that the finite self finds its bliss in realising fully that it is the accessory (*śeṣa*) of the Lord, its principal (*śeṣin*), which is a fundamental feature of his definition of embodiment. Here we might want to consider the question of the presence of the 'holy' as well as the 'true' in Rāmānuja's account. Moreover, the idea that the world may be thought metaphorically to be the body of God strikes me as being a very powerful resource for the enrichment of the theological imagination and hence of spiritual experience. An encounter with Rāmānuja's account is not simply a matter of reasoning, of working out conceptual similarity and dissimilarity. Reading Rāmānuja's texts, in which his concept of embodiment is developed, along with those of Aquinas is also an act of *collectio*, a meditational exercise that forms its own extended pedagogy, feeding and expanding my religious imagination as it seeks to intuit the closeness and delight that is being created and being destined to know God, as I learn to see myself as the body and accessory of God.

5. Conclusions

In this article I have argued that there are certain concerns within the Catholic community in Britain, which, unless addressed, are likely to militate against any greater acceptance and appreciation of the new comparative theology and I have suggested that the retrieval of classical models might serve to meet these concerns. I have explored one particular model, that of Thomas Aquinas, as a classical theological account that enjoys a very great prestige in the Catholic tradition.

Other comparative theologians may well feel the force of these concerns less strongly. Disagreement on this matter, however, would I hope not detract form appreciation of the ongoing value of classical models in themselves for the contemporary exercise of comparative theology, which I have wanted to explore and promote. For its part, Aquinas' approach is one that is supports a sustained and fruitful engagement with the thought of non-Christian traditions. The general principles of the relationship of nature and grace and the affirmation of the universality and unity of truth provide a useful theological justification for having confidence in such an engagement. Moreover, as I mentioned at the beginning, it brings a number of important contributions to the discipline of comparative theology. First, the process of transformation, captured by the image of water turning into wine, and the three ways in which this occurs, is helpful as an analysis of cross-religious encounter, one that is true to what is involved in any theological engagement across religious traditions. In concrete theological engagements some such transformation always takes place, if the thought of another tradition is actually assimilated into one's own, and if one is learns from another tradition within the terms of one's own identity. Such theological engagement is, of course, rather different from the methods and concerns of comparative religion, where the phenomena of religions are simply compared.

Aquinas' approach, then, is simply a good model for how to do comparative theology, when taken and developed further to meet contemporary Catholic reflection on other religions as well as the distinctive emphases of new comparative theologians. At the same time, for those concerned with such issues, it does also have the power to unite the academy with the *ecclesia* and hence serves the interests of Catholic theologians who want to explore such cross-religious encounters without becoming dislocated from the accepted norms and traditions of their church community. Thus it can support a form of new comparative theology that is manifestly *tradition with a new identity*.

Conflicts of Interest

The author declares no conflict of interest.

References and Notes

1. Pope Benedict XVI. Address to the Roman Curia, December 22, 2005. "Ad Romanan Curiam ob omnia natalicia." *Acta Apostolicae Sedis* Vol. XCVIII (6 Januarii 2006); Libreria Editrice Vaticana, 2006, pp. 40–53.
2. Burrell, David B. "Thomas Aquinas and Islam." *Modern Theology* 20 (January 2004): 71–89.
3. Burrell, David B. *Towards a Jewish-Christian-Muslim Theology*. Oxford: Wiley-Blackwell, 2011.
4. Forder, Jim, and Frederick C. Bauerschmidt, eds. Aquinas in Dialogue: Thomas for the Twenty-First Century. Malden, MA: Blackwell Pub., 2004.
5. Roy, Louis O.P. "Medieval Latin Scholasticism: Some Comparative Features." In *Scholasticism*, Cabezón, edited by José Ignacio. New York: State University of New York Press, 1998, pp. 19–34.
6. D'Costa, Gavin. *Theology and Religious Pluralism*. Oxford: Blackwell, 1986.
7. D'Costa, Gavin. *Christianity and World Religions: Disputed Questions in the Theology of Religions*. Oxford: Wiley-Blackwell, 2009.
8. D'Costa, Gavin. *The Meeting of Religions and the Trinity*. London: T&T Clark, 2000.
9. D'Costa, Gavin, ed. *The Catholic Church and the World Religions*. London: T&T Clark, 2011.
10. D'Costa, Gavin. *Theology in the Public Square: Church, Academy and Nation*. Oxford: Blackwell Publishing, 2005.
11. Keating, Daniel A. Book review of Clooney, Francis. "The Truth, the Way, the Life: Christian Commentary on the Three Holy Mantras of the Śrīvaiṣṇava Hindus." *Nova et Vetera* 10 (Winter 2012): 283–6.

12. Kiblinger, Kristin Beise. "Relating Theology of Religions and Comparative Theology." In *The New Comparative Theology: Interreligious Insights form the Next Generation*, edited by Clooney; London: T&T Clarke, 2010.
13. Panikkar, Raimon. *The Unknown Christ of Hinduism*. London: Darton, Longman & Todd, 1964.
14. Thomas Aquinas. *Summa Theologiae*. Latin text and English Translation. Translated by Gilby, Thomas, et al. 60 vols. London: Eyre and Spottiswoode, and New York: McGraw–Hill, 1964–73.
15. MacIntyre, Alisdair. *Whose Justice? Which Rationality?* London: Duckworth, 1988.
16. Thomas Aquinas. *Thomae de Aquino Super Boetium De Trinitate*. Textum a Bruno Decker Lugduni Batauorum 1959 editum ac automato translatum a Roberto Busa SJ in taeniis magneticas denuo recognovit Enrique Alarcón atque instruxit. *Corpus Thomisticum: Index Thomisticus*, edited by Busa, R., S.J., et al. Latin text. Web edition by Bernot, E. and Alarcón E. Fundación Tomás de Aquino, Pamplona, Spain, 2000–12.
17. Preller, Victor. O.G.S. "Water into Wine." In *Grammar and Grace: Reformulations of Aquinas and Wittgenstein*, edited by Jeffrey Stout and Robert MacSwain. London: SCM, 2004.
18. Jordan, Mark. *Rewritten Theology: Aquinas after His Readers*. Oxford: Blackwells, 2006.
19. Bonaventure. *Collations on the Six Days* in *The Works of Bonaventure*. Translated by de Vinck, J. Patterson: St Anthony Guild Press, 1960–1970.
20. Gilson, Etienne. *History of Christian Philosophy in the Middle Ages*; Sheed & Ward Ltd.: London, UK, 1980
21. McGrade, A.S., ed. *Cambridge Companion to Medieval History*. Cambridge, UK: Cambridge University Press, 2003.
22. Augustine. The Trinity. Translated by Hill, Edmund. O.P. New York: New City Press, 1991.
23. Ganeri, Martin. Catholic Encounter with Hindus in the Twentieth century: In Search of an Indian Christianity. *New Blackfriars* 88 (July 2007): pp. 410–32.
24. Rāmānuja, *Śrī Bhāṣyam*. Sanskrit text Laksmithatachar, edited by M.A. Chief. Critical edition in four volumes. Melkote: Academy of Sanskrit Research, 1985–1991.
25. Clooney, Francis Xavier. *Comparative Theology: Deep Learning across Religious Borders*. Oxford: Wiley-Blackwell, 2010.
26. Grant, Sara R.S.C.J. *Śaṅkarācarya's Concept of Relation*. Delhi: Motilal Banarsidass, 1999.
27. Grant, Sara. R.S.C.J. *Towards an Alternative Theology:Confessions of a Non-Dualist Christian*. Notre Dame: University of Notre Dames Press, 2002.
28. Burrell, David B. *Towards a Jewish-Christian-Muslim Theology*. Oxford: Wiley-Blackwell, 2011.
29. Ganeri, Martin. "Two Pedagogies for Happiness: Healing goals and healing methods in the *Summa Theologiae* of Thomas Aquinas and the *Śrī Bhāṣya* of Rāmānuja." In *Philosophy as Therapeia*, edited by Ganeri, Jonardon and Clare Carlisle. Cambridge: Cambridge University Press, UK, 2010.

Reprinted from *Religions*. Cite as: Khorchide, Mouhanad, Topkara, Ufuk. "A Contribution to Comparative Theology: Probing the depth of Islamic Thought." *Religions* 4 (2013): 67-76.

Article

A Contribution to Comparative Theology: Probing the Depth of Islamic Thought

Mouhanad Khorchide [1] and Ufuk Topkara [2,*]

[1] Center for Islamic Theology, University of Münster, Hammerstr.95, Münster 48153, Germany; E-Mail: khorchide@uni-muenster.de

[2] Center for Comparative Theology, University of Paberborn, Warburgerstr.100, Paderborn 33098, Germany

* Author to whom correspondence should be addressed; E-Mail: utopkara@mail.upb.de.

Received: 5 December 2012; in revised form: 25 January 2013 / Accepted: 28 January 2013 / Published: 31 January 2013

Abstract: Muslim theologians, as much as ordinary Muslims, will immediately agree with the characterization of God as all compassionate. However, it remains rather opaque how God's compassion can be fully explained in terms of comparative theology. How can Muslims relate to God's compassion? What role does God's compassion precisely play in the Quranic revelation and the daily practice of Muslims?

Keywords: Islamic theology; theology of compassion in Islam; comparative theology; Islamic thought; compassion and mercy in Islamic theology

1. Laying the Foundation

Islamic theology currently faces a challenging phase of its ongoing development. Whereas the global Muslim community is engaging global modernity in the political, cultural, economic and social arenas, Islamic theology remains—aside from individual examples few and far between—somewhat reluctant to participate in new forms of comparative discourses. Only a handful of theologians across the world seem to have realized how fundamentally important this is for the future of Islamic theology.[1]

Ignoring the intellectual and philosophical challenges that modernity poses to any set of beliefs is essentially a hopelessly isolationist stance and one that Islamic theology can no longer afford to hold. More importantly, this kind of intellectual stagnation fails to reflect the historically rich self-perception and scrutiny of Muslim theologians across the centuries, who have often analyzed and engaged new intellectual frontiers in the past. As proven at multiple points in its long history, Islamic theology only grew stronger by juxtaposing its ideas and beliefs against those of other traditions.

Engaging modernity does not invalidate the Islamic past. To the contrary, it is absolutely necessary to reiterate the Islamic tradition in its multifarious manifestations and introduce all strands to a new discourse fueled by modernity. Muslim theologians should be held accountable for nothing less than establishing a series of critical comparative explorations. In fact, as much as it is essential for the Muslim community to probe Islamic heritage, the same value and significance should be devoted to the studies of modern day philosophies and intellectual inquiries from other religious, as well as secular traditions.

A historical example of such a comparative effort makes this point very clearly. One of the most intriguing and intellectually stimulating scholars in Islamic history is Muhammed Abu Hamid Al-Ġhazālī. Only very few scholars can claim to have had as far reaching an impact on both the practices and beliefs of Muslims across centuries. Certainly, Al-Ġhazālī's scholarly work was, to some extent, promoted by the Seljuk Wazir Nizam Al-Mulk for political reasons. However, the extensive impact of Greek philosophy on Muslim scholars and contemporary debates influenced Al-Ġhazālī's scholarly work. From Al-Kindi, to Al-Farabi and Ibn-i Sina, many Muslim scholars incorporated Greek philosophy into their thinking and reasoning, leaving the door wide open for both criticism and agreement between these two broad schools of thought as a form of comparative theology.

Al-Ġhazālī was among those who criticized the influence of Greek philosophy on Muslim theology, pointing out the incompatibilities between the two. He did so not only because the political authorities demanded this of him, but because of his critique on his own intellectual convictions and beliefs [1]. We can draw this conclusion from an incredibly audacious biographical work in which Al-Ġhazālī guides the reader on his journey through philosophy and faith. The reader accompanies Al-Ġhazālī through various stages of doubt and self-reflection, to the point at which he finally reaches a coherent answer to his central inquiry of how to access or experience divinity. Some Muslim scholars argued (and some even still hold this position today) that Al-Ġhazālī has responded to the central claims of philosophy by means of philosophy, itself, and thereby undermined any legitimacy of philosophical thought for theology *per se*. As much as this extreme claim cannot be taken seriously, we simultaneously have to underline the fundamental differences between 12th century and 21st century understandings of philosophy.

---

[1] These theologians represent a wide range of interests and scholarly work. However, their work is particularly stimulating, as it broaches the disciplines intellectual frontiers by engaging idea(l)s of modernity. The list includes, but it is not limited to: Khaled Abou El Fadl, Ebrahim Moosa, Farid Esack, Sherman Jackson, Mohammed Arkoun.

Like many of his contemporaries, Al-Ġhazālī viewed Greek philosophy as an intellectual threat to Muslim beliefs. What sets him apart, however, is that instead of simply refuting philosophy, as a whole, he thoroughly engaged it. Essentially, Al-Ġhazālī provided a blueprint from which we can derive both an epistemology and a critical methodology, a method that is applicable to the set of inquiries we are facing in our own contemporary situation. Like Al-Ġhazālī in his time, present-day Muslim theologians should not hesitate to investigate and examine other strands of critical thought that could help us understand our faith more deeply [2].[2] As Al-Ġhazālī showed us, Islamic theology can develop an epistemology and critical methodology born from and based upon its own traditions and, yet, in analytical dialogue with others; an epistemology and methodology able to coherently and constructively respond to intellectual challenges to our faith.

2. Comparative Theology

There are multiple points of entrance through which Islamic theology can join modern comparative theological discussions. However, one particular debate Islamic theology will have to address sooner or later is the paradigmatic shift in modern philosophy that was introduced by Immanuel Kant. Certainly, contemporary Muslim scholars are by and large aware of the most important currents of Western philosophy. Many Muslim scholars have, in fact, reflected on modern Western philosophy.[3] However, we still believe that levels of engagement and even the very meaning of "engaged" are contested. It is legitimate that Muslim scholars' fundamental stance toward modern philosophy, as a Western non-Muslim way of thinking, is to be highly critical. But this should not prevent them from examining Western modern thought thoroughly.

Until recently, there has been no comprehensive scholarly work, relying upon a Muslim perspective, dealing with the critical assessments of Kant's description of the relation of reason and philosophy and the status of religion in modern thinking. For instance, in comparison to the breadth and depth of Christian scholarly work devoted to Kant's paradigmatic Enlightenment reflections, Muslim scholars' engagement with Western philosophy has been rather insufficient and scattered.[4]

Whereas the confrontation with modern-day philosophy remains to be seen, the remainder of this essay will focus on a particularly intriguing contemporary theological debate in which Islamic theology is beginning to engage comparative theology.

Even a cursory look at the numerous modes of expression of religious groups in the present-day leaves us overwhelmed. A highly diverse and heterogeneous group of communities believe, in one way or another, in a deity. Comparative theology emerged in this theological realm, seeking truth in and through various religious and non-religious traditions. More precisely, comparative theology holds that a believer in one tradition can seek understanding, and perhaps even a measure of truth, in and

---

[2] Ebrahim Moosa's work on Al-Ġhazālī is a profound example of how the tradition can be engaged critically and applied to current debates.

[3] The list includes, but is not limited to, Sir Muhammed Iqbal, Seyyed Hossein Nasr, Tariq Ramadan and Hassan Hanafi.

[4] Kant's "critique of reason" is not directed against Christianity or any specific denomination. It rather develops a coherent theory of epistemology, which fundamentally challenges perceptions of the relation between reason and faith.

through other religious traditions. It is important to underline that comparative theology is not directed to challenging a particular faith *per se*, but is rather concerned with creating new means of understanding the other, and through that process, the self.[5] In other words, comparative theology could help Islamic theology develop a greater reflective and reflexive understanding. Through comparison with other cultures and traditions, we could develop new means of communication, in our attempts to addressthe divine.

Speaking about the divine and the ways in which the believer reaches out to the divine (including practices) requires a specific frame of linguistic and cultural references. Any community of believers shares these references internally. However, they remain rather opaque to anyone outside of the community who is trying to grasp their meaning. As long as one cannot fully understand what the shared practices and linguistic references actually mean, it is simply inconceivable to fully comprehend the strands of communication with the divine defined by these cultural references. However, it is not entirely impossible to overcome these limits on our understanding. Comparative theology holds that by long and patient study, the outsider could become somewhat of an insider. Truly, this requires quite a bit of a scholarly and personal effort. Nevertheless, the depth of understanding one can possibly achieve is equally rewarding.

On a different note, broader understanding of those linguistic references could help us to decipher the underlying strands of communication of each and any religious tradition. Still, one might ask why would we want to understand those peculiar and alien categories of communication with the divine? Why would we want to understand how a different religious group is addressing its deity in the first place? As simple as it may sound, by engaging in this process, we might be able to explore and distinguish fine nuances in our own communication with the divine. Moreover, it could also be seen as an attempt to read God's signs, which the Qur'an emphasizes on multiple occasions ([3], Q 2:164; Q 3:190).

By engaging with a community and its linguistic and cultural references, we can discover ourselves both in and through the other. This would not only allow us to detect shared practices of belief; it could also enrich our own practice or deepen our faith. In many ways, it would exemplify the Quranic claim that God has created us in different tribes and that we are supposed to get to know each other [3].[6] The verb used in the verse goes beyond the notion of simple acquaintance or friendly relationship. It rather implies a sincere attempt to understand the other, in all of the other's complexities and contradictions to what we see, feel or know as truth ([4], pp. 605–07).

---

[5] For a thorough description of comparative theology, see in this volume: Klaus von Stosch, Comparative Theology as Liberal and Confessional Theology.

[6] The Qur'anic verse reads ([3], Q 49:13) "People, We created you all from a single man and a single woman, and made you into races and tribes **so that you should recognize one another**. In God's eyes, the most honoured of you are the ones most mindful of Him: God is all knowing, all aware."

3. How Can Comparative Theology Contribute to Islamic Theology

Islamic theology has not been predominantly concerned with responding to modernity. Essentially, Islamic theology is preserving and conveying an understanding of and a belief in God, outlined and defined in the Qur'an and the life of the Prophet Muhammed. However, this does not mean that Islamic theology is merely operating within a restricted theological arena isolated from the rest of the world. An insular existence of Islamic theology, of its reasoning about God or its faith seeking understanding, is neither intended nor encouraged [5]. Comprehension and understanding of the divine are fostered in networks of shared knowledge and references. Thus, Muslims and their belief are as much intertwined with other cultures as those are with the Muslim world. Throughout the history of the Muslim world, Muslims have been exposed to many experiences, cultures and theologies. Consequently, learning from other cultures was perceived as both necessary and enriching for its own understanding. Even if Muslim scholars considered other traditions, faith based or not, to be flawed or in some ways inferior and unacceptable, they still did not hesitate to study and learn from them. By doing so, Muslim scholars not only extended the horizon and depth of Muslim thinking, they also acted in accordance with the prophetic teaching that striving for knowledge is considered an obligation for every Muslim.

We have already mentioned some of the intellectual challenges ahead for Islamic theology, *i.e.*, the philosophical inquiries surrounding the belief in a supremely powerful and compassionate deity. Whereas a wide range of different topics can be addressed, one particular debate continues to attract special interest. The question is fairly old, yet still very persistent. Considering all of the misery, poverty, suffering and sorrow in this world, how can we still believe in an all-merciful, all-compassionate God? While Christianity, for example, embraced this inquiry, which is usually defined as theodicy, as part of its theological discourse, Muslim scholars remain somewhat silent on the issue. Muslim scholars, in general, seem to be reluctant to devote any attention to this question, claiming that it has no relevance for Islamic theology.

However, not all Muslim scholars can easily ignore the question of theodicy. Currently, we are witnessing the emergence of Islamic theology as an academic discipline in Germany. The German government has endowed several universities across the country in order to encourage the emergence of Islamic theology within their theological faculties. Muslim students have thus already started to study their religion through intellectually sophisticated and compelling comparative theological reflection.

Even though the faculty and the students of these departments are devoted to preserving and discovering their own religious heritage, Islamic theology will no longer remain isolated within an intellectual vacuum. Muslim theologians will have to engage meaningfully the vast and long-lasting tradition of German thought and philosophy. Ultimately, they will help forge an understanding of Islam that will be open to academic and modern philosophical scrutiny. Therefore, it is very unlikely that Muslim theologians in Germany will be able to avoid the question of theodicy any longer. Comparative theology could provide them with a series of tools for tackling this particularly challenging issue.

Also, as stated above, Christianity embraced this question and developed a set of arguments that explain why Christians can and should believe in God, even when the world is haunted by great suffering and sorrow. We believe that Muslim theologians can learn a great deal by familiarizing themselves with the relevant discourse shaped by Christian theologians. This is, moreover, true not only related to this particular question of theodicy. The study of comparative Christian theology and its peculiar engagement with Western philosophy could help Muslim theologians comprehend and evaluate theological reasoning that meets modern global philosophical scrutiny.

Secondly, as we have previously pointed out, seeking a divine truth is an endeavor that Muslims share with many religious groups. However, some traditions are closer in theory and practice to us than others. Judaism, Christianity and Islam are viewed as the three Western monotheistic cultures or Abrahamic religions. The Qur'an mentions time and again that following Abraham's teachings and the teachings of all other prophets who came after him is mandatory to establish Islam: "So [you believers], say, 'We believe in God and in what was sent down to us and what was sent down to Abraham, Ishmael, Isaac, Jacob, and the Tribes, and what was given to Moses, Jesus, and all the prophets by their Lord. We make no distinction between any of them, and we devote ourselves to Him'" ([3], Q 2: 136).

Given this practice of engaging the other Abrahamic religions, it is rather bewildering how dismissive contemporary Muslim theologians can be when it comes to evaluating, for instance, Moses or Jesus based on respective Jewish or Christian sources. This is a relatively new phenomenon, as Jewish sources were, at times, relied on in such areas as seeking knowledge about the prophets during the early stages of Islam. In fact, a whole genre called Isra'iliyat [7] was introduced into early Islamic writings. The Isra'iliyat also proves useful for our time, serving as an excellent example of how differently the process of transmitting knowledge can be perceived. The Isra'iliyat was a focused attempt to understand the history of the prophets through the eyes of Jewish scholars or in light of Jewish sources. It served as historical evidence, incorporated into the oeuvre of Islamic writings. One might assume that those beliefs were considered only as long as they did not oppose or violate the theological position of Islam in any essential way.

In other words, Muslim scholars could essentially gain compelling insight into Jewish sources if they would engage historical material based on the criteria of comparative theology discussed above. More precisely, connecting the Isra'iliyat with Jewish theology would certainly help us better understand this specific inherent and embedded set of comparative beliefs. The same would be true for any attempt to appreciate the life of Jesus based on Christian sources and Christian theology [7]. Consequently, Muslim history offers us a legacy; namely engaging Jewish and Christian theological reasoning as part of what Islamic intellectual discourse has incorporated throughout history.

---

[7] Wahb ibn Munabbih was a specialist in this kind of knowledge and was reputed to be the first to write a book in the genre. Wahb lived from 34 to 110 Hijri (654–728 CECE) and was famous for his vast knowledge of religious texts and stories relating to the pre-Islamic prophets and past nations (*Isra'iliyat*). See, for further information, the Jewish Encyclopedia under WAHB IBN MUNABBIH (Abu 'Abd Allah al-Ṣana'ani al-Dhimari); Another example for heavy influence of *Isra'iliyat* in Islamic writing is "The History of the Prophets" written by Ahmet Cevdet Pasha, 1912.

However, we should be aware that this kind of approach would not receive overwhelming support from many Muslim thinkers. On the contrary, many will object to the historical reliability and authenticity of Jewish and Christian sources, claiming that the Qur'an has actually refuted them [8–10].[8] Others will argue that the Christian perception of Jesus is diametrically opposed to the Muslim belief and the Quranic statement about his prophethood. We cannot now engage this point in greater detail, but it should be underlined that perceptions that are not grounded in a deeper reflection, essentially prevent us from unlocking meaningful trails of understanding and appreciation of both the other and ourselves.[9]

4. The Theology of Mercy in Islam: A Contribution to Comparative Theology

As we elaborated earlier, engaging with comparative theology can be a mutually beneficial process for both Muslims and non-Muslim theologians. Islamic theology could not only seek to unveil new insights, but at the same time inspire and stimulate thinkers of other religious denominations. We believe, for instance, that the theology of mercy in Islam is suited to nurture a deeper perception of God.

Muslims believe that the Qur'an is utterly divine. Muslims also believe that by engaging the Qur'an, *i.e.*, reciting and contemplating its meaning, they actually engage in and are somehow touched by the divine. The Qur'an, therefore, resembles a particularly decisive experience in the realm of Muslim life. One can hardly imagine how fundamentally and deeply this impacts Muslims' perceptions of the relationship of God and humanity, the role of the created *versus* the creator and, most importantly, the supreme attributes of God in Muslim belief.

Before we ask how Muslims perceive God, it seems necessary first to ask how God is described in the Qur'an. Given the above-explained importance of the Qur'an, reflecting about God through the Qur'an resembles both the point of departure and the ultimate goal of Muslim theological reasoning.

Based on the Qur'an, we can therefore make the following statement: Muslims can identify God, because He describes himself in the Qur'an "He is God: there is no god other than Him, the Controller, the Holy One, Source of Peace, Granter of Security, Guardian over all, the Almighty, the Compeller, the Truly Great; God is far above anything they consider to be His partner. 24 He is God: the Creator, the Originator, the Shaper. The best names belong to Him. Everything in the heavens and earth glorifies Him: He is the Almighty, the Wise." ([3], Q 59:23–25).

Many attributes are listed in the above-mentioned verse. However, one attribute is emphasized in the Qur'an more than others—God's mercy. The Qur'an states "'Grant us good things in this world and in the life to come. We turn to You.' God said, 'I bring My punishment on whoever I will, but **My mercy encompasses all things**.'" ([3], Q 7:156).

---

[8] The corruption and/or misreprsentation of the Bible has long prompted Islamic theological debates. However, in contrast to the common perception, some Muslim theologians (e.g., Süleyman Ateş) argue to re-evaluate the issue based on revised hermeneutical access to the Qur'an.

[9] Klaus von Stosch (in this volume): The quality of a comparative theology is not dependent on the number of internalized theories, but rather on its capacity to create networks and to be in dialogue with other perspectives, *i.e.*, searching for truth in different contexts.

Muslim theologians, as much as ordinary Muslims, will immediately agree with the characterization of God as all merciful and compassionate. However, it remains somewhat unclear how God's mercy can be fully explained and scrutinized. How can Muslims relate to God's mercy? Or is it a rather figurative or descriptive term? What precise role does God's mercy play in the Quranic revelation and the daily practice of Muslims?

In attempting to define God, Khaled Abou El Fadl elaborates "God is too infinite, too grand, and too limitless for any human being to presume to know or to possess the one and only way of unlocking the secrets of our moral universe. {...} It is in the very nature of things that each of us searches for a way, that each group of people that believes in an idea will search for a way, and what matters is that they become convinced or persuaded that their way is correct" ([6], p. 226). Abou El Fadl outlines basically the context in which the search for God unfolds. "Believing in an idea" expresses the notion about how each group of people arrive at their conclusions about God. In Islamic theology, these conclusions are based on the revelation of God, the teachings of the Prophet Muhammed and the long lasting tradition of Islamic thought. In the modern world, as stated above, we can likewise enrich our understanding by directing our attention to non-Muslim perceptions of the divine. Additionally, we can also explore new paths of understanding by engaging our own tradition differently, aided by a comparative approach to religious truth.

Hence, we believe that there is much reason to acknowledge God's mercy as a promising way to contextualize God. God Himself highlights in the Qur'an that He can be held accountable on the grounds to be merciful: "Say, 'To whom belongs all that is in the heavens and earth?' Say, 'To God. **He has taken it upon Himself to be merciful**. He will certainly gather you on the Day of Resurrection, which is beyond all doubt. Those who deceive themselves will not believe'" ([3], Q 6:12).

There are a series of other observations that support this assumption. First of all, "mercy" is the attribute by which God describes himself most often. No other attribute is cited as much as mercy. 113 out of 114 chapters of the Qur'an start with the formula "In the name of God the allforgiver, and merciful." Secondly, the Qur'an even goes one step further, and not only describes God as merciful, but equates the attribute of mercy with God and states that there is an essential connection between them [3].[10] God's mercy is also described as a place of refuge: "Say, '[God says], My servants who have harmed yourselves by your own excess, do not despair of God's mercy. God forgives all sins: He is truly the Most Forgiving, the Most Merciful" ([3], Q 39:51). The concept of mercy is therefore both the hope that God will always bestow his mercy upon us and also a promise that we can rely on his mercy.

We would like to briefly examine one particular field in which some might detect a contradiction or tension of sorts. How does the theology of mercy relate to the numerous accounts of God's wrath? Indeed, God describes Himself in many instances as wrathful ([3], Q 16:106 and Q 20:81). The divine wrath should not, however, be evaluated as a simple act of vengeance for not obeying God's rules. It should rather be perceived as a call to mankind to uphold the divine incentives of mercy, justice and

---

[10] The Qur'an states in 17:110 "Say [to them], 'Call on God, or on the Lord of Mercy–whatever names you call Him, the best names belong to Him."

compassion. It is the divine mercy that reminds us constantly not to violate the prime directives that God has framed for us in his revelation. Here, we can clearly establish a strong connection between the concept of mercy and its implication in our lives. The divine mercy is not merely a theoretical concept restricted to the Qur'an. Additionally, it is not an arbitrary notion derived from the Qur'an. Moreover, the divine mercy establishes interdependency between our hopes and actions. The Muslim is asked to enact in his own life the same kind of mercy he expects to receive from the divine.

God's mercy does not only manifest itself in the Quranic revelation. It actually reaches into our everyday life. God's mercy is, therefore, all encompassing and cannot be restricted. It is also not reserved solely for those who believe in God. Mercy is passed on to any being that has been created by God. Engaging with God's mercy means both giving and receiving. It does not only indicate receiving mercy from God. Rather, Muslims are asked time and again to initiate mercy themselves, to act upon mercy and, thus, to fuel God's mercy. Consequently, we should understand the Quranic revelation as a communicative, dialogical process, in which the Muslim actively engages with God. By doing so, he instantly receives God's mercy, while at the same time he also reflects upon it, spreads it and directs it back to God.

Still, no matter how much we elaborate the issue of mercy, we will always fall short of fully grasping what God's mercy finally entails. As Khaled Abou El Fadl says, "God is too infinite, too grand, and too limitless for any human being to presume to know or to possess the one and only way of unlocking the secrets of our moral universe." As a consequence, drawing on all manifestations of God's mercy can help us to intensify and strengthen our comprehension. A brief analysis of Christian theology, for instance, will reveal that Biblical texts often refer to God's mercy. Comparing Christian with Muslim understandings of God's mercy might help us observe how it is bestowed upon mankind. This is not unfamiliar to Islam anyway, since Jesus' teachings are incorporated into our set of beliefs. However, can we really claim to have a thorough idea of what Jesus taught or how God's mercy was conveyed through Jesus? By and large, Muslims only relate to the Quranic references about Jesus. Taking Christian sources into account would improve our understanding quite directly.[11] It stands to reason, however, that we would likely detect the same God speaking to us through the Qur'an and the teachings of the Prophet Muhammed as the God who spoke through Jesus.

On the other hand, Christian theology can also derive insight into God's mercy by exploring the life of the Prophet Muhammed. Addressing the prophet's role, the Qur'an states "A Messenger has come to you from among yourselves. Your suffering distresses him: he is deeply concerned for you and full of kindness and mercy towards the believers" ([3], Q 9:128). This is the only instance in which a divine attribute, namely mercy, is being assigned to the Prophet. Therefore, the life and the teachings of the Prophet became not only thoroughly intertwined with divine mercy, but the Muslim community based on this Quranic verdict also evaluates all records about the Prophet by reference to divine mercy.

---

[11] Engaging the Biblical accounts on Jesus and the concept of mercy in Christianity as part of a comparative learning process is impossible here; however, we intend to devote appropriate attention to this topic and will employ the issue of divine mercy in Biblical accounts in a forthcoming essay.

Muslims are therefore convinced that God exemplified his mercy in the Prophet Muhammed's life and, by doing so, gave us a human role model.

Without too much debate, we can conclude that mercy is one of the overarching themes of the Quranic revelation. A theology of mercy could help us shift the gravity of Islamic theology and, consequently, enable Muslims to investigate a relatively unexplored field of theological reasoning, comparative theology. At the same time, it could also inspire other religious groups to reflect on and dialogue with Islamic thinking in a broader sense—and to seek to bring new insights into their own reasoning about the divine.

Conflicts of Interest

The authors declare no conflict of interest.

References and Notes

1. Marmura, Michael E. *Al-Ġhazālī, Abū-Ḥāmid Muḥammad. The Incoherence of the Philosophers = Tahāfut al-falāsifah: A Parallel English-Arabic Text*. Provo: Brigham Young University Press, 1997.
2. Moosa, Ebrahim. *Ghazali and the Poetics of Imagination*. Chapel Hill: North Carolina Press, 2005.
3. Abdel Haleem, M. A. S. *The Qur'an, A New Translation*. Oxford: Oxford University Press, 2005.
4. Wehr, Hans, and J. Milton Cowan. *The Hans Wehr Dictionary of Modern Written Arabic*. Wiesbaden: Harrassowitz, 1994.
5. Abou El Fadl, Khaled. Speaking, killing and loving in God's name. *The Hedgehog Review*, Spring 2004, 71–77.
6. Abou El Fadl, Khaled. "Reading the Signs: The Moral Compass of Transcendent Engagement." In *Herausforderungen an die islamische Theologie in Europa- Challenges for Islamic Theologie in Europe*. Edited by Mouhanad Khorchide and Klaus von Stosch. Freiburg: Herder, 2012.
7. Ayoub, Mahmoud, and Irfan A. Omar, eds. *A Muslim Looks at Christianity: Essays on Dialogue*. New York: Orbis Books, 2007.
8. Michel, Thomas F. *A Muslim Theologian's Response to Christianity. Ibn Taymiyya's Al-Jawab al-Sahih*. New York: Caravan Books, 1984.
9. Accad, Martin. Corruption and/or Misinterpretation of the Bible-The Story of Islamic usage of Tahrif. *Theological Review* 24 (2003): 67–97.
10. Schreiner, Stefan. "Der Koran als Auslegung der Bibel-die Bibel als Verstehenshilfe des Korans." In *Nahe ist dir das Wort ...": Schriftauslegung in Christentum und Islam*. Edited by Hansjörg Schmid, Andreas Renz and Bülent Ucar. Regensburg: Pustet Friedrich KG, 2010.

Cite as: Schmidt-Leukel, Perry. "Scholars in Europe on the New Comparative Theology. A Pluralist's Rejoinder." In *European Perspectives on the New Comparative Theology*, edited by Francis X. Clooney and John Berthrong. Basel: MDPI, 2014, 163-176.

Scholars in Europe on the New Comparative Theology. A Pluralist's Rejoinder

Perry Schmidt-Leukel

Institute for Religious Studies and Inter-Faith Theology, Evangelisch-Theologische Fakultät, University of Münster, Universitätsstraße 13-17, Münster 48143, Germany; E-Mail: perrysl@uni-muenster.de

1. Some Terminological Misgivings

1.1. What Is Meant by "European Perspectives"?

Though choosing the title "European Perspectives on the New Comparative Theology", the editors of this collection are fully aware that "our authors do not speak with a single 'European voice'" (p. 1). One wonders, however, what the Europeanness of such a voice or perspective—whether single or multiple—might be. First of all, Europe doesn't speak (quite literally) with one voice or language. There is little, often no, exchange between the Anglophone countries, the Francophone ones, the German speaking ones, the Scandinavian countries, the Mediterranean ones, the Eastern European countries or those on the Balkan.[1] Not many theological books are translated these days[2] and English has not (yet?[3]) become the European *lingua franca*. Not many German theologians are aware of theological developments and controversies taking place in English or vice versa and I'm afraid that this is not much different in France or Spain, Italy, Greece, Poland, Hungary, *etc.*—though I don't know for sure, which in itself might be taken as evidence that there is not too much theological exchange between Europe's different language zones. A brief look at the contributors in the present

---

[1] I think this judgment is fair despite the laudable efforts to the contrary – at least within Roman Catholic Theology—by the 1989 founded *European Society of Catholic Theology (ESCT)/Europäische Gesellschaft für Katholische Theologie (EGKT)/Association européenne de Théologie Catholique (AETC)*.

[2] Regarding the translation of New Comparative Theology publications, I am only aware of the recent translation of Clooney's "Comparative Theology" into German [1], one of his older works into French [2] and the volume edited by von Stosch and Bernhardt [3] containing some fresh papers of Neville, Ward and Fredericks translated into German.

[3] The two most efficient bodies in the field of Intercultural Theology (*European Society for Intercultural Theology and Interreligious Studies, ESITIS*, established in 2005) and Buddhist-Christian Studies (*European Network of Buddhist Christian Studies, ENBCS*, established in 1996) made English their working language.

collection shows that seven come from German speaking countries, three from the United Kingdom and two from the Benelux states. This is at most a snippet of Europe. Yet even within these narrow boundaries the contributors form a small and by no means representative group: UK contributors aside, the rest are united by the fact that they (though to different degrees) follow, and partly participate in, theological debates in English. And precisely this makes our small group of authors not very "European" (as it is, presumably, not typically "American" to follow theological debates in German). Otherwise the authors would not have to say much about the "New Comparative Theology", because, I'm afraid, they would not know what that is. There is neither a single European discourse on theology, nor—as far as I can see—is the "New Comparative Theology" a central topic in Europe's different theological discourses. The positive aspect of this, however, is that what the contributors to this volume have to share should not be taken as merely of regional relevance. It is rather a collection of voices from scholars in Europe contributing to a global theological discourse on "Comparative Theology".

There might, however, be one aspect that perhaps indicates at least one particularly "European" feature, as suggested by *Ulrich Winkler*. It concerns the Vatican's (after all, a European state[4]) role in European theology. Within the confinements of the Roman Catholic Church, one might assume, the influence and/or control exerted by the Vatican should be equally strong around the world (at least in theory). In some European countries, however, particularly (though not exclusively) in the German speaking ones, its influence extends over parts of public universities, primarily (but by no means exclusively) over departments or institutes of Roman Catholic Theology (see [8]). In various European states theology is taught at public Universities as denominational theology in strictly separate institutional units (faculties, departments, institutes). The University of Munich, for example, has one large faculty of Roman Catholic Theology, one only slightly smaller faculty of Protestant Theology and a middle sized unit of Orthodox Theology. Do they have Ecumenical Theology as well? Yes, of course: a Catholic one, a Protestant one and an Orthodox one. It is the Churches, neither the universities nor the state, who have the last say on who is allowed to teach and who is not, and what they are allowed to teach and what not. *Winkler*, *Bernhardt* and *Drew* all make the point that the discussion about the New Comparative Theology, and in particular about its relation to a Pluralist Theology of Religions, is not only restricted, but predetermined and at times massively distorted by ecclesial control. *Winkler*, courageously (though still a bid hidden in his first endnote) points to the fact that there exists a whole genre of theological publications produced only on the demand of Vatican congregations, the authors being forced to establish their orthodoxy—or to explicitly reject what the Vatican currently perceives as not fully orthodox. If scholars do not comply, they will not get the academic post they are looking for, or even lose their present one—a situation that is as personally saddening and morally appalling as it is academically scandalous. In fact, the conditions hinted at by *Winkler* are well suited to cause students keeping their fingers off before they might get them burnt.

---

[4] Though, for various reasons, not a member of the European Union—one reason being that it would not fulfill the "Copenhagen criteria" which require members of the EU to be democracies.

The censor's objective is most fully accomplished when mental self-censoring begins even before the censor needs to take any further action.

Fortunately this situation does not prevail at all European universities. There are countries, as for example England and Scotland, where theology, at public universities, is in a position to proceed freely, restricted only by the rules and methods of good scholarly practice. Yet one should note that there are voices, as that of *Gavin D'Costa*, rendered (with endorsement?) in *Ganeri*'s contribution which in relation to theology departments at UK universities deplore the "loss of Church control over the institution" (Ganeri, p. 135) and purport that a revision of this situation would also "promote ... the study of other religions" (*ibid.*). The experience of the German speaking countries, however, shows that under Roman Catholic control, there is no free discussion and research on how to understand the religions theologically and the vision of studying religions under authentic scholars from different religious traditions within one and the same faculty or department appears rather illusory (as pointed out by *Winkler*). Yet, precisely the latter is possible in various theology departments in the UK, or at some other academic places in Europe, as, for example, at the Free University of Amsterdam or the Academy of World Religions at the University of Hamburg which are beyond the reach of the Vatican.

This leads to the question as to where Comparative Theology is practiced in Europe (with or without restrictions). The answer to this question hinges on what exactly we mean by "Comparative Theology".

1.2. What Is Meant by "Comparative Theology"?

In my mind, the basic issue in characterizing or defining Comparative Theology is its relation to interreligious dialog. These days, interreligious dialog is often taken as a political and social tool, as a pragmatic instrument for precaution against, and management of, interreligious conflict. Yet the pioneers of interreligious dialog had conceived it as a new *locus theologicus*, as a source of fresh theological insight and understanding. In this light, one may rightly see Comparative Theology—as stressed by *Dehn*, *Drew*, *Moyaert* and others—as a form of interreligious dialog. Perceived in any narrow sense, one would have to state that Comparative Theology is done at only very few places within Europe (Paderborn, Salzburg, ...?). Yet, if understood in a broad sense as theological interreligious dialog, plenty of Comparative Theology has been and is being done in Europe though not under that specific label. For commitment to theological interreligious dialogue, particularly to Christian-Jewish and Christian-Muslim dialog or Abrahamic trialog, but also to Christian-Buddhist and, to a somewhat lesser degree, Christian-Hindu dialog, is present and found at various theological centers across Europe (with regional variations). Taking a closer look at the theological work that is being done in Europe on and within interreligious dialog, one will easily see that this abounds with comparative topics. I must confess that I am sometimes puzzled why those who present and understand themselves as "Comparative Theologians"—and now I am not only talking about Europe—do not make more out of the abundance of comparative work that has already been done in interreligious dialogue of a theological nature.[5] Could anyone, for example, sensibly assume that Comparative Theology involving Buddhism and Christianity began with the writings of James Fredericks? How could any Comparative Theologian in that specific field responsibly ignore all the efforts and fruits of theological exchange between Buddhism and Christianity over the last five or six decades? This applies equally well to all the other areas of interreligious exchange. Hence *Dehn* rightly asks: "What purpose does C.T. serve beyond that which dialogical research has previously served for a long time? What is the surplus of saying 'comparative' instead of 'dialogical'?" (Dehn, p. 44).

Perhaps, one might be inclined to answer, Comparative Theology brings a new methodology to interreligious dialog, one that has not been followed by previous attempts and, hence, promises new insights and fruitful results. But to what extent is this correct? As far as I can see, a specific methodology of how to do Comparative Theology has not yet been agreed among the New Comparative Theologians. Surprisingly, even the methodology of comparison itself is far from being at the center of the discourse among the New Comparative Theologians. While comparative method enjoys meticulous attention and reflection in *Robert Neville*'s "Comparative Religious Ideas Project" [4], the meaning of "comparison" remains deliberately vague and broad in *Clooney*'s remark that "*comparison is a reflective and contemplative endeavor by which we see the other in light of our own, and our own in light of the other*" ([5] p. 11). This uncertainty about the understanding and specific method of comparison in Comparative Theology makes method a rather weak candidate for giving Comparative Theology a clearer profile against or within theological interreligious dialog.

The desideratum of a sharper methodological profile within the New Comparative Theology is strongly expressed in *von Stosch*'s contribution. In his own suggestions, however, he is ready to pay a fairly high price for it, that is, rejecting that whole strand of Comparative Theology which tends towards a "global" or "interreligious theology" (as exemplified in the work of *Keith Ward*, *Robert Neville*, *John Thatamanil* and others) and confining "Comparative Theology" exclusively to small scale case studies—a strategy that he associates with the work of *Clooney* and *Fredericks*. Yet even in this respect it is, according to *von Stosch*, necessary "to develop this 'micrological' kind of inquiry in a more systematic way" (von Stosch, p. 34). That is, the selection of case studies must not be arbitrary, but "geared to anthropological and theological problems", it "must engage questions about sense, salvation and truth" in order to avoid the comparison of "irrelevant subjects" (*ibid.*). Yet do these very sensible suggestions not somehow work against the preferred "micrological" approach? How can you establish what would have to count as a relevant case study, if you are not more or less familiar with the religious tradition as a whole—including its various contexts? Precisely the decision of what to compare with what can lead to the most grave distortions if it does not follow carefully elaborated hermeneutic rules. The major religious traditions form large reservoirs of highly impressive and highly repulsive cases when it comes to anthropological and theological problems. Massively imbalanced

---

[5] Apparently that was different in the early days of the "New Comparative Theology". See, for example, how more or less the whole field of interreligious theological dialog was taken as Comparative Theology in Clooney's review article of 1995 (see [7])

impressions can easily be produced just by selecting suitable (or rather unsuitable) cases for one's case studies. This insight emerged strongly from decades of research when the phenomenology of religion and its comparative methods dominated the Science of Religion. I fully agree with *von Stosch*'s judgment "that comparative theology needs an ideologically critical process in determining both its research areas and methods" (p. 36). But I think that precisely for this reason Comparative Theologians should take to their heart *Bernhardt*'s advice "that interreligious comparisons are to be conducted by the standards of religious studies" (p. 28). Comparative Religion has to offer much expertise on both the pitfalls and pathways of interreligious comparison from which theologically motivated comparisons could and should learn.

My critical remarks do not infer that so far no fresh methodological approaches have emerged from the New Comparative Theology. Apart from the helpful reflections in *Neville*'s Comparative Religious Ideas Project, which I already mentioned, I would like to highlight in this respect the innovative genre[6] of cross-religious commentarial writing that we find in the series, edited by *Catherine Cornille*, "Christian Commentaries on Non-Christian Sacred Texts".[7] Interestingly this series, as far as I can see, is not mentioned in any of the contributions to the present volume which might perhaps indicate that its volumes are not perceived as works of Comparative Theology. The volumes in this series point to an aspect of Comparative Theology that is rightly associated by *Jacques Scheuer* with what *Raimon Panikkar* in 1978(!) had called the "*intra*-religious dialogue" (Scheuer, p. 125). *Scheuer*'s observation is much in line with the way *Clooney* distinguishes Comparative Theology from interreligious dialog, saying that the Comparative Theologian "will begin to theologize as it were from both sides of the table, reflecting personally on old and new truths in an interior dialogue" ([5] p. 13). Important as this kind of "interior" or "*intra*-religious" dialog is, it runs the risk, as indicated by *Reinhold Bernhardt* in a recent review article, that the real voice of the religious other is made redundant ([10] p. 195). This danger can only be averted if Comparative Theology remains firmly embedded in interreligious dialog so that, for example, despite the contrary intention of *Cornille*, cross-religious commentaries are not merely written for one's own religious community but with the deliberate intention of eliciting a response from members of those traditions to which the scriptures commented on belong.

2. Comparative Theology and the Theology of Religions

In distinguishing the New Comparative Theology from Comparative Religion as practiced within the Science of Religion or *Religionswissenschaft,* supporters of the first seem unanimously clear that their approach differs from the latter in its explicit theological interest in religious truth. Yet, if any aspects of the Christian faith are studied in comparison (however broad or narrow the comparative methodology might be) with aspects of the faith of other religious traditions under the perspective of the possible, hoped for, confessed, *etc.* truth of the faith, this inevitably raises the question of whether

---

[6] Though not absolutely new. In China, under the influence of the "Harmony of the three teachings"-doctrine, the writing of cross-religious commentaries has been a widespread practice [33].

[7] On the editor's concept of the series see [9].

(1) the possible truth on the one side excludes the truth on the other side or, if not, whether (2) it might surpass it, or (3) might be more on a par with it, e.g. by constituting a variant or by being in some way complementary. Carrying out interreligious comparisons with a deliberate theological interest will necessarily lead into the realm of those kinds of questions as are discussed in the so-called theology of religions, as the three questions just indicated mirror the three basic options in the theology of religions: That is, such questions will emerge, not in addition or even competition to, but precisely from particular and specific case studies. However, the New Comparative Theology is propagated since the middle of the 1990s as "an alternative to a theology of religions"—as was the title of *Frederick*'s 1995 manifesto.[8] Though this claim was neither shared by all representatives of Comparative Theology (e.g., not by *Keith Ward*) nor presented with equal radicality—*Clooney* always took it more as a plea for a moratorium in the theology of religions debate—it promised to open a new pathway for theological engagement with other religions without entering the dogmatic minefield of the theology of religions.

As a pluralist, I find it particularly interesting to see how this claim has fared about twenty years after it was first propagated. Looking at the contributions to this volume, one hardly finds much or strong support for it, but plenty of excellent refutations. *Bernhardt*, *Winkler*[9], *Hedges* and *Drew* all demonstrate persuasively that Comparative Theology is not, and cannot be, free from making the kind of theological assumptions that are explicitly discussed in the theology of religions. The alleged alternative, therefore, does not really relate to the New Comparative Theology and the theology of religions as such, but to one particular option within the theology of religions, the pluralist one, which is quite frankly admitted by *Dehn* when he identifies the pluralist theology of religions as the "major antagonist to C.T." (Dehn, p. 44). Yet, is this antagonism symmetrically perceived from both sides or does it reflect a one-sided perception from the side of (some) Comparative Theologians? Religious pluralists do not have any problems at all with doing theology comparatively. *John Hick* produced a pioneering comparative study on "Death and Eternal Life" [13], *Wilfred Cantwell Smith* contributed pioneering comparative work on "Faith and Belief" [14] and on the understanding of scripture within different traditions [15]—all three works as detailed, specific and, most of all, as knowledgeable as anything produced in the New Comparative Theology. And a number of pluralists became pluralist through comparative considerations in the course of interreligious dialog.[10] Pluralists don't see an antagonism with Comparative Theology, but just question whether it is a realistic option, as some supporters of the New Comparative Theology claim, that one can seriously perform comparative interreligious studies while at the same time refraining from any theological evaluation.

As *Bernhardt*, *Hedges* and *Drew* convincingly argue, Comparative Theology, if it involves the idea of theological learning from other faiths, is carried out on the assumption or hope that theologically relevant truth can be found outside Christianity (see Bernhardt, p. 24f. & 28; Hedges, p. 55f; Drew, pp. 73–76). *Rose Drew* thus rightly states: "…comparative theology cannot emerge from exclusivism"

---

[8] See [11] and my critical discussion in [12], pp. 90–104.
[9] See also his recent book [32].
[10] For an overview on the various strands and different roots of pluralist theologies of religions see [24].

(Drew, p. 73). Or, as expressed by *Martin Ganeri*: The comparative theologian will not merely "equate 'non-Christian thought' with 'natural human reason,' but be genuinely open to the presence of the 'holy' as the expression of the universal action of the Spirit…". Yet with this kind of openness, one is already "clearly … in the area of theology of religions" (Ganeri, p. 146). The inevitable consequence is—to quote *Drew* again—that Comparative Theology "must proceed from provisional inclusivist or pluralist assumptions" (Drew, p. 73). *Paul Hedges* even accuses those who continue to claim that the New Comparative Theology is "different and somehow 'beyond'" the theology of religions as being immune to "the compelling critiques" (Hedges, p. 56). But are such claims still perpetuated? *Francis Clooney* identified himself several times as an inclusivist (e.g. [16] p. 194f; [5] p. 16) and so recently did *James Fredericks* (see [17] p. xv).

Now, if Comparative Theology of religions cannot successfully abstain from adopting a specific position in the theology of religions, and if these can only be of either an inclusivist or pluralist nature, are there any specific arguments against a pluralist position that would make inclusivism the preferred or most natural option of Comparative Theology? Within the present collection, the strongest polemics against theology of religions in general, and the pluralist position in particular, is found in *Marianne Moyaert*'s chapter, as, for example, when she accuses pluralism and particularism (exclusivism) "as exponents of a desire for control", whereas "comparative theology can be regarded as a form of vulnerable theology" (Moyaert, p. 103). Her more sober arguments against religious pluralism come down to the following two well-known objections: *first*, pluralism's assessment of the religious other is *aprioristic* and does not emerge from a detailed and patient engagement with the other; *second*, pluralism is dominated by a *homogenizing tendency* which reduces all differences to sameness and ignores the real otherness of the other. Both accusations are interconnected in the imputed desire for control in as much as, by means of the aprioristically "presupposed commonalities", the other is not allowed to speak for himself (Moyaert, p. 114). I am not going to reply to *Moyaert*'s imputation of a hidden desire for control on the side of the pluralists (being happy to leave this psychological or postcolonial clairvoyance to her). If we don't speak about imputations but about the more manifest forms of any desire for control, we observe this—see above—in the actions of the Vatican, which is hardly dominated by religious pluralists. So let me confine my reply to the alleged apriorism and homogenizing tendency of pluralism.

It is a well-known fact that both, *Karl Barth* and *Karl Rahner*, explicitly acknowledged the aprioristic nature of their exclusivist and inclusivist theologies (though at least *Karl Rahner* expressed an interest in seeing his views confirmed by the findings of the "history of religions"). This, however, was very different to pioneers of pluralism, as *Raimon Panikkar*, *Wilfred Cantwell Smith* and *John Hick*. Both, *Hick* and *Smith* began as exclusivists, while *Panikkar* took off with a sort of Rahnerian type of inclusivism. As in the case of a number of other pluralists (including myself), it was their long, intensive and theologically serious encounter with, and study of, the religious other that led them to change their theological presuppositions and develop pluralist approaches. Hence the accusation of apriorism is hardly justifiable. It is rather a converse question that emerges, namely whether the supporters of the New Comparative Theology are equally open to possibly revise their theological views if propelled by their comparative work. In this respect, I fully agree with *Ulrich Winkler*'s maxim that the openness for at least a "partial and potential pluralistic theology of religions is an indispensable precondition for comparative theology" (Winkler, p. 13). Throughout her contribution, *Moyaert* invokes a kind of openness to the religious other which she terms "vulnerability". But does she tell us what that vulnerability consists in? According to *Hans Joachim Margull* who introduced the term "vulnerability" to the theological debate on interreligious dialogue as early as in 1974, it explicates the various claims to religious absoluteness and superiority to be wounded in this encounter [18].[11] Yet apparently this is not the sense that *Moyaert* has in mind. For she speaks of a vulnerability that leaves one's confessional convictions intact, or at least forbids to transform them to the point where one would have to surrender traditional superiority claims and adopt a pluralist position. This leaves one wondering who could be more justly accused of "apriorism".

The problem of openness to revision is, in my view, a crucial issue when we inquire about the innovative force of Comparative Theology. The spectrum is perhaps best represented by the positions of *Frank Clooney* and *Keith Ward*. At the one end is *Clooney*'s understanding of Comparative Theology as a confessional discipline: "acts of faith seeking understanding ... rooted in a particular faith tradition but which, from that foundation, venture into learning from one or more other faith traditions" ([5] p. 10). At the other end we find *Keith Ward*'s concept of Comparative Theology as not confessional but "as an intellectual discipline which enquires into ideas of ultimate value and goal of human life, as they have been perceived and expressed in a variety of religious traditions" ([6] p. 40). The latter implies a concept of "theology" that is not in any generic sense Catholic, Anglican or Christian, but seen as a "discipline of reflection upon ideas of the ultimate reality and goal of human life, of God, and of revelation" which "can be undertaken by people of many diverse beliefs" ([6] p. 46). Thus for *Ward* too, the Comparative Theologian will be rooted in a particular religious/confessional tradition but he or she "seeks to extend one's tradition as it encounters new understandings" [6] p. 47). Where *Clooney* and *Ward* meet is the centrality of interreligious learning; where they differ is the extent to which this learning is permitted to involve revision. For *Clooney,* Comparative Theology remains "intelligently faithful to tradition even while seeking fresh understanding outside that tradition" ([5] p. 11), while for *Ward* the Comparative Theologian needs "being prepared to revise beliefs if and when it comes to seem necessary" ([6] p. 48). So *Moyaert*'s version of a more restricted and less open form of Comparative Theology is at least not representative of all who work under that label. Yet if one takes her emphasis on "vulnerability" seriously, one should follow *Margull* and relate this vulnerability to religious superiority claims.

So what about *Moyaert*'s second objection against pluralism as an allegedly homogenizing approach that cannot be open to the religious other's otherness? To cut a long answer short, the issue is not that pluralists would ignore, deny or neglect differences, but that they suggest an alternative interpretation and evaluation of at least some (not all) differences. Somewhat simplifying, one can say that the exclusivist takes difference and otherness as indicative of falsity. That is, the religion of the

---

[11] Through Margull the term entered the WCC's *Guidelines on Dialogue* (1979) where it appears under no. 21 as a central attitude in dialog.

other is false *because* it differs from one's own. The inclusivist takes difference as indicative of inferiority. That is, the religion of the other is inferior to one's own *to the extent* it differs from one's own. The pluralist suggest that some differences, in particular some of those regarding images/concepts of the Ultimate, can be interpreted as equally valid despite being different, e.g., by understanding the differences as compatible or even complementary. *John Hick*, for example, did not subscribe to the theory that the different *personae* and *impersonae* of the Ultimate are just different expressions of the same experience, but that they are imbedded in different systems and relate to *different experiences* of the *same ultimate reality*. If one, however, denies, from a Christian perspective, that the religious other is at all in some form of contact with the same ultimate reality, that is, with that reality to which we refer by the term "God", then one has simply adopted an exclusivist stance. However, it is not at all the case that only exclusivists would take religious otherness seriously. They just suggest a different interpretation of that otherness, as does the inclusivist and the pluralist. So why should the pluralist be accused of diminishing the otherness of the other simply because he or she interprets that difference as a different form of relation to the Ultimate? If *Moyaert*—as she apparently does—reckons with truth and wisdom in other faiths which are not merely of a human nature, she could also be accused of diminishing the otherness of the other, namely in case a radical exclusivism would be right, that is, if the otherness or the other would indeed consist in not being related to God at all. In accusing pluralism of neglecting or denying differences, *Moyaert* distorts not only the pluralist position but also the real issue at stake, which is about different interpretations and evaluations of religious differences.[12]

A third objection, raised against theology of religions in general, takes us back to the issue of revision. It is mentioned briefly by *Dehn* when he blames any theology of religion, whether exclusivist, inclusivist or pluralist, of inadequately and improperly essentializing "religions as monolithic entities" (Dehn, p. 45). According to *Dehn*, religions are too complex, too diversified and too much subject to constant flux as to become, in any meaningful way, subject to large scale theological assessments, as is, according to *Dehn*, inevitably the case in all three theology of religions options. (By the way, how then could *Wilfred Cantwell Smith* have been a pluralist? Was he not the first who vigorously argued against an essentialist misunderstanding of religious traditions?) Anyway, *Dehn* sees Comparative Theology in this respect in a much more favorable position in so far as its narrowly limited case studies can focus on specific dialogical situations without making overall judgments on religious systems or traditions as a whole. This argument plays a prominent role in the way *von Stosch* takes Comparative Religion as an alternative to the theology of religions—not in his contribution to this volume but in his other publications. *Von Stosch* combines this objection with his specific recourse on Wittgenstein's language game theory by relating religious truth claims to the practical dimension within particular narrowly confined contexts and reinterpreting them as expressing "grammatical" rules. Relating religious truth claims to the metaphysical realm is rejected by *von Stosch* as a somewhat backward and outdated "metaphysical realism" (see [20], p. 226). One might, I suggest, harbor some justified doubts whether that Wittgensteinian reinterpretation of

---

[12] This point is further elaborated in [19].

religious truth claims is really in line with how these claims are understood by those who make them (allegedly *von Stosch*'s primary *locus* of all theological reflection in this field). Yet there is another, perhaps more weighty counter argument: There is absolutely no need to assess a religious tradition in its totality in order to make responsible judgments in the theology of religions. For example, the exclusivist claim that salvific truth is found in only one religion, or one religious sub-sect, is already falsified if one identifies just one single instance of salvific truth outside the group's borders. Similarly, the inclusivist claim of the unique superiority of salvific truth as taught within one's own group is falsified if one identifies just one single case outside in the light of which such claimed superiority is no longer credible. I should add that I use the term "falsified" here not in any strong epistemological sense, but in the limited sense of a "falsification" *under the premises of faith* and *on the basis of criteria accepted by, and in, faith*. Nevertheless I presuppose that under such premises the law of rational consistency enables indeed such forms of "falsification". At least it can be shown how high the costs would be to immunize one's beliefs against such "falsification". If, for example, the occurrence of genuine love would count as knowledge of God (1 John 4:7), one single case of a loving non-Christian—inspired and nurtured in this love by his or her non-Christian faith—would suffice to falsify exclusivist claims. To immunize exclusivism against that kind of falsification would require either to drop the premise of genuine love being evidence of knowledge of God or to hold that all love in the case of a non-Christian is not genuine or, at least, is not what is meant by Christian *agapé*.[13] Yet why would Jesus then have had *agapé* illustrated by the behavior of a non-Christian, well, even a non-Jew? So the first alternative of avoiding falsification might be too costly and the second too implausible. This is just to illustrate how, through comparative theological work, the positions of exclusivism, inclusivism and indeed pluralism too can be either strengthened or weakened without having to assess religious traditions as a whole in each and every respect. So *Clooney*'s more recent suggestion "that the theology of religions and comparative theology mirror and imply one another, and even help one another" ([22], p. 196) can and should indeed be taken as constructive advice.

There is one more crucial aspect to this debate that I would like to address. If exclusivism assesses the other's religion as false because it is different, and if the inclusivist sees it as inferior to the extent it differs, both exclusivism and inclusivism are unable to accord any genuine theological value to religious difference and hence to religious diversity. This can also be shown by the following thought experiment: If you believe that your own religion is in an objective sense the only true religion in the world, you will naturally harbor the wish that ideally all human beings should become members of this one and only true religion. Similarly, if you believe that your own religion is in an objective sense uniquely superior to all other religions, you will wish that ideally all human beings should become members of this uniquely superior religion. For it would be immoral to hold the idea that only "we" should enjoy the exclusive or superior truth while our neighbors should be satisfied with either none or

---

[13] This was George Lindbeck's strategy: Whatever a Buddhist does under the name of "Buddhist compassion", it is "radically ... distinct" from "Christian love" for the love of non-Christians is not (yet) "shaped by the message of Jesus' cross and resurrection" (see [21] pp. 40 and 60).

lesser forms of salvific truth.[14] Yet if ideally all humans should become members of one's own religion, by implication all other religions should ideally disappear. Exclusivism and inclusivism has no room for a positive view of religious diversity—yet pluralism does. Now, if practicing Comparative Theologians demonstrate in and through their theological work that they do in fact accord theological value to religious diversity, and that they do not harbor the ideal of Christianity swallowing up ("fulfilling") all other religions, are they then something like "anonymous" or "practicing pluralists", as Paul Knitter suggested [23]? Could it be the case that their resistance against taking a clearer stand in the theology of religions debate is triggered—at least if they are Roman Catholics—not that much by theological arguments, but by well-founded concerns over ecclesial consequences as *Bernhardt* (p. 25f) and *Drew* suggest (p. 81f.)? The answer has to be left to those concerned.

3. Comparative Theology and the Global Quest for Truth

If the "deep learning across religious borders" (*i.e.*, the subtitle of [5]) that Comparative Theology aims at takes place within several religious traditions and if this process should not be isolated from the living dialogical exchange, the result would be, as *Drew* points out, a global and "permanent interreligious colloquium" (Drew, p. 81) as had been envisioned by *Wilfred Cantwell Smith*. Indeed, some representatives of the New Comparative Theology understand their work precisely as a contribution to this development. *John Thatamanil* speaks of it as "a common inquiry about ultimate matters" ([24], p. xii). This interest is shared with the increasing efforts towards an intercultural or global philosophy.[15] I agree with *Claudia Bickmann* when she highlights that a prominent challenge for intercultural philosophy arises from the fact that philosophy in contemporary Europe has become largely atheist or non-religious while "most non-European traditions still cling to the idea of a highest metaphysical entity or a highest divine being" (Bickmann, p. 99). Hence, if Western philosophy will not choose the easy route of considering all non-Western philosophies as simply underdeveloped, it is confronted through comparative philosophy with the need of grappling with religious and metaphysical claims all over again. This insight may also warn against making Comparative Theology too closely dependent on just one or some modern or post-modern philosophical systems of the West. Comparative Theology challenges theologians not only to question their traditional theological presuppositions, but also their philosophical inclinations. This does not necessarily make comparative work easier but certainly more realistic—and once more points to the need of firmly embedding it in interreligious and cross-cultural exchange.

In this context, it evokes an interesting issue (and a further good topic for comparative analysis) as to which reasons might motivate adherents of other religions to engage themselves in interreligious

---

[14] This, by the way, is the crux of Dupuis' suggestion that the uniquely superior revelation is found only in Christ, but that God nevertheless wants to have an enduring(!) plurality of religions. For this would imply that God wants the majority of human beings to be lastingly satisfied with lesser forms of revelation—a kind of inclusivist version of the exclusivist double-predestination view.

[15] For three paradigmatic examples of using a comparative approach within "global" or "world philosophy" see [26], [27] and [28].

dialog and/or Comparative Theology and what kind of theology of religions is behind their motives.[16] An example is offered in the contribution of *Mouhanad Khorchide* and *Ufuk Topkara*. They explicitly raise the question why Muslims should be interested in studying other faiths and give the very constructive answer that this is "an attempt to read God's signs, which the Qur'an emphasizes on multiple occasions" (Khorchide/Topkara, p. 156). Even stronger: understanding different communities is a human duty, rooted in the plan of the creator who created diversity with the purpose of making the effort of mutual understanding a human task (*ibid.*). I fully agree, not only with this line of theological thinking, but also with how this is further spelled out by *Khorchide* and *Topkara*: Engaging in Comparative Theology can help Muslims to get a better understanding of the other and thereby of themselves. This is also true of central aspects of belief, as they briefly explain with the example of understanding divine mercy. This belief can be deepened by learning how God's mercy has manifested itself among other religious communities (p. 161) and can be strengthened by learning from others how they dealt with the major challenge of this belief, the problem of evil (p. 157). *Khorchide*'s and *Topkara*'s emphasis that this kind of learning about, and from, the religious other has to be based on the study of the authentic scriptural sources of other faiths is highly significant (p. 158). I also agree when they hold that interreligious learning could and should occur in both directions, that is "Christian theology can also derive insight into God's mercy by exploring the life of the Prophet Muhammed" (p. 161). This further confirms that Comparative Theology should best be seen as a form of interreligious dialog within the broader context of a global interreligious colloquium.

In 1990,[17] some years before the first manifestos for Comparative Theology were published, *Clooney* wrote an article that foreshadows much of his later development: his skepticism about the theology of religions and his sympathy for a theology that is somewhat fuzzy, unpredictable, focusing on the particular, "rich in examples, modest in systematizations", a "practice of 'thinking Christianity' with a set of resources that includes non-Christian elements" ([30], 488). And yet there is a noticeable difference between this and his later "confessional" stance; as in 1990 *Clooney* presented the theologians that are most apt to practice this "new theology" as people with a fluid religious identity. They have not exclusively been formed as Christians or Catholics but have also been exposed to the influence of non-Christian religions (*ibid.* 487). Interreligious dialog is for them nothing that takes place between clearly distinguished groups: "The new theologians involved in such encounters are likely to have elements from multiple traditions within their proper store of theological resources, even before the dialoguing begins..." (*ibid.* 490). As an example, *Clooney* presents *Panikkar* who has "spoken for decades of the possibility of sinking roots into multiple religious traditions". Also, *Clooney* suggests that "this possibility will now become a normal rather than extraordinary one" (*ibid.* 490, fn. 11). I think it is quite wholesome to remember that at least one of the roots of the New Comparative Theology lies in this (*Clooney*'s personal?) experience of a multi-religious identity which demands to be expressed and reflected in new theological forms. Here we see why Comparative Theology in *Clooney*'s work recalls strong associations with *Panikkar*'s concept of *intra*-religious

---

[16] For a survey of pluralist attitudes in Judaism, Islam, Hinduism and Buddhism see [29].
[17] It was published in 1991 as [30].

dialog. The multi-religious individual—as the natural host of *intra*-religious dialog—can be understood as a microcosmic image of our global situation, as has been argued by *Rose Drew* as a result of her groundbreaking research on Buddhist-Christian dual-belonging ([31] pp. 224–27). If this is a valid interpretation, and I think there is much to speak in favor of it, then the global interreligious colloquium to which Comparative Theology contributes may be understood as humanity's "*intra*-religious dialog" on a collective, corporative, world-wide level.

References

1. Francis X. Clooney S.J. *Komparative Theologie. Eingehendes Lernen über religiöse Grenzen hinweg*. Paderborn: Ferdinand Schöningh, 2013.
2. Francis X. Clooney S.J. *Sagesse Hindoue: Pour qui cherche Dieu*. Bruxelles: Editions Lessius, 2004.
3. Reinhold Bernhard and Klaus von Stosch, eds. *Komparative Theologie. Interreligiöse Vergleiche als Weg der Religionstheologie*. Zürich: TVZ, 2009.
4. Robert Neville, ed. *The Comparative Religious Ideas Project*. Vol. 1: The Human Condition; vol. 2: Ultimate Realities; vol. 3: Religious Truth. Albany: SUNY, 2001.
5. Francis X. Clooney S.J. *Comparative Theology. Deep Learning across Religious Borders*. Chichester: Wiley Blackwell, 2010.
6. Keith Ward. *Religion and Revelation. A Theology of Revelation in the World's Religions*. Oxford: Clarendon Press, 1994.
7. Francis X. Clooney S.J. "Comparative theology: A review of recent books (1989–1995)." *Theological Studies* 56 (1995): 521–50.
8. Adrian Loretan, ed. *Theologische Fakultäten an Europäischen Universitäten. Rechtliche Situation und Theologische Perspektiven*. Münster: LIT-Verlag, 2005.
9. Catherine Cornille. "Interreligiöse Theologie und die Bescheidenheit des Ortes." In *Interreligiöse Theologie. Chancen und Probleme*, Reinhold Bernhardt and Perry Schmidt-Leukel, eds. Zürich: TVZ, 2013, 161–79.
10. Reinhold Bernhardt. "Komparative Theologie." *Theologische Rundschau* 78 (2013): 187–200.
11. James Fredericks. "A universal religious experience? Comparative theology as an alternative to a theology of religions." *Horizons* 22 (1995): 67–87.
12. Perry Schmidt-Leukel. *Transformation by Integration. How Inter-faith Encounter Changes Christianity*. London: SCM Press, 2009.
13. John Hick. *Death and Eternal Life*. Basinstoke: Macmillan, 1990 (1st ed. 1976).
14. Wilfred Cantwell Smith. *Faith and Belief*. Princeton: Princeton University Press, 1979.
15. Wilfred Cantwell Smith. *What Is Scripture? A Comparative Approach*. London: SCM Press, 1993.
16. Francis X. Clooney S.J. *Theology after Vedanta. An Experiment in Comparative Theology*. Albany: SUNY, 1993.

17. James L. Fredericks. "Introduction." In *The New Comparative Theology. Interreligious Insights from the Next Generation*, Edited by Francis X. Clooney S.J. London–New York: T&T Clark, 2010.
18. Hans-Joachim Margull. "Verwundbarkeit. Bemerkungen zum Dialog." *Evangelische Theologie* 34 (1974): 410–20.
19. Perry Schmidt-Leukel. "Religious Pluralism and the Need for an Interreligious Theology." In *Religious Pluralism and the Modern World. An Ongoing Engagement with John Hick*, Sharada Sugirtharajah, ed. Basingstoke–New York: Palgrave Macmillan, 2012, 19–33.
20. Klaus von Stosch. *Komparative Theologie als Wegweiser in der Welt der Religionen*. Paderborn: Ferdinand Schöningh Verlag, 2012.
21. George Lindbeck. *The Nature of Doctrine. Religion and Theology in a Postliberal Age*. Philadelphia: Westminster Press, 1984.
22. Francis X. Clooney S.J. "Response." In *The New Comparative Theology* (as ref. [19]), 191–200.
23. Paul Knitter. "Virtuous Comparativists Are Practicing Pluralists". In *Religious Pluralism and the Modern* (as ref. [21]), 46–57.
24. Perry Schmidt-Leukel. "Pluralisms. How to Appreciate Religious Diversity Theologically." In *Christian Approaches to Other Faiths*, Alan Race and Paul Hedges, eds. London: SCM Press, 2008, 85–110.
25. John J. Thatamanil. *The Immanent Divine. God, Creation, and the Human Predicament*. An East-West Conversation. Minneapolis: Fortress Press, 2006.
26. Hajime Nakamura. *A Comparative History of Ideas*. London–New York: Kegan Paul International, 1992.
27. David A. Dilworth. *Philosophy in World Perspective. A Comparative Hermeneutics of the Major Theories*. New Haven–London: Yale University Press, 1989.
28. Hans P. Sturm. *Weder Sein noch Nichtsein. Der Urteilsvierkant (Catuṣkoṭi) und seine Korollarien im östlichen und westlichen Denken*. Würzburg: Ergon Verlag, 1996.
29. Perry Schmidt-Leukel. "Pluralist Approaches in some Major Non-Christian Religions." In *Twenty-First Century Theologies of Religions: Retrospection and New Frontiers*, E. Harris, P. Hedges, and S. Hettiarachi, eds. Amsterdam–New York: Rodopi, 2014 (forthcoming).
30. Francis X. Clooney S.J. "The Study of Non-Christian Religions in the Post-Vatican II Roman Catholic Church." *Journal of Ecumenical Studies* 28 (1991): 482–494.
31. Rose Drew. *Buddhist and Christian? An Exploration of Dual Belonging*. London–New York: Routledge, 2011.
32. Ulrich Winkler. *Wege der Religionstheologie. Von der Erwählung zur komparativen Theologie*, Innsbruck–Wien: Tyrolia Verlag, 2013.
33. Joachim Gentz. "Religious Diversity in the Three Teachings Discourses." In *Religious Diversity in Chinese Thought*, Perry Schmidt-Leukel and Joachim Gentz, eds. Basingstoke–New York: Palgrave Macmillan, 2013, 123–39.

MDPI AG
Klybeckstrasse 64
4057 Basel, Switzerland
Tel. +41 61 683 77 34
Fax +41 61 302 89 18
http://www.mdpi.com/

Religions Editorial Office
E-Mail: religions@mdpi.com
http://www.mdpi.com/journal/religions

www.ingramcontent.com/pod-product-compliance
Lightning Source LLC
Chambersburg PA
CBHW061357010526
44107CB00012B/965